Improving Student Engagement and Development through Assessment

With a unique focus on the relationship between assessment and engagement, this book explores what works in terms of keeping students on course to succeed.

Against a backdrop of massification and the associated increase in student diversity, there is an escalating requirement for personalized, technology-driven learning in higher education. In addition, the advent of student fees has promoted a consumer culture resulting in students having an increasingly powerful voice in shaping curricula to their own requirements. How does one engage and retain a group of students of such diverse culture, ethnicity, ambition and experience?

Using examples from a variety of institutions worldwide, this edited collection provides a well-researched evidence base of current thinking and developments in assessment practices in higher education. The chapters discuss:

- staff and student views on assessment
- engaging students through assessment feedback
- assessment for learning
- assessing for employability
- interdisciplinary and transnational assessment
- technology-supported assessment for retention.

Improving Student Engagement and Development through Assessment draws together a wealth of expertise from a range of contributors, including academic staff, academic developers, pedagogical researchers, National Teaching Fellows and Centres for Excellence in Higher Education. Recognizing that a pedagogy which is embedded and taken for granted in one context might be completely novel in another, the contributors share best practice and evaluate evidence of assessment strategies to enable academic colleagues to make informed decisions about adopting new and creative approaches to assessment. This interdisciplinary text will prove an invaluable tool for those working and studying in higher education.

Lynn Clouder is Director of the Centre for Excellence in Learning Enhancement (CELE) at Coventry University, UK.

Christine Broughan is Head of Applied Research at Student Services, at Coventry University, UK.

Steve Jewell is Senior Lecturer in Strategy and Applied Management at Coventry University, UK.

Graham Steventon is Senior Lecturer in Criminology at Coventry University, UK.

Improving Student Engagement and Development through Assessment

Theory and practice in higher education

Edited by
Lynn Clouder, Christine Broughan,
Steve Jewell and Graham Steventon

Routledge
Taylor & Francis Group

LONDON AND NEW YORK

First published 2012
by Routledge
2 Park Square, Milton Park, Abingdon, Oxon OX14 4RN

Simultaneously published in the USA and Canada
by Routledge
711 Third Avenue, New York, NY 10017

Routledge is an imprint of the Taylor & Francis Group, an informa business

British Library Cataloguing in Publication Data
A catalogue record for this book is available from the British Library

Library of Congress Cataloging in Publication Data
Library of Congress Control Number: 2012937598

ISBN: 978-0-415-61819-9 (hbk)
ISBN: 978-0-415-61820-5 (pbk)
ISBN: 978-0-203-81752-0 (ebk)

Typeset in Galliard
by Taylor & Francis Books

MIX
Paper from
responsible sources
FSC
www.fsc.org   FSC® C004839

Printed and bound in Great Britain by
TJ International Ltd, Padstow, Cornwall

Contents

List of illustrations

Figures

Tables

Notes on contributors

Chi Baik is a lecturer in higher education at the Centre for the Study of Higher Education, University of Melbourne, Australia. Her research focuses on university assessment practices and the internationalization of university curricula. In the past few years, she has conducted various projects for government and the University of Melbourne.

Greg Benfield is an educational developer (Learning Technologies) at Oxford Brookes University in the Oxford Centre for Staff and Learning Development (OCSLD). He supports e-learning tutors on the Postgraduate Certificate of Teaching in Higher Education, and delivers national workshops on e-learning and assessment.

Alex Bols is Head of Education and Quality, National Union of Students. He is a member of the UK team of Bologna Experts and sits on many sector committees including Quality in HE Group, HE Public Information Steering Group, HE Better Regulation Group and HEFCE's Teaching, Quality and Student Experience Strategic Advisory Committee.

David Boud is Professor of Adult Education in the Faculty of Arts and Social Sciences, University of Technology, Sydney. He has written extensively on teaching, learning and assessment in higher and professional education. Recently he has focused on assessment for learning in and beyond courses.

Christine Broughan is Head of Applied Research within Student Services at Coventry University. She teaches Psychology for the University of Oxford and the Open University. Christine has a key role in working with partners to develop an inclusive approach to improving teaching, learning and assessment in higher education.

David Carless is an Associate Professor in the Faculty of Education, University of Hong Kong. His main research interest is in how assessment can be reconfigured to stimulate productive student learning. His books include: *How Assessment Supports Learning: Learning-Oriented Assessment in Action* and *From Testing to Productive Student Learning: Implementing Formative Assessment in Confucian-Heritage Settings.*

Mark Childs is a senior research fellow for e-learning at Coventry University. Since 1997, he has worked on close to 30 projects involving technology-supported learning – as a researcher, consultant, evaluator, manager and principal investigator, at Coventry and in previous posts at the Universities of Wolverhampton and Warwick.

Lynn Clouder is Professor of Professional Education and Director of the Centre for Excellence in Learning Enhancement at Coventry University. She was awarded a National Teaching Fellowship in 2007. Her PhD thesis focused on the professional socialization of health professionals and her research interests include reflective practice, work-based learning, professional and interprofessional learning.

Anthony Cook is Emeritus Professor of Teaching and Learning at the University of Ulster. He was Director of the STAR (Student Transition and Retention) project which documented practices designed to ease the transition of new students into higher education. Trained as a biologist, he developed interests in early decision-making in new students.

Heather Conboy is ELT Co-ordinator in the Faculty of Art, Design and Humanities and part of the Centre for Enhanced Learning through Technology at De Montfort University, Leicester, UK. Her research interests include peer communication in online learning and her PhD research examines online discourse in a creative writing programme.

Glenda Crosling is an Associate Professor and Director of Education Quality and Innovation at Monash University Sunway Campus in Malaysia, where she is responsible for educational quality assurance and improvement. She has researched and published widely on the enhancement of the quality of teaching and learning in higher education, in books, chapters and journal articles.

Mark Davies is Professor of Bioscience at the University of Sunderland. Mark has worked for many UK HE sector organizations, including the QAA, UUK and the Higher Education Academy, and was heavily involved in the FDTL4 *Student Transition and Retention* ('STAR') project. Mark is also a National Teaching Fellow.

Phil Davies has been lecturing in computing at the University of Glamorgan for the past 25 years. In the past few years he has integrated the development of digital stories into his teaching and assessment, and made use of his CAPODS tool to support the peer assessment of students' stories.

Norman Day is Head of Careers and Employability at Coventry University and has worked in a range of settings across school, further and higher education sectors. His research interests include measuring the impact of careers interventions and access to the professions for students from lower socio-economic groups.

Frances Deepwell is an educational development consultant at Oxford Brookes University. She leads a course for associate teachers and tutors on the Postgraduate Certificate in Teaching in Higher Education. Her research interests include the evaluation of educational processes, and she supports the continuing professional development of academic and learning support staff.

Palitha Edirisingha is a lecturer in e-learning at the University of Leicester. His research and supervision interests include the use of digital devices and web-based technologies for formal and informal learning in developed and developing countries. Research projects include IMPALA (podcasting), WoLF (m-learning), MOOSE (3D virtual worlds), GIRAFFE (wikis), and PELICANS (Web 2.0).

Ron Edwards is a professor and Vice President – Academic at Royal Melbourne Institute of Technology University's campus in Vietnam. He has published extensively in the field of international business and has made contributions to the associated field of international education. From 2000 to 2005, he was Course Coordinator for Monash University's first 'international' degree, and from 2006 to 2010 he led the largest school at Monash University's Sunway campus in Malaysia.

Ed Foster is Study Support Co-ordinator at Nottingham Trent University, helping students manage the transition into higher education. His primary research interests are the transition into higher education, student retention and engagement. Ed leads on a HEFCE/Paul Hamlyn Foundation Project exploring effective strategies for improving student retention in higher education.

Clinton Golding is a senior lecturer at the Higher Education Development Centre, University of Otago, New Zealand. He takes a philosophically-based interdisciplinary approach to education for thinking, interdisciplinarity, dialogue, inquiry and problem-solving across the disciplines. Previously he worked at the Centre for the Study of Higher Education, University of Melbourne.

David Grantham is a higher education consultant specializing in reflective practice, work-based learning and student development. His recent experience is with postgraduate students including colleagues on PG Certificate programmes. He was awarded a National Teaching Fellowship in 2001 and is currently researching curriculum design encouraging student personal and intellectual growth.

Phil Gravestock is Head of Learning Enhancement and Technology Support at the University of Gloucestershire. Phil is a National Teaching Fellow with an interest in inclusion and flexible learning. He was Director of the 'Enhancing

Students' Reflection through the use of Digital Storytelling' Pathfinder Project.

Richard Hall is De Montfort University's e-Learning Co-ordinator, and a research associate in the Centre for Computing and Social Responsibility. He is a National Teaching Fellow and Reader in Education and Technology. His current research focuses upon the place of technology in the idea of the twenty-first-century university.

Sara Hammer works in learning and teaching design at the University of Southern Queensland, Australia. Her specialist support domain is assessment and assessment practice. Her recent research includes topics such as the development of critical thinking, embedding graduate attributes, and assessing students with a disability.

Marie Hardie is the Faculty MBA Director at Coventry Business School and introduced Company Internships to the Coventry Masters Programmes. Her research interests include employability within the UK and China, employer engagement and graduate recruitment.

Christina Hughes is a professor and Chair of the Faculty of Social Sciences, University of Warwick. Her recent research has focused on analyses of pleasure in pedagogical processes. She has also published widely on methodological issues, the most recent of which are concerned with quantitative approaches within feminism.

Lynne Hunt is Professor Emeritus who won the 2002 Prime Minister's Award for Australian University Teacher of the Year and a 2009 Australian Executive Endeavour Award to study quality assurance in university teaching. She co-edited *The Realities of Change in Higher Education* (2006) and served as a Director on the Board of the Australian Learning and Teaching Council until 2008.

Martin Jenkins is Manager, Centre for Educational Development, Christchurch Polytechnic Institute of Technology, New Zealand. Previously he was Academic Manager, Centre for Active Learning, University of Gloucestershire. His current interests include digital storytelling and learning design for programme development and sharing practice. He was awarded a National Teaching Fellowship in 2004.

Steve Jewell is a senior lecturer at Coventry Business School and teaches research methods, the dissertation and the internship. His research interests include assessment, employability and factors that influence student performance.

Steve Larkin is a professor and Pro Vice Chancellor for Indigenous Leadership at Charles Darwin University, Australia, and currently chairs the National Indigenous Higher Education Advisory Council to the Australian Government. As an Aboriginal academic, Steve has worked for over 30 years in Australian Aboriginal affairs, mainly in health, education and public policy.

Sarah Lawther is part of the Learning Development Team at Nottingham Trent University and lead researcher on the HERE Project. Sarah is particularly interested in the use of mixed methods in research and has extensively researched student transition, retention and engagement. She is currently working to use these findings to improve the learning and teaching experience for students.

Liz McDowell is Professor of Higher Education at Northumbria University. Her research focuses on relationships between assessment and learning and students' experiences of assessment. She is the founder of an influential international conference series on assessment. Liz was Director of the National Centre for Excellence in Assessment for learning, 2005–10.

Jane McNeil is Director of Academic Development at Nottingham Trent University. She leads a team of specialists who support the university's academic development and quality strategies. She is an experienced academic with research interests in assessment, feedback, academic writing and the use of technology to enhance learning and teaching.

Martin Oliver is Reader at the London Knowledge Lab, a research centre of the Institute of Education, University of London. His work focuses on the use of technology in higher education. He is currently Chair of the Association for Learning Technology and editor of *Learning, Media and Technology*.

Margaret Price is Professor in Learning and Assessment at Oxford Brookes University and a National Teaching Fellow. Her research interests include: student engagement with assessment and feedback, how staff and student come to understand assessment standards, and peer support for learning. She is currently Director of the Business School Pedagogic Research Centre (including ASKe, the Assessment Standards Knowledge exchange).

David Sadler is Professor Emeritus in Higher Education at Griffith University, Brisbane, Australia. Since 1973, his research has focused on formative and summative of learning. Widely cited, his current work is focused on grading, academic achievement standards, and assessment that leads to improved learning and student capability.

Michael Sankey is currently the Director of Learning and Teaching Support at the University of Southern Queensland, Australia. He specializes in e-learning pedagogies, multimodal design, visual and multiliteracies. He is particularly interested in how aesthetically enhanced learning environments can better transmit concepts to students from diverse backgrounds.

Ormond Simpson worked at the UK Open University for 30 years and then at the Open Polytechnic of New Zealand as a visiting professor. He has written two books: *Supporting Students in Online Open and Distance Learning* and *Student Retention in Online Open and Distance Learning*.

Ian **Solomonides** is Associate Professor and Director of the Learning and Teaching Centre at Macquarie University, Sydney, Australia. Formerly from the UK, he moved to Australia in 2006. Ian has a strong research interest in student engagement and is an Executive Member, Council of Australian Directors of Academic Development.

Graham Steventon is a senior lecturer in Criminology at Coventry University. His use of creative, student-centred teaching and learning methods stems from a background in architecture and urban design, and he teaches and researches using technologies, such as podcasting and immersive worlds, to inform dynamic approaches to curriculum delivery.

Sue Thompson is Professor of Academic Development and Director of Teaching and Learning Development at Liverpool John Moores University, UK. Her professional interests are focused on promoting and supporting excellence in teaching and learning. As National Teaching Fellow, she is leading a research project investigating the second year experience.

Philip Watland is an Instructor of Learning Technology at Olds College, Canada. His interest lies in researching individuals' experiences of teaching and learning in technology-supported learning environments. His role includes supporting faculty in the use of learning technologies in both classroom and online environments.

Mantz Yorke's career includes senior management and educational research at Liverpool John Moores University, UK, and a secondment to the Higher Education Quality Council. He is currently Visiting Professor in the Department of Educational Research, Lancaster University. His research and publications span employability, the first year experience, retention and assessment.

Foreword

Assessment of students in higher education is crucial for the integrity, validation and quality not only of programmes of study, but also for individual institutions and the system overall. In more recent times, the centrality of assessment in student learning has been resoundingly endorsed in the pedagogical literature, emphasizing its role in encouraging students to take what should be effective approaches to their study so that they can achieve success with the learning outcomes that are embedded in assessment processes. Significantly, assessment is also a means of reinforcing higher order thinking, which is the hallmark of higher education.

Another important theme, particularly in these times of student diversity, is that of student engagement in their learning. Perceived as integral to academic success, engaged students are more likely to be motivated to study for meaning and understanding, rather than merely doing what is required to pass an exam or assignment. In combination, these two pivotal themes of assessment and student engagement as essential components in successful academic outcomes result in a strong approach to enhancing the quality of learning and teaching. This book provides an important opportunity to explore the synergy of these themes; it seeks to investigate from a range of perspectives the ways in which student engagement can be enhanced through assessment, and the ways that assessment also can be enhanced by assisting students to engage in their learning. Furthermore, the interaction of these themes not only represents best practice, but also advances the boundaries of practice more generally into yet unexplored domains, opening the field for further progress. For the benefit of students in our diverse higher education systems, curriculum developers, teachers, quality assurance practitioners and policy-makers, this book's exploration should be a valuable and useful resource. I commend it to such staff regardless of their particular role or setting.

Glenda Crosling
Monash University Sunway Campus
Malaysia

Introduction

Lynn Clouder and Christina Hughes

This book is set in the context of current challenges in higher education: massification, student diversity, an escalating demand for personalized learning driven by developments in information technology and pressure on marking turnaround times, to name but a few. The advent of student fees is promoting a consumer culture in which students are becoming 'customers' with an increasingly powerful voice in shaping curricula to their own requirements. Likewise employers are exerting pressure on higher education institutions to turn out students with workplace skills. In this context, assessment is key; student retention, completion and employability are hard outcomes linked to assessment targets in a target-driven world and used as indicators of success.

Yet assessment is challenging for academics as well as students. Mention assessment and feedback in any higher education institution in the UK and the spectre of the National Student Survey (NSS) springs to mind. Whether one sees the NSS as a robust research tool or not, it does reveal that assessment and feedback are consistently the aspect of their course with which students are least content. In response, this book acknowledges the need to 'do better' in terms of student satisfaction.

There are also inevitable dangers in an over-zealous approach in making assessment central to the resolution of these political, reputational and financial imperatives facing educators and managers. The contemporary drive toward assessment-led curricula can produce excessive, and overly complex, approaches that impede rather than support students' learning (Heywood 2000) – assessment on, rather than with and for, students. It can create an emotional climate for the student that is anxious, nervous, or simply, but damagingly, disinterested. In jeopardy is the joy of learning (Quinn 2010) and at risk a focus on assessment as primarily a tool of enablement. Quinn critiques the dominance of regulatory ideas and practices in higher education, which lead to reductionist and fragmented approaches and overly technological solutions that constitute a pedagogic loss rather than gain. Along with others (see Clayton *et al.* 2009; Tamboukou 2010; Hughes 2011) she recognizes the spirit of pleasure that is necessary in capturing imaginations and fostering creative and engaged responses to learning. What is too easily forgotten is that many students entering higher education not only expect, but look forward to, some independence and a different kind of learning and approach to assessment, than that experienced at school. Student aspirations may be directed ultimately toward employment and the class of degree now necessary for securing this, but they still aspire to develop their love of subject matter and to experience the disruptive rapture when understandings shift in significant ways.

Acknowledging the truism that assessment drives learning, well-conceived and implemented assessment can play an important part in making learning enjoyable and meaningful and therefore more engaging. Notwithstanding institutional measures of success, the contributors to this book focus specifically on assessment and its potential to enable students to engage with peers and tutors, to gain personal insight, to feel valued and supported, and above all feel they 'fit in' as part of a learning community, and, as such, can succeed in higher education. Perhaps the book's most important message is that neither top-down nor bottom-up strategies work effectively in isolation. Grass-roots interventions can have a positive impact on student engagement, but without a strategy that targets the whole institution, improvements will be piecemeal.

The structure of the book

The chapters in this book are arranged to form three key themes: (1) setting the broader context of assessment from the perspectives of students, staff and institutions; (2) outlining specific assessment interventions; and (3) a focus on strategic change at an institutional level. Critical friend commentaries following each chapter provide an external reference point allowing readers unfamiliar with the terrain to gain a sense of how the ideas fit into wider debates.

This collection provides a well-researched evidence base of current thinking and developments in assessment practices in higher education, drawing on both applied and theoretical research. A particular strength of the book is its interdisciplinary nature, which enables similarities and differences between disciplinary demands and needs to be accommodated. It gathers together a wealth of expertise from academics, academic developers, pedagogical researchers, National Teaching Fellows and Centres for Excellence in Higher Education, from Australia, New Zealand, Malaysia and the UK. Recognizing that a particular pedagogic strategy that is well embedded and taken for granted in one context might be completely novel in another (King *et al.* 2007), the aim is to inspire academics and managers not only to critique their own practice, but also to be brave and imaginative in creating new or different assessment possibilities.

References

Clayton, B., Beard, C., Humberstone, B. and Wolstenholme, C. (2009) 'The jouissance of learning: evolutionary musings on the pleasures of learning in higher education', *Teaching in Higher Education*, 14(4): 375–86.

Heywood, J. (2000) *Assessment in Higher Education: Student Learning, Teaching, Programmes and Institutions*, London: Jessica Kingsley.

Hughes, C. (2011) 'Pleasure, change and values in doctoral pedagogy', *Studies in Higher Education*, 36(3): 1–15.

King, V., Clouder, L., Deane, M., Deepwell, F. and Ganobcsik-Williams, L. (2007) 'Reflections on the First International iPED Conference, Coventry TechnoCentre, UK, 10–11 September 2006', *Teaching in Higher Education*, 12(3): 425–33.

Quinn, J. (2010) *Learning Communities and Imagined Social Capital*, London: Continuum.

Tamboukou, M. (2010) *In the Fold Between Power and Desire: Women Artists' Narratives*, Newcastle Upon Tyne: Cambridge Scholars Publishing.

Chapter 1

Student views on assessment

Alex Bols

Introduction

When graduates think back to their university days, it is often the assessments that stick in their minds – cramming for that final exam, staying up all night drinking coffee to finish a report or essay on time or frantically rushing around to get their dissertation bound – and, for many, these reminiscences are often associated with rising stress levels and feelings of dread. There has been a growing academic discourse in recent years that assessment, and the feedback that students receive as part of this process, are a key part of the learning process. However, when I speak to students, many of them consider assessments to simply be a hurdle that they have jump over on the way to getting a qualification. This chapter will provide an overview of what students think about assessment and suggest some ways of improving this experience.

The views of students are being taken ever more seriously in the higher education community. In part, this may be due to recognition of the active nature of learning, with students at the centre of this process; something they do *for* themselves, not something done *to* them. This recognition of the active nature of learning gives greater weight to their views about the way in which they are taught and assessed, and has given rise to the discourse of 'student engagement' with students as co-producers of the education in a community of learning (Streeting and Wise 2009). However, student engagement is not the only show in town; it is also recognized that as students have started to contribute ever larger amounts of their own money towards the cost of their education, they have become more like 'consumers' (Cuthbert 2010) of their education, or at least they exhibit consumer traits. In many ways, these discourses of students as consumers and co-producers of their education reflect opposing ends of a spectrum – but either way the expectations and experiences of students in relation to their assessment are becoming an increasingly important factor in the modern higher education sector.

The importance of receiving the views of students has given rise to a growth industry of how to engage students and get the views of student consumers. This ranges from improved representation structures to course evaluation surveys and even a National Student Survey. The National Student Survey (NSS) carried out in the United Kingdom is an annual survey of final year undergraduate students with over 250,000 responses every year. In the first five years of the NSS, feedback and assessment have stubbornly remained the areas of least satisfaction among students. While around 80 per cent of students claim overall satisfaction, those satisfied with their assessment and feedback have been a good 15–20 points below this. Although satisfaction levels have increased from 59 per cent in 2005 to 66 per cent in 2010, there has not been a step change in improvement to suggest that this issue has been addressed satisfactorily.

Whether we consider students to be consumers or active participants in their education, one thing is clear, that on every previous occasion when the costs have been passed on to students, it has resulted in higher expectations about their experience and the quality of their course. After the 1998 introduction of full-time undergraduate fees and then their further increase in 2006, we saw year-on-year increases in the number of students making complaints and appeals (Office of the Independent Adjudicator 2009), campaigns on feedback turnaround times (NUS 2010a), and even protests at some universities about the number of contact hours that students received (Grimston 2009); in other words, students are becoming increasingly critical and demanding of their education. The reforms in England following the 2010 Parliamentary votes to raise undergraduate tuition fees up to £9,000 are likely to affect this focus still further, not least because for many courses students will not just be contributing to the costs of the course, but will also be funding the cost of teaching entirely. Therefore, how institutions respond to the expectations of students in relation to this key area of feedback and assessment will be increasingly important.

Feedback and assessment are topics on which many students unions have been doing a considerable amount of work in recent years, and a recent survey of students unions showed that 71 per cent of respondents said that it was their priority area for the year. NUS has also provided resources for students unions including a Charter on Feedback and Assessment, 10 Principles on Feedback and on Assessment, and many other resources, such as research, action plans and campaign materials through the Feedback and Assessment Campaign Toolkit (FACT) (NUS 2010b). This chapter will look at what students think about assessment, bringing together data from the NSS (The Higher Education Funding Council for England 2010) and the NUS/HSBC Student Experience Report (NUS/HSBC 2009), as well as highlight some of the demands that students are beginning to make in relation to their assessment and feedback. The activity of NUS and students unions has provided an insight into some of the key priority areas that students have identified, and from this material I have developed a handy acronym for the five key issues, FINALS: Feedback; Innovative; Anonymous; Learning; Submission.

What do students think?

There is a wide range of evidence to suggest that both assessment and feedback are important issues for many students and in part this reflects why so many students unions have focused on this issue in recent years. In this section I will give a flavour of the research available by looking at the Oakleigh research (Oakleigh Consulting and Staffordshire University 2010) into what information students need when applying to university and the national surveys of student opinion, the NSS and the NUS/HSBC Student Experience Report.

Information for prospective students

In the first half of 2010, HEFCE commissioned Oakleigh and Staffordshire University to identify the key pieces of information required by students when applying to go to university. As part of their research, they identified 16 key pieces of information that students need to help inform their decision (ibid.). The 16 key pieces of information include a wide variety of topics including the 'proportion of students employed in a full-time professional or managerial job one year after completing this course' and the 'average salary in the first year after completing this course', as well as inquiring about the costs of accommodation and bursaries available. It is therefore interesting to note that these fairly instrumental pieces of information also include two that specifically relate to feedback and assessment, emphasizing the importance of this issue to students, even before they go to university and in making their decisions about whether and where to study.

The NUS/HSBC Student Experience Report (NUS/HSBC 2009) also asked students what information they needed to help make their choice, with 11 per cent of students citing information about the 'course marking scheme including exams and other assessment procedures'. The prominence of information relating to assessment and feedback in both pieces of research highlights not just the interest of students in these issues but also suggests that these issues will feed into informing their expectations and where they eventually decide to study.

The National Student Survey (NSS)

The NSS surveys students on various aspects of their learning experience, including the quality of teaching, academic support and organization and management. The survey also asks students about their experiences in relation to feedback and assessment, such as judging whether 'assessment arrangements and marking have been fair' and whether 'the criteria used in marking have been clear in advance'. While the responses to these two questions are above the average in the feedback and assessment section average, with 70 per cent and 72 per cent respectively, this is still well below other sections within the survey.

It is partly the result of the significantly lower levels of satisfaction, highlighted by the NSS, which has given rise to the focus on the issue in recent years. The HEFCE (Higher Education Funding Council for England 2008) report, *Counting What Is Measured or Measuring What Counts?* suggests that many institutions have tackled the issue of feedback and assessment, at least in part, because of the fact that the NSS is now incorporated into several national newspaper league tables.

NUS/HSBC Student Experience Report

In addition to the NSS, the NUS also undertakes an annual survey of student experience. The NUS/HSBC Student Experience Report (NUS/HSBC 2008) explores a wider range of aspects relating to the student learning experience and has gone into greater depth into the issue of assessment. The research is based primarily on an online survey, which runs in June, and in which the respondents are selected via a student panel. In 2010, a total of 3,863 students took part in the survey, fulfilling a variety of interlocking quotas including year of study, institution type and gender. The final results are weighted to ensure representativeness.

The NUS/HSBC research presented students with three statements about the assessment that they receive and asked them to state on a seven-point Likert scale how much they agreed/disagreed with these statements. The statements looked at whether assessment highlights areas to focus on, whether it is part of the learning process, or whether it is just a way of measuring what they have learnt. The results can be seen in Figure 1.1.

There are high levels of dissatisfaction in relation to assessment, with 39 per cent disagreeing with the statement that assessment I receive 'helps highlight areas that I need to focus on' (increasing to 78 per cent if you include those that neither agree nor disagree), and 27 per cent disagreeing with the statement that assessment I receive 'is part of the learning process' (increasing to 74 per cent, if you include those that neither agree nor disagree). With respect to the latter, it would be interesting to consider the extent to which this is because students do not believe that assessment is integral to learning or because they have not been told of the role that assessment can play in the learning process as part of their

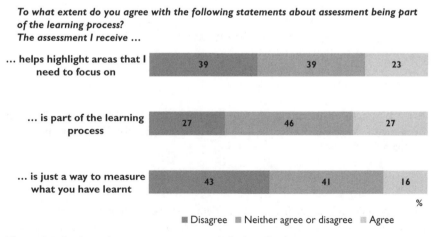

Figure 1.1 Student views on assessment and the learning process

academic induction process. The most positive response was with respect to the statement that assessment is 'just a way to measure what you have learnt' with 43 per cent of students disagreeing with this statement. Although the largest section again, 41 per cent, was those that neither agreed nor disagreed.

What do students want? FINALS

The NSS, NUS/HSBC Student Experience Report and the Oakleigh public information research, as well as much academic research, highlight a wide range of student concerns in relation to assessment. Based on this research, and the activity of both students unions and NUS, I have identified five key areas relating to student expectations that I will explore in more detail in this section using the FINALS acronym.

Feedback

Feedback is the area of greatest challenge and would be worthy of its own chapter, or even book, of what students think and want. Feedback has been identified as one of the most important elements in supporting learning (Nicol and Macfarlane-Dick 2006; Price *et al.* 2007; NUS 2008). The research emphasizes that students want feedback because it helps them to improve their understanding of what they got right or where they went wrong, so that they are able to learn from this for the future. However, the complaints from students often are that the comments they receive are not useful. As part of the NUS Great Feedback Amnesty I gathered quotes from students about what they thought about their feedback. A few of these quotes from students really give a flavour of the usefulness of feedback:

> All I get is a grade next to my matriculation number without any indication on how I'm actually doing.
> I got an essay back where the only comment was 'use a bigger text size', there was nothing on how to improve my grade.
> For a rather lengthy scientific report, the feedback I received consisted of a mere two ticks and a question mark.

I will therefore concentrate on four key points that are most commonly raised by students regarding feedback: timely, face-to-face feedback, format and exam feedback.

Timely

The timeliness of the feedback that students receive is often the most common complaint that students have. The NUS/HSBC Student Experience Report (NUS/HSBC 2011) shows almost 25 per cent of students have to wait five weeks or more on average to receive feedback. This clearly does not match Benne *et al.*'s definition of feedback that it should be 'provided as close in time to the behaviour as possible' (cited in Falchikov 1995: 159). Students also express irritation that they have to hand their assessment in on time otherwise they are penalized, whereas tutors can hand their feedback whenever they want.

The key issue for most students in relation to the timeliness is that they know when they are going to get feedback. This has resulted in many institutions setting time-limits within which students should receive their feedback (NUS 2010b). This management of students' expectations is a useful way of improving satisfaction but if we truly consider feedback to be an integral part of the learning process, then we should also consider how we can meet, rather than just manage, their expectations.

The NUS has called for generalized feedback of the key learning points to all students within a week of the assessment – ideally this would be given before the assessment is submitted – and then more personalized feedback within three weeks.

Face-to-face feedback

For feedback to be useful as part of the learning process, students need to be able to read it, understand it, and learn from it. It is sometimes commented by some academic staff that students do not actually want feedback and demonstrate this by saying that some students do not pick up their essays from the departmental office, especially if they have already received the grade online: 'it is not inevitable that students will read and pay attention to feedback even when that feedback is lovingly crafted and provided promptly' (Gibbs and Simpson 2002: 20). However, the perception that students do not collect written feedback highlights that even if all students were to get lengthy feedback on all their assessments in a timely fashion, it still would not truly meet the needs of all students. What will really support the student's learning is developing a dialogue between the student and the academic. For a discussion of this point, see the Osney Grange Group's *Feedback: An Agenda for Change* (2009).

The NUS calls for all students to have 'face-to-face' feedback for at least the first piece of assessment each academic year (NUS 2010b).

Format of the feedback

The NUS/HSBC Student Experience Report (NUS/HSBC 2011) compares the way in which students currently receive feedback and how they would like to receive it. This builds on the previous section about face-to-face feedback, finding that significantly more students want to receive feedback verbally than currently do so, with only 24 per cent currently receiving verbal feedback and 67 per cent wanting verbal feedback in an individual meeting with their tutor. However, as students also want greater ownership of their own learning process, engaging them in deciding the form of feedback would also potentially improve satisfaction and engagement.

Many academics are looking at different ways of presenting feedback, especially through the use of new technologies such as electronic feedback or via video message. Such innovations, as long as discussed and agreed with students, are to be welcomed. In addition, it is worth considering how students themselves are supported to critique their own work and that of other students. This peer-to-peer feedback will provide a very real learning opportunity for students as they begin to understand the connections between the assessment criteria and their own work (Osney Grange Group 2009). It is important as part of the induction process to emphasize the benefits of this approach to students as they may not value the opinions of other students, especially if they think that they have paid for the feedback of an expert.

The NUS believes that all students 'should be given the choice of format for feedback'. This choice of format is especially important for those students studying flexibly, whether distance learning, part-time or other flexible learning method (NUS 2010b).

Exam feedback

The final type of feedback that students want is feedback on exams. This is especially important for those courses that are almost entirely assessed through exams. Another topic for consideration should be how academics provide some form of formative feedback on exams. This might be specific exam preparation sessions, but involve more than just looking at past papers. This process should emphasize exam technique and key learning points from previous years.

When asked in the NUS/HSBC research what feedback students currently receive on exams, only 27 per cent receive online feedback, only 13 per cent receive written comments, and only 5 per cent receive verbal feedback individually or in a group. There is therefore still a long way to go to meet the expectations of the 90 per cent of students who say that they want feedback on their exams.

Innovative

Innovation in assessment is an important area that can be overlooked when putting together a programme specification and getting a new course ready for validation. It is sometimes quite easy just to use the form of assessment that you were assessed with at university or that has always been used in your department, and there is also sometimes the perception that trying something new will either be frowned on by the Quality Assurance Agency (QAA) or be harder to get approved. However, using different forms of assessment can be both exciting and engaging for students, and with many schools now using assessment for learning and innovative approaches these students will increasingly come to expect innovation.

Innovation in assessment should particularly look at the ways in which new technologies are integrated into the assessment methods; with the pace of change of technology many new interesting possibilities will become increasingly available. Zimbardo (2010) suggests that the amount of time young people spend playing computer games has had a fundamental impact on the hard-wiring of their brains and they are now used to learning through a try and try again approach of re-playing each level of a game until they have completed it. This experimentation approach differs from the more traditional form of learning based on knowledge and reading round a topic. It is therefore important to consider new forms of technology as a way of being able to fully assess the knowledge and learning of young people.

Innovation should also include looking at the ways in which students themselves are engaged in the process of developing and designing their assessment. One of the most interesting statistics that jumped out at me when I first saw the data from the first NUS/HSBC Student Experience Report in 2008 was in relation to the extent to which students currently felt engaged and the extent to which they wanted to be engaged. The question probed not just superficial engagement but the extent to which they wanted to be involved in shaping the 'content, curriculum and design' of their course. In the most recent NUS/HSBC Student Experience Report (NUS/HSBC 2011), only 29 per cent of students felt that they were currently engaged in this compared to 58 per cent of students who said they wanted to be involved. Some institutions have trialled this approach of engaging students in designing their assessment and it is interesting to note that students did not simply try and design an easy form of assessment (Birmingham City University 2011). In fact, in many cases, the assessment that they designed was significantly more testing than the previous form of assessment – such as using interviews – and as they were involved in designing it, they felt real ownership and were therefore generally more engaged in learning on the course.

The NUS believes that students should be provided with a variety of assessment methods and calls for greater use of innovation in assessment, including the use of technology and involving students in designing their own assessment (NUS 2010b).

Anonymous

One of the main campaigns that many students unions have run in relation to assessment over the past decade has been in relation to anonymous marking. Research (NUS 1999, cited in NUS 2010b) suggests that, at the very least in terms of the perceptions of students, there is discrimination if the marker is able to see the name of the person whose work they are marking. In the research, 44 per cent of students unions believed that discrimination and bias played a part in the way that students' work was assessed and addressed. Explanations might be complex but one quote that resonates with what we hear from students is: 'I would have got a higher mark, but he's never liked me.' There is some research into the impact of anonymous marking on success of minority groups of students (NUS 1999, cited in NUS 2010b), although this is still a largely under-researched area. However, Brennan's (2008) research (cited in NUS 2010b) suggests that marks for some groups change if they are marked anonymously. For example, he shows that at the University of Wales, following the introduction of anonymous marking, the number of women awarded firsts increased by 13 per cent.

It should also be stressed that anonymous marking campaigns are not accusing academics of discrimination, but by introducing anonymous marking, it helps to remove the suspicion of bias. However, I would also encourage universities to carry out their own research across their institution and between similar universities, examining the impact of anonymous marking on under-represented groups and on students' perceptions of fairness in relation to assessment methods. Clearly, it is not possible for all assessments to be marked anonymously, especially in the arts and music disciplines, but where this is not possible, there might be other approaches, including using double marking, that can help mitigate the perception in these disciplines.

The NUS believes that there should be 'anonymous marking for all summative assessment'. This is important in relation to the perception of fairness, even if there is not research at your institution to prove discrimination.

Learning

Going back to Figure 1.1, the most positive aspect revealed by the survey was that 43 per cent disagreed with the statement that assessment is just a way of measuring what they have learnt. This would therefore imply, and this is reinforced by speaking to students, that at least to a certain extent students recognize the importance of assessment as a part of the learning process. Some students realize that if they are going to get the most out of their education, then they will have to truly engage with it. The induction process is a key part of ensuring that students are engaged in their learning and understand the benefits of investing time and effort into not just passing exams but developing a real understanding of their field. Passing an exam may be important in terms of getting a first job, something that more students are likely to consider a priority; however, in terms of developing and deepening the skills and aptitudes necessary for a future career, investment at this early stage will pay dividends for a long period.

The use of formative assessment is an integral part of the learning process. Formative assessment can enable the student to reflect on their own learning, encourage and stimulate learning and also identify levels of student understanding by the lecturer and so enable either a speeding up or a repeating of various aspects.

NUS believes that 'formative assessment and feedback should be used throughout the programme', calling for formative assessment and feedback to be integrated into the curriculum in a strategic way.

Submission

The last element of the FINALS acronym relates to the submission of assessment. This is something that, while it does not seem like the most important issue, is actually one that can be very frustrating to students. It is often the smallest things in life that cause the most annoyance! The issue of electronic assessment is something that resonates widely with students. Many students will have written the assessment on a computer and then not to be able to submit it online just seems perverse. As a part-time student myself, I have found it bizarre that I would write my essay on my laptop at home, download readings and notes from the Institution's virtual learning environment or through Athens, but then when the essay was finished, I would then need to physically print it out and go in to the office to hand it in and receive a receipt from the administrator.

In the UK, Bucks New University students union developed an education campaign in 2009/10 highlighting ten key points relating to the student learning experience. They highlighted electronic submission as one of the key points of the campaign, as Chris Clark, Vice-President (Education) at the union said:

> In our universities there are more part-time students, commuting and distance learners than ever before. At the same time, communications technologies that were once difficult to use are now mainstream and intuitive. These students find it an inconvenience to travel to campus simply to submit a piece of assessment, which sometimes means having to take time off from work.
>
> (NUS 2010a)

There might be some practical issues with electronic submission such as how to provide an electronic receipt, although there are some examples of where this has been resolved, and other practical issues of what happens if a student sends work electronically but it is not received. But these are only that, practical issues that will need to be resolved. As Chris Clark goes on to say, 'Can there be a justification at this moment in time for failing to offer students a slick, reliable and integrated electronic method of submitting work and receiving feedback and results?'

Student expectations

In the introduction, I touched on the dichotomy between students as consumers or co-producers of their education and it would be true to suggest that

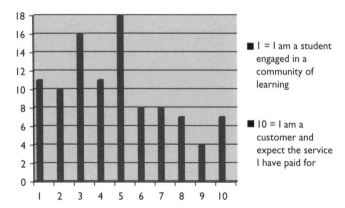

Figure 1.2 Percentage of students identifying with the consumer/co-producer dichotomy

some of the individual demands made by students would be expected by students for different reasons depending on how they identify themselves in relation to this spectrum. The NUS/HSBC Student Experience Survey asked students to plot themselves on a ten-point Likert scale as to whether they considered themselves to be 'a student engaged in a community of learning' or 'a customer and expect the service I have paid for', the results of which are shown in Figure 1.2. It was interesting to note that 37 per cent of students rated themselves in the 1–3 category; in other words, they strongly agreed with the statement about being in a community of learning. This compares with 18 per cent who rated themselves 8–10; in other words, they strongly positioned themselves as a customer. The NUS/HSBC (2009) report also showed that 65 per cent of students thought that their expectations would rise if they were paying more and so this identification with being a consumer is likely to increase.

There were also interesting differences in the way in which students considered themselves by subject discipline, and so when tackling feedback and assessment it is worth considering the expectations that students have and how these may differ according to the background of the student or the discipline that they are studying. The induction process will be key to preparing students for their learning experience.

Conclusion

In conclusion, what students want is FINALS:

• Feedback that is timely, incorporates a face-to-face dialogue, delivered in a format that they can choose, and with feedback on their exams.
• Innovative approaches to assessment that incorporate new forms of technology and engage students in the process of designing the assessment.

- Anonymous marking in assessments to remove the perception of bias and provide reassurance to students.
- Learning-focused assessment that is a part of the learning process, including appropriate use of formative assessment.
- Submission of assessment that makes life easier for students, especially those studying flexibly, including greater use of electronic submission.

FINALS brings together both the expectations of students, which could be seen as relatively reactive, but also looks at how they can be more proactively engaged with their learning processes, which could help counter the creep towards consumerization, develop deeper learning and understanding and also engage students with their learning, thus helping to aid retention.

References

Birmingham City University (2011) *Students Academic Partners*. Available at: http://www2.bcu.ac.uk/celt/forming-learning-partnerships/sap (accessed 15 March 2011).

Cuthbert, R. (2010) 'Students as customers?', *Higher Education Review*, 42(3): 3–25.

Falchikov, N. (1995) 'Improving feedback to and from students', in P. Knight (ed.) *Assessment for Learning in Higher Education*, London: Kogan Page, pp. 157–66.

Gibbs, G. and Simpson, C. (2002) *Does Your Assessment Support Your Students' Learning?* Available at: http://isis.ku.dk/kurser/blob.aspx?feltid=157744 (accessed 15 March 2011).

Grimston, J. (2009) 'Students at top university revolt over teaching standards', *Sunday Times*, 10 May. Available at: http://www.timesonline.co.uk/tol/life_-and_style/education/article6256503.ece (accessed 15 March 2011).

Higher Education Funding Council for England (2008) *Counting What Is Measured or Measuring What Counts? League Tables and their Impact on Higher Education Institutions in England*. Report to HEFCE by the Centre for Higher Education Research and Information (CHERI), Open University, and Hobsons Research. Available at: http://www.hefce.ac.uk/pubs/hefce/2008/08_14/ (accessed 15 March 2011).

——(2010) *2010 Teaching Quality Information Data*. Available at: http://www.hefce.ac.uk/learning/nss/data/2010/ (accessed 15 March 2011).

Nicol, D. and Macfarlane-Dick, D. (2006) 'Formative assessment and self-regulated learning: a model and seven principles of good feedback practice', *Studies in Higher Education*, 31(2): 199–218.

NUS (2008) *The Ten Principles of Good Feedback Practice*. NUS Briefing, The Great Feedback Amnesty, London: NUS.

——(2010a) *HE Focus Assessment 5*. Available at: http://www.nusconnect.org.uk/news/article/6010/665/ (accessed 15 March 2011).

——(2010b) *Feedback and Assessment Campaign Toolkit*. Available at: http://www.nusconnect.org.uk/campaigns/highereducation/learning-and-teaching-hub/feedback/campaigntools/ (accessed 15 March 2011).

NUS/HSBC (2008) *Student Experience Report: Teaching and Learning*. Available at: http://www.nus.org.uk/PageFiles/350/NUS_StudentExperienceReport.pdf (accessed 25 August 2011).

——(2009) *Student Experience Report: Teaching and Learning*. Available at: http://www.nusconnect.org.uk/resourcehandler/797d8465-c46d-48a8–93ed-979d508f4863/ (accessed 25 August 2011).

——(2011) *Student Experience Report: Teaching and Learning*. Available at: http://www.qmsu.org/pageassets/academic/projects/NUS-HSBC-Student-Experience-Report.pdf (accessed 28 January 2011).

Oakleigh Consulting and Staffordshire University (2010) *Understanding the Information Needs of Users of Public Information about Higher Education*. Report to HEFCE. Available at: http://www.hefce.ac.uk/pubs/rdreports/2010/rd12_10/rd12_10b.doc (accessed 15 March 2011).

Office of the Independent Adjudicator (2009) *Annual Report*. Available at: http://www.oiahe.org.uk/media/13808/oia-annual-report-2009.pdf (accessed 30 July 2011).

Osney Grange Group (2009) *Feedback: An Agenda for Change*. Available at: http://www.brookes.ac.uk/aske/documents/OGG%20agenda%20for%20change.pdf (accessed 15 March 2011).

Price, M., O'Donovan, B. and Rust, C. (2007) 'Putting a social-constructivist assessment process model into practice: building the feedback loop into the assessment process through peer review', *Innovations in Education and Teaching International*, 44(2): 143–52.

Streeting, W. and Wise, G. (2009) *Rethinking the Values of Higher Education: Consumption, Partnership, Community?* Available at: http://www.qaa.ac.uk/Publications/InformationAndGuidance/Documents/Rethinking.pdf (accessed 30 July 2011).

Zimbardo, P. (2010) *The Secret Powers of Time*. Available at: http://www.youtube.com/watch?v=A3oIiH7BLmg (accessed 15 March 2011).

CRITICAL FRIEND COMMENTARY

Margaret Price

One certainty in the current turmoil within higher education is that raising student fees will drive up student expectations of experience, satisfaction and pay-off. Institutions are looking afresh at clarifying, managing and meeting those expectations. The work undertaken by the NUS is a good place to start as they were raising the student voice and debating issues of assessment and feedback long before the spectre of increased tuition fees. There is much to agree with in their conclusions but there are some factors that come into play in the complexity of the assessment that cannot be ignored in its practice.

Consumer or co-producer? This is the key question. While it is encouraging to see that the majority of students are at the co-producer end of the spectrum (Figure 1.2), the data also shows that the largest group of respondents locate themselves in the middle. Does this mean that they are unsure of their role and agency in the learning process? Before we unquestioningly move to meet all student expectations, should we not stop and ask ourselves the question 'Is the customer always right?' For students to play the role of co-producer effectively, they need to have a good understanding of the learning process and be assessment-literate. Figure 1.1 illustrates well that students' assessment literacy is not well developed, considerable uncertainty about the role and nature of assessment being evident. I do not point this out to denigrate students; why should they have a sophisticated understanding of assessment (indeed, staff without the benefit of pedagogic training and effective staff development also lack understanding of assessment)? For students to become effective co-producers, they need to be assessment-literate. It is the educators' responsibility to provide opportunities that deliberately develop assessment literacy within and beyond the formal curriculum.

Like other literacies (for example, language, academic, digital, information), assessment literacy takes time to learn and needs plenty of practice to achieve proficiency. In this chapter there is an emphasis on the role of induction in preparing students for study and developing know-how about assessment. Indeed, early introduction to assessment expectations is really important but not enough. Induction needs to be followed through with orientation and a programme-wide commitment to development that recognizes the importance of assessment literacy and supports the slowly learnt nature of some its attributes.

Assessment is a key driver of learning and needs to be pushed in the right direction. So students need to understand much more about the purposes, design and processes of assessment and feedback. Most importantly, they need to understand the role assessment can play in their learning. The more students understand the factors that come into play in assessment, the more staff and students can work together to make the assessment process work well. However, the issue of resourcing cannot be ignored. Choices have to be made about how and when to use resources. Students need to understand and participate in making those choices. Would they really expect a choice of feedback methods if it meant less feedback overall? Perhaps, but they need to understand the trade-offs in assessment and feedback.

One such trade-off relates to anonymous marking. The use of anonymous marking certainly has its place in summative assessment but caution is needed. Anonymous marking means that it is much more difficult for feedback to be part of a learning dialogue between teacher and student. Perhaps this is appropriate for purely summative assessment, but, in practice, summative and formative work are often conflated. In these circumstances, the non-assessment-literate student (or staff member) cannot separate the two aspects and the summative aspect often over-shadows the formative one and the learning is lost.

Like assessment, feedback does not lend itself to simple blanket solutions because the context is of such importance. While rules may be designed to achieve compliance with beneficial initiatives they can also misdirect limited resources. So when the NUS calls for face-to-face feedback, I applaud and recognize its importance in the early stages of a programme, but prescribing the very first assessment is a step too far. Staff need to be allowed to make judgements about the needs and wishes of students in deciding when best to provide face-to-face feedback in anticipation of the greatest gain for learning.

What is very clear from this chapter is that students must be invited to fully participate in higher education institutions' communities, thereby fostering assessment literacy and enabling the co-producer role to be played out in practice.

Chapter 2

Trained for the high jump; asked to do the long jump

Does first year assessment promote retention?

Anthony Cook

Introduction

To benefit from any experience, an individual must be involved in it. In the context of higher education, this manifests itself as students attending academic and social activities associated with the course, actively engaging with the other participants and, of course, completing and submitting tasks designed to demonstrate the extent to which they have benefitted. A proportion of students, for a variety of reasons, do not engage with these educational processes and either underperform or, in extreme cases, drop out entirely. Those who leave do so because they believe it is the right thing for them to do at that time.

The loss of students from a course before completion is essentially an institutional problem. It results in a loss of income, a diminished reputation when institutional metrics are published and increased recruitment costs to replace lost students. Non-completion is a student's solution to their problems. Examination of institutional statistics in the United Kingdom shows that increased non-completion is associated with high proportions of students with poor entry qualifications and from under-represented groups (lower socio-economic classes, low participation neighbourhoods) (Higher Education Statistics Agency 2011). Widening participation and increasing non-completion rates are essentially, therefore, pulling in opposite directions. The extent to which this is seen as a problem rather depends on the political and funding environment. In the past, open enrolment (access to higher education to all who had graduated successfully from secondary education) in some continental European countries appeared as an extension of the right to education. The extent to which all students would be able to complete a programme of study was secondary to their right to attempt to do so. In the absence of selection, the supply of places, at least in year one, has to match or exceed demand.

Selection

In the UK, student selection has been the norm and the demand for places in higher education has always exceeded supply. Selection is based almost entirely on academic qualifications, although in recent years a lack of discrimination at the high end of the grade range of pre-entry qualifications has resulted in other criteria being employed. As the size of the higher education (HE) sector expanded and its associated costs increased, the necessities of controlling expenditure resulted in political questions being asked about value for money from a system which failed a proportion of its students (Public Accounts Committee 2008). Offering opportunities to a broader range of students was only seen as economically justified if those students subsequently succeeded. While we all obviously focus on withdrawal, it should be noted that the survival of students in the UK educational system is relatively high. Over 90 per cent of British students proceed to a second year of study in higher education (National Audit Office 2007). International comparisons are difficult because different countries measure different things and different admission policies inevitably result in different retention patterns. Nevertheless, the UK compares favourably with other developed countries in the proportion of its students that proceed to the second year of study.

The reasons for student non-completion

Many studies of the causes of student non-completion have concluded that it is a multi-factorial problem and that students do not complete their courses for a wide variety of reasons (Yorke 1999). It is, however, necessary to make generalizations for the purposes of discussion. Students leave early for two reasons. First, poor research or misleading information may have led them to apply for the wrong course in the wrong institution. Anecdotally one hears of students who left a marine biology course in a university in the English Midlands because it was not by the sea, or of those who had been led to believe that once qualified as a psychologist, a career in criminal profiling would await them. These are extreme examples of a general feeling that the course was not what they had expected, and rather than persist with something they did not want to do or could not lead to their final goal, they chose to leave. The extent to which this generalization is true is unknown but factors associated with disappointment are seen in the high frequency of responses in national surveys to questions like 'I chose the wrong course' (Yorke and Longden 2008). The second reason is more appropriate to this book. Some students cannot cope with the change which occurs between their prior experience and that in year one. The misalignment between prior experiences and year one is multidimensional and includes aspects of social as well as academic activities (Cook and Leckey 1998).

Yorke's work conducted in 1999 and then repeated a decade later in 2008 (Yorke 1999, 2008) shows that the factors associated with non-completion are many and their relationships complex. In general, factors associated with teaching methods, staff support, etc. are major contributors to early leaving. The extent to which poor assessment practices impact on student early leaving is problematic. Yorke and Longden (2008), in a UK-wide survey of students who had not completed their first year, included questions about their assessment experience. In a ranking of popularity these questions were ranked 15th (the quality of feedback) and 25th (the speed of feedback) as contributors to a decision to leave. It should be noted, however, that 'The way the course was taught did not suit me' may also relate to assessment and this was ranked 2nd. Australian research reported by Kift and Moody (2009: 1) argues that 'intentional first year curriculum design has a critical role to play in enhancing first year student engagement, success and retention'. A fundamental component of the first year curriculum design is a transitional approach to student assessment. This approach is designed to wean new students from teacher-dependent teaching and assessment styles to independent learning and research-based assessments. In a qualitative study of student interviews in the UK, Luan (2010) identified student involvement in Higher Education (HE) and being able to identify and solve problems, such as assessment, as key characteristics of persisting students. The reasons for early leaving therefore are associated with poor decision-making prior to entry, and the teaching, learning and assessment environment at university not meeting students' expectations or needs. Other factors will be significant for some students but in general the critical factors are as outlined above.

Information

Given that one of the persistent reasons for early leaving is students claiming to have joined an inappropriate course or not liking the teaching methods, it is perhaps surprising that greater encouragement has not been given to students to research courses more thoroughly. Universities could also publicize their courses more comprehensively and promote a greater level of public awareness of what a university education is like. This is especially true when the higher non-completion rates are seen in universities with a widening participation agenda, and which are recruiting many students whose parents are less likely to have gone to university themselves and who will therefore have minimal familial knowledge of tertiary education (Gorard et al. 2006). It has been shown that students' expectations of university are largely derived through inertia from their secondary school experience (Cook and Leckey 1998). They expect university to be much like school and their greatest unresolved fear is the prospect of having to work independently. Students tend to stop researching courses once they have been awarded a place. Thus their research is conducted to discriminate between courses and to inform choices rather than to find out more about the eventual choice made. Further, the information used is predominantly that supplied by the institutions themselves as part of their marketing effort (Higher Education Funding Council for England 1999). Where continued contact (for example, through newsletters or mentors) has been maintained after acceptance, it has been shown to be effective in better preparing students for their course (McKillop and Walker 2006; Bennett 2009; Slee et al. 2009).

In other jurisdictions, considerable research effort has been put into identifying aspects of the transition between secondary and tertiary education. Thus, in the Australian context, Pargetter, McInnis, James, Evans, Peel and Dobson (1998) identify a range of factors of which a student may be unaware on entry. These include: a lack of immediate goals on entry compared with the focus placed on gaining the entry qualifications; a lack of understanding of the different standards expected of work at the two levels; the inaccurate understanding of university education and of course content developed in the final years of school; the comparative lack of clarity and transparency in university assessment objectives; and a lack of appreciation of the support structures possible in a large institution compared to the relatively small institutions from which they have come.

Although not derived from UK research, many of these factors will have resonance with UK academic staff. It may be possible for prospective students to learn about these and other differences prior to entry provided they know that they might present potential problems. It may also be possible for academic staff to address these issues during induction but this also assumes that academic staff are also well versed in potential issues of student transition. It is perhaps more practical to design a transitional pedagogy which starts utilizing the skills and expectations of new students as they actually are, but which rapidly changes to develop and exploit research skills, independence, collaborative learning and the more adventurous expectations of the later years of the university experience.

Incongruence

The mismatch between prior qualifications and the first year university experience is often cited as a cause of non-continuance (Cook 2009). In some cases, the mismatch is based on subject choice, for example, those cited by Yorke and Longden (2008), or may refer to the ways in which the curriculum is delivered and assessed (Cook 2005).

Misalignment between the content of prior qualifications in the UK and first year degree programmes is inevitable, given the diversity of degrees offered and a minimum entry qualification of two subjects at GCE A level (General Certificate of Education, Advanced level). Some programmes specify merely the number of UCAS (University and College Application System) tariff points required rather than the subjects studied. These degree programmes assume no detailed prior knowledge but only a range of study and intellectual skills. In practice, it is often only languages and the science and engineering subjects which specify particular subject-based qualifications for entry. Only about 30 per cent of university applicants have taken any form of science and this restricts the numbers of potential science undergraduates. Thus the restricted requirements for university entry and the early subject choices made by potential students have given rise to concerns related to the development of science-based industries in the UK (Royal Society 2011).

The GCE A level is a national standard of achievement at the end of secondary education. There are many individual subjects within this examining system, of which students normally take three. A minimum of two is normally required for university entrance. There is no maximum number, although five would be unusual. GCE is held in high esteem by the general public, students and teachers (Smith *et al.* 2006) and other end-of-secondary qualifications are measured by reference to it as exemplified by the construction of the University and College Admission Scheme tariff points system (UCAS 2011). The qualification currently has a diversity of uses including university entrance, vocational training and a performance indicator for the quality of secondary education.

GCE is the final step in testing associated with the National Curriculum in the UK. Prior to the introduction of the National Curriculum in 1989, school and university teachers could find common cause in the pursuit of curriculum development and teaching. After this date, however, the school and university agendas started to diverge. Developments at secondary level have been driven by the statutory assessment instruments associated with the National Curriculum and the perception of competition between schools occasioned by published league tables (Knights 2004). The university sector, on the other hand, became driven by the needs of the Research Assessment Exercise (RAE) and the expansion of student numbers without commensurate increases in resources. Political control of the secondary sector remained under a department of education in various guises while that of the university sector passed to a department of business, again under various names. Divergence between the sectors therefore can be seen in the forces which drive their development and, as a consequence, in what they have had to do to meet their targets and measures.

Student performance in the GCE is a measure of school performance as well as a qualification in its own right. Schools can select which subject their students will take under which examining board. There is therefore competition between examining boards for candidates. Market forces would dictate that schools select that examination board which is likely to give the best results, in terms of grades, for their pupils. This may not favour those attributes best suited to success at university. It is worth asking therefore whether the assessment instruments used at GCE and the teaching methods associated with maximizing student performance in that qualification represent an appropriate preparation for university.

Comparison of the published curricula for the secondary and tertiary sectors shows a number of fundamental differences. First, the secondary curriculum defines the maximum assessment requirements. Details of the assessment schemes are highly specified and the syllabi are illustrated with extensive teachers' notes. Examination questions and associated mark schemes are published each year. Comparison of the mark schemes with the published materials shows that the expected answers rarely stray beyond the information provided by the examining board (Cook 2005). As a consequence, there is little need for students to learn anything other than that which is published by the examining board. Indeed, to do so would be a waste of time as far as the examination performance is concerned. As Torrance, Colley, Garratt, Jarvis and Piper (2005) have observed, the detailed specification of assessment criteria has resulted in an increased instrumentalism in which the achievement of individual outcomes has become a substitute for holistic, deep learning. Tertiary curricula, on the other hand, are expressed as programme specifications, the framework for which is outlined by the Quality Assessment Agency (QAA). They are statements of what all successful students will have achieved (QAA 2006). By implication, therefore, they represent the minimum assessable curriculum. Knowledge and skills acquired beyond this minimum will often gain credit as a result of the judgement of individual academic staff. The difference is essentially that between a high jump in which success is merely clearing the bar and a long jump in which success is determined by jumping as far as one can. The secondary high jump attitude can carry over to the early years of university. Luan (2010: 90), in a study of what success means to students, recorded the following comment from a year 1 student:

> I am not too worried about getting the top grade as long as I can get into the second year ... Well, I analyzed the criteria for the marking – the marking criteria. And based on what grades I wanted, I put that much effort in.

This is a product of criterion-referenced assessment in which knowledge of the criteria serves to limit student effort. Although HE assessments are also criterion referenced, the achievement of the highest 'grade' is typically at a relatively low mark (70 per cent), leaving plenty of room 'above the bar' for high achieving students. Second, in the secondary system, the teacher is rarely the assessor except in small elements of coursework, in which case their judgements are closely monitored. The teacher therefore is free to work closely with the students to prepare them for the assessment. Indeed, the trend has become for the curriculum to be completely controlled by the teacher. Cook (2005: 113) quotes one teacher: 'Teachers ensure at all times that pupils remain "on message". All pupils submit at least two drafts. Some enter their coursework project in January and re-submit it in June to secure an improved mark.'

It may also be significant that students from public schools in the UK do less well at university than would be predicted on the basis of their GCE grades (HEFCE 2003). This is interpreted as indicating the effect of coaching and the experience of specialized teachers in preparing students for particular examinations. This further emphasizes the different attributes required to be successful in the two systems. In the tertiary system the teacher sets and marks the assessment and this militates against a close liaison between teacher and students in the preparation for assessment.

Third, the balance between coursework and examination changes between secondary and tertiary systems, sometimes abruptly. At GCE, formal coursework is relatively rare except in some vocational qualifications. The emphasis is often on unseen examinations. These examinations are highly structured in most subjects and while the structure does not, of course, give the answer, it does imply the extent of the answer required. The necessity for extended writing is limited. This is changing with the introduction of more free response questions and the allocation of specific marks for the quality of English. Nevertheless, in science subjects at least, the structure of the question dictates the structure of the answer to an extent which rarely gives incentives for more expansive writing. The assessment schemes in university courses vary but would normally involve extensive coursework as well as examinations. Coursework may involve a broad variety of activities while examinations may be longer and less structured than any previously experienced. With modularization and the summative assessment of some modules immediately after Christmas in year one, first year students have to adjust from one system to the other in relatively few weeks.

These differences in teaching and assessment are reflected in the attitudes of teachers towards their role. In comparing responses of teachers in Higher Education with those in Further and Secondary sectors, Crabtree, Roberts and Tyler (2007: 342) cite the following:

> The role of the teacher [in secondary education] … 'is to understand the nature of the syllabus, to reach classes effectively using a variety of different teaching styles and to make sure students make progress'. In contrast, a university tutor replied to the same question by saying 'We are responsible for the student's learning experience. It's up to us to engender an interest in the subject and to ensure that students receive adequate direction about how to access information. It's our job to give them the opportunities even though we can't make them use these.'

As far as the promotion of initiative, independence and coherent writing are concerned, changes in newer versions of the pre-entry curricula are in the wrong direction from the university viewpoint. Thus, in reviewing curriculum 2000 (the latest iteration of the GCE), the Office for Standards in Education (Ofsted) reported that one unintended consequence of the changes was that the ways in which learning was often organized resulted in students following a teacher-determined programme and consequently students had little opportunity to express their own opinions (Ofsted 2003). Torrance *et al.* (2005) report that the avoidance of extended writing tasks sometimes motivates the choice of post-16 qualifications. As Cook (2005: 112) has succinctly put it, many new students have been educated in a 'teacher-dependent, risk-averse learning culture'.

The opinions of students

Surveys of student opinion are many and varied. The UK National Student Survey (NSS) is open to all graduating students and their opinion is sought on various aspects of their experience. Student opinions of assessment methods are almost universally poorer than of other aspects of provision (Williams and Kane 2008). Table 2.1 compares the top three with the bottom three universities in

Table 2.1 Comparison between universities at the extremes of the *Guardian* league
tables in terms of aspects of assessment in Biology drawn from the National
Student Survey

University	Overall satisfaction	Assessment criteria	Detailed comments	Prompt feedback
University A	90	80	69	80
University B	97	74	70	74
University C	94	69	69	69
University X	79	90	48	55
University Y	93	71	53	57
University Z	71	74	52	67

Source: *Guardian* (2011).

Key: Data refer to the percentage of students responding positively to the following
prompts:
Overall I am satisfied with the quality of my course
The criteria used in marking have been clear in advance
I have received detailed comments on my work
Feedback on my work has been prompt
Data derived from National Student Survey
University ranking derived from the *Guardian* league tables

the *Guardian* league tables (*Guardian* 2011) with respect to aspects of assessment. While there is a distinction between the top and bottom of the table, these
are not as stark as the position of these courses at the extremes of a league table
might lead one to expect. Overall satisfaction far exceeds that normally accorded
to the various measures of assessment.

A lack of personal engagement and a lack of staff contact, both of which may
be related to assessment, figure in the top ten reasons given by students who have
left university early (Yorke and Longden 2008). In reporting the free responses
of students who had left university, these authors report none related directly to
assessment and the disparity between secondary and tertiary experience comes
over as related to the relationship between staff and the student concerned, for
example: 'My personal tutor was intimidating, uncaring and cold. I felt that that
sort of experience for the next three years was not worth the debt I would face
when I left' (ibid.: 27). And to the teaching styles: 'I felt quite isolated in terms
of studying. Lecturers spoke during lectures and then would leave the room with
no time for questions' (ibid.: 26).

Conducting interviews with students who have left appears to extract different
information to that gained by open-ended questions in questionnaires. In contrasting the views of staff with those of students, Young, Glogowska and Lockyer
(2007) report that students were more likely to identify aspects of the course as
reasons for early leaving than were the staff. Just under half of the students
interviewed identified the 'leap' from pre-degree to degree work as a significant
contributor to their leaving, while about one-third mentioned an aspect of

assessment such as a lack of clear guidance and/or inadequate feedback. Students appear not to mention poor choices or courses not meeting their expectations unless prompted (ibid.) and prefer to focus on aspects of poor course provision. In contrast, staff identify student deficits as causes of non-completion.

In a study of why students persist in their course Luan (2010: 159) concluded that students continue on their course because they are achieving some personal goals. The most commonly cited academic achievement relating to persistence was 'passing assessment and grades'. Thus, externally validated success is an important motivation in persistence. Equally, a poor assessment experience, particularly associated with the feedback received in year one can hinder the progress of even good students and influence views on the usefulness of feedback received, and impact on academic engagement and approaches to learning (Potter and Lynch 2008).

Conclusion

The secondary and tertiary sectors in the UK have different political masters and different objectives and targets. This has resulted over the past 30 years in a divergence in aims and teaching and assessment methods which is getting wider and does not serve the needs of those students who have to traverse the gap between them. The best students will always cope with the difference. Indeed, many will thrive because of the difference (Lowe and Cook 2003). Some, however, will falter and either fail to proceed or leave early.

As Young et al. (2007) point out, if policy direction is determined largely by staff opinion and attitudes, then it is inevitable that solutions to the student non-completion problem will be focused on remedies which attempt to make students better rather than those which modify the course and its assessment regimes to better suit the needs and talents of incoming students. Viewed cynically, most students new to HE have spent the previous 13 years being indoctrinated in educational systems designed to meet targets and improve institutional positions in league tables. To expect to change student behaviour in the first few months of their first year at a time when they are having to adjust to a range of other changes in their lives is unrealistic. Equally, for teaching staff to continue to do the same things and expect different outcomes is foolish. Change is inevitable and since the secondary assessment system has shown itself to be remarkably popular and resistant to change, it will have to be the university sector which initiates that change.

Change will have to be of two types. Torrance et al. (2005: 2) have recognized an important trend in assessment:

> We have identified a move from what we characterize as assessment *of* learning, through the currently popular idea of assessment *for* learning, to *assessment as learning*, where assessment procedures and practices may come

completely to dominate the learning experience, and 'criteria compliance' comes to replace 'learning'.

Criteria compliance is the inevitable consequence of increased transparency of criteria and using student assessment as a measure of institutional performance. The first change therefore will need to be to resist a trend towards assessment as learning. While this may be a valid element in a balanced assessment strategy, its dominance needs to be questioned.

The second change will have to be for universities to modify their assessment regimes to more closely match those to which new students have become accustomed. University staff then have to take responsibility for the transition to university-style assessments. It does not matter what procedures have to be used in year one to introduce new students to new ways of working, provided that at the end of the qualification standards have been maintained and graduate qualities have been achieved.

One of Crabtree *et al.*'s (2007: 343) higher education interviewees put it thus: 'I want people to give me answers that aren't simply from my handouts and lecture notes.' This aspiration will not be widely met without a conscious change in the ways in which students are prepared for assessment.

References

Bennett, D. (2009) 'Student mentoring prior to entry: getting accurate messages across', in A. Cook and B. S. Rushton (eds) *How to Recruit and Retain Higher Education Students: A Handbook of Good Practice*, New York: Routledge.

Cook, A. (2005) 'Responding to changes in pre-entry qualifications', paper presented at Science Learning and Teaching Conference, 2005.

——(2009) 'The roots of attrition', in A. Cook and B. S. Rushton (eds) *How to Recruit and Retain Higher Education Students: A Handbook of Good Practice*, New York: Routledge.

Cook, A. and Leckey, J. F. (1998) 'Do expectations meet reality? A survey of changes in first year student opinion', *The Journal of Further and Higher Education*, 23: 157–71.

Crabtree, H., Roberts, C. and Tyler, C. (2007) *Understanding the Problems of Transition into Higher Education*, in *Proceedings of the 4th Education in a Changing Environment Conference*. Available at: http://www.ece.salford.ac.uk/proceedings/papers/35_07.pdf (accessed 17 February 2011).

Gorard, S., Smith, E., May, H., Thomas, L., Adnett, N. and Slack, K. (2006) *Review of Widening Participation Research: Addressing the Barriers to Participation in Higher Education*, York: Higher Education Academy.

Guardian (2011) *School League Tables*. Available at: http://www.guardian.co.uk/education/interactive/2011/jan/12/gcse-alevel-league-tables (accessed 16 February 2011).

Higher Education Funding Council for England (1999) *Providing Public Information on the Quality and Standards of Higher Education Courses*. Available at: http://www.hefce.ac.uk/pubs/hefce/1999/99_61.rtf (accessed 24 February 2011).

——(2003) *Schooling Effects on Higher Education Achievement.* Available at: http://www.hefce.ac.uk/pubs/hefce/2003/03_32.htm (accessed 22 February 2011).

Higher Education Statistics Agency (2011) *Performance Indicators in Higher Education in the UK (2008/9).* Available at: http://www.hesa.ac.uk/ (accessed 22 February 2011).

Kift, S. M. and Moody, K. E. (2009) 'Harnessing assessment and feedback in the first year to support learning success, engagement and retention', in *ATN Assessment Conference 2009 Proceedings, 19–20 November 2009,* RMIT University, Melbourne.

Knights, B. (2004) 'Building bridges: traversing the secondary tertiary divide', *English Subject Centre Newsletter,* Issue 6, York: Higher Education Academy.

Lowe, H. and Cook, A. (2003) 'Mind the gap: are students prepared for higher education?', *The Journal of Further and Higher Education,* 27: 54–76.

Luan, Y. (2010) 'Understanding first year undergraduate achievement in a post 1992 university science department', unpublished thesis, University of Wolverhampton.

McKillop, A. and Walker, A. (2006) 'Surestart: developing contacts with applicants to an e-learning course', in K. A. Macintosh, A. Cook and B. S. Rushton (eds) *Informing Students: Quality Information,* Coleraine, Northern Ireland: University of Ulster, pp. 77–86.

National Audit Office (2007) *Staying the Course: The Retention of Students in Higher Education,* London: National Audit Office.

Office for Standards in Education (2003) *Curriculum 2000: Implementation,* London: HMI.

Pargetter, R., McInnis, C., James, R., Evans, M., Peel, M. and Dobson, I (1998) *Transition from Secondary to Tertiary: A Performance Study.* Available at: http://www.dest.gov.au/archive/highered/eippubs/eip98-20/contents.htm (accessed 15 February 2011).

Potter, A. and Lynch, K. (2008) Quality feedback on assessment: apple for the teacher? How first year student perceptions of assessment feedback affect their engagement with study, in *Proceedings, 11th Pacific Rim First Year in Higher Education Conference, Hobart, 30th June–2nd July 2008.* Available at: http://www.fyhe.com.au/past_papers/papers08/FYHE2008/content/pdfs/3e.pdf (accessed 16 February 2011).

Public Accounts Committee (2008) *Staying the Course: The Retention of Students on Higher Education Courses.* Available at: http://www.publications.parliament.uk/pa/cm200708/cmselect/cmpubacc/322/322.pdf (accessed 22 February 2011).

Quality Assurance Agency (2006) *Guidelines for Preparing Programme Specifications,* Gloucester: Quality Assurance Agency.

Royal Society (2011) *Preparing for the Transfer from School and College Science and Mathematics Education to UK STEM Higher Education,* London: Royal Society.

Slee, P., Watts, C. and Thomas, M. (2009) '"I'll be there for you": the impact of Northumbria "Friends" on recruitment and retention', in A. Cook and B. S. Rushton (eds) *How to Recruit and Retain Higher Education Students: A Handbook of Good Practice,* New York: Routledge.

Smith, K., Varnai, A. and Clark, S. (2006) *GCSEs and A Level: The Experiences of Teachers, Students, Parents and the General Public,* London: QCA. Available at: http://www.ipsos-mori.com/Assets/Docs/Archive/Polls/qca2.pdf (accessed 16 February 2011).

Torrance, H., Colley, H., Garratt, D., Jarvis, J. and Piper, H. (2005) *The Impact of Different Modes of Assessment on Achievement and Progress in the Learning and Skills Sector*, Learning and Skills Development Agency. Available at: http://www.itslifejimbutnotasweknowit.org.uk/files/AssessmentModesImpact.pdf (accessed 17 February 2011).

University and College Application System (2011) *UCAS Tariff.* Available at: http://www.ucas.com/students/ucas_tariff/ (accessed 22 February 2011).

Yorke, M. (1999) *Leaving Early: Undergraduate Non-completion in Higher Education*, London: Falmer Press.

Yorke, M. and Longden, B. (2008) *The First Year Experience of Higher Education in the UK*, York: Higher Education Academy.

Young, P., Glogowska, M. and Lockyer, L. (2007) 'Conceptions of early leaving: a comparison of the views of teaching staff and students', *Active Learning in Higher Education*, 8: 275–87.

Williams, J. and Kane, D. (2008) *Exploring the National Student Survey: Assessment and Feedback Issues*, York: Higher Education Academy.

CRITICAL FRIEND COMMENTARY

Mark Davies

Without doubt, retention in higher education has become a global issue, one that even our most prestigious institutions have to tackle. This chapter makes strong, convincing and perhaps relentless links between retention and assessment. The chapter takes a balanced view of the available literature, which is not in great supply, and insightfully covers all the main articulation points. I found the work accessible and a useful summary of the current position. Essentially, this chapter is a clarion call for work to overcome the issues identified, which are not trivial. Non-completion is a complex problem and so the solutions will not be simple but will be difficult to achieve. Research has told us that solutions will likely be context-specific and only transferable to a limited extent. But they will be worth it, at least in a financial sense, given the considerable loss to any university of a single student dropping out. That each loss might be a personal tragedy is a motivating factor in working in this area, but universities may well be more persuaded by the financial argument.

Assessment has to serve many purposes and is pulled in many directions, and yet, in general, the literature dealing with definitions of assessments is out of alignment and consists of fragmented discourses. In part, this lack of consistency, at a global level, has its roots in a single discontinuity: those working on and in the compulsory sector and those working on and in higher education. It may be that the consequent differential development of theoretical frameworks of assessment has driven and/or widened the practice gap between schools and universities. This chapter relates to this notion square-on. The athletics analogy not only applies as Cook states, but also in that school assessment tends to be bite-sized, well specified, and immediately completed, while university assessment operates in the longer term, with goals that might be more vague, or at least communicated in that way. A separation of political masters cannot be good.

Cook rightly points out that unexpected and/or unmanageable change is the key to the issues identified and that the causal link to assessment has not been well made. Indeed, it would be difficult to establish such causality, not least because students might be unwilling to indicate that they dropped out because of problems with assessment – it marks them as a failure in a system that they have succeeded in for so long. Does this lack of causality mean that we should abandon thoughts of tinkering or changing the system? Absolutely not! Students have been coming into higher education for many years from an 'assessment culture', or as Cook reminds us, 'assessment as learning'. Assessment is in their bones and there is no doubt that the high jump/long jump discontinuity exists and it is at that interface that attention should focus.

A focus could be on information and Cook notes that it is 'surprising' that greater encouragement has not been given to prospective students to research more about their potential courses and universities. However, this assumes that the information provided is accurate, complete and honest, which is not always the case, and that students can be influenced in this way. That they are relatively young and newly-independent may factor in. They may be keen to assert their independence and so only learn through experience; but that is cold comfort for the student who has dropped out. Schools could have a role here, but they would need an incentive. Cook points to evidence that establishing dialogue between universities and their potential students increases students' preparedness for university so that their expectations and reality are more closely matched. Topics related to assessment could be included in the discourse. But again the direct link to retention is unclear. What is clear is that the students are happier for the contact. It might be that such inclusivity through contact and dialogue is the key and the information transmitted back and forth is largely irrelevant.

A better focus may be on weaning and that could be in the form of Cook's 'transitional pedagogy', which he locates in the universities. But given that most students studying A levels in the UK are aiming to enter higher education, could that pedagogy not be located in schools, where it might provide some understanding of higher education practice to schoolteachers? Could students be assessed as part of A levels in their preparedness for life at university? I use 'assessed' because then students and staff would give it the attention it deserves. Nevertheless, the arguments for locating the weaning in universities are strong, and although that might involve considerable costs associated with staff development, they would be pump-priming and subsequently reduced. Assessment is a difficult subject with complex drivers and goals but surely there is room for a 'conscious change' in the ways students are prepared for assessment in order to aid retention. Is there not a moral imperative?

Chapter 3

Exploring new students' conceptions of engagement and feedback

Ed Foster, Jane McNeil and Sarah Lawther

Introduction

If assessment is the 'engine that drives learning', as Phil Race (2006: 74) wrote, then 'feedback is the oil that lubricates the cogs of understanding'. Both aspects of this epigram can be seen in numerous studies and in the daily experience of lecturers. It seems clear that assessment can hold students' attention and help them focus on their studies (Solomonides and Swannell 1996; Gibbs and Simpson 2004). Allied to this, feedback appears to play a crucial role in helping students to reflect on the work they have done and to learn from the experience of doing so (Sadler 1989; Black and Wiliam 1998; Juwah *et al.* 2004).

This chapter will focus primarily on the role of feedback in helping students to engage with learning at university. However, it must be acknowledged that giving, receiving and using feedback are fraught with difficulties. There are reports of mismatched perceptions of the process and purpose of feedback (see, for example, MacLellan 2001; Carless 2006; Crisp 2007). There appear to be contrasting practitioner and student experiences of feedback, highlighted year after year in National Student Survey findings. There is also evidence that the feedback process can be stressful for staff (Stough and Emmer 1998; Hartney 2007) and bewildering to students (Bailey 2009). The latter is particularly the case for first year students, whose prior experience of feedback is very different to that encountered in higher education. This chapter will, therefore, pay particular attention to the experience of first year students as they strive to make the transition from learning in post-16 education to university.

Completing assessments = student engagement?

Students engage with assessment. They sit examinations; they plan coursework, submit it and receive feedback about it. They have to engage with multiple assessment points to complete each level of study, and in the United Kingdom over 90 per cent of students do progress from the first to the second year (National Audit Office 2007). Clearly, these students are engaging in some way with the assessment and feedback process. However, for many students, the extent to which this constitutes *meaningful* engagement with their studies is debatable. As Hand and Bryson (2008) ask, are they engaged, or merely busy?

Many writers have tried to define what constitutes meaningful student engagement. Kuh, Cruce, Shoup, Kinzie and Gonyea (2008: 555) describe it as 'the quality of effort students themselves devote to educationally purposeful activities that contribute directly to desired outcomes'. Hand and Bryson (2008: 9) characterize it as a continuum of effort, finding in their interviews with students a range of reported effort, from highly engaged to more perfunctory attitudes to assessment. They describe *'false engagement'*, where students adopt an instrumental approach, seeking only to maximize their grades, and *'disengagement'*, where students undertake the minimum of work they judge will allow them to pass the assessment. This seems not unlike the *strategic* and *surface* tactics described in the large body of work on approaches to study, which has made a strong case for an association between conceptions of learning, approaches to study and achievement in assessment (see, for example, Prosser and Trigwell 1999; Ramsden 2003). Another view of engagement is Adam's model (1979, cited in Willis 1993). This categorizes *'accountable performance'* (the completion of assessed coursework) as the lowest and least sophisticated of four types of engagement. Finally, Mann (2001) suggests that when students perceive assignments as outputs to be produced, they are more likely to be alienated than engaged. If students do perceive assignments as finished products, they may see little benefit in reading tutor feedback.

It appears, therefore, that students can engage with assessment and not be meaningfully engaged with their studies or subject. McInnis (2005) argues that engagement is more than simply the completion of assessment tasks, but is a broader concept in which students also understand and adopt the institution's values and approaches to study. The process by which this happens is complex; Bryson, Cooper and Hardy (2010: 2) situate it in socially constructed ideas and expectations about, and the experience of, becoming a university student, arguing that: 'Engagement is both a pre-requisite for learning to occur and a binding agent that allows learning to keep occurring.' Assessment can, therefore, focus students' minds, but does not necessarily engender student engagement.

The first year

The first year at university is very influential in shaping students' engagement throughout the rest of their studies. Their early encounters with assessment and feedback are central in this. Students encounter a very different environment at university to the one they experienced in the final year of post-16 education. They are also expected to *engage* in higher education in a different way to their prior studies. For example, Thomson (2008) cites a study with history students conducted while they were studying for their school Advanced Level qualifications and later at university. During A level study, the students had believed they were developing independent learning skills but when reflecting on this experience at university, they changed their view to one of having been largely 'spoon fed'. In another study, Foster and Brittain (2010) interviewed university lecturers who had shadowed students in a further education college and a sixth form college. The lecturers were surprised by a number of key differences, particularly about what they considered the high level of guidance students were offered to develop a 'correct' answer.

The lecturers in the Foster and Brittain study had expected to see evidence of more preparation at college for the independent learning required at university. Considered as the stage between secondary and higher education, post-16 education has an important role in this. However, a National Audit Office report (2002: 21) indicated that university staff believe post-16 education is 'increasingly becoming a continuation of pre-16 education', rather than preparation for higher education. If this is the case, then one response is to design the first year of university study to help students develop the skills and approaches needed for higher level learning. This transitional approach itself is sometimes perceived as 'spoon-feeding'. For example, Thomson (2008) reported that some academics felt frustrated at the prospect of having to provide what they perceived as remedial support to new students. However, if we accept that all students are, as Leask (2006: 187) describes them, '"cultural others" seeking acceptance into the academic cultural community', then the transitional approach is only making explicit what would otherwise be the implicit 'rules' about studying in higher education.

Feedback

Feedback plays a central role in helping students develop their approaches to university study. Or, at least, it should. Straightforward models of feedback have a beguiling appeal for the educator: the student is advised by the expert about their progress and modifies their approach accordingly. Ideas such as Argyris and Schön's (1974) single and double loop learning, and Kolb's (1984) experiential learning cycle are widely taught to new lecturers and, inasmuch as any idea can be, they feel inherently 'right'. However, context is all. For example, the authors of this chapter received formative feedback at several stages of the writing, which, in turn, led us to reflect, discuss and develop the argument. This process maps well to either feedback model cited above. So far, so good, but we are familiar with this process and the expectations for reviewer and writer; we also have an understanding of the subject, and could interpret and use the feedback accordingly. In this context, then, the conditions for learning from feedback are fulfilled: the student must understand what is expected of them, have a sense of the quality of their work, and be able to determine what they need to do to improve in subsequent work (Sadler 1989).

The context for many students new to higher education is that they have not yet developed the necessary approaches to effectively exploit feedback. For example, Jessen and Elander (2009) found that students in post-16 education overestimated how prepared they were for writing in higher education. Although the writing tasks in higher education looked ostensibly similar, there were some profound differences of approach and methodology that the students in post-16 education simply did not yet appreciate. This is problematic if a first year student does not receive feedback about the standard of their work until their second term at university.

Furthermore, there are differences between the two education sectors in the actual process of giving and receiving feedback. While formative feedback is widely used in both, students receive it at different points in relation to developing their work. Sadler (1989) argues that the difference between formative and summative feedback is not timing, but intent. Formative feedback provides students with guidance about ways to improve their work; summative informs them about how well they have achieved the required standard. Crucially, Yorke (2003: 117) argues that formative feedback is different because it is *'dialogic'*. However, this chapter suggests that *timing* is a very important distinction between the feedback practices in post-16 and higher education, and that a dialogue through formative feedback is much harder to achieve at university. Students in post-16 education appear to receive far more formative feedback *during* the production of a piece of work; in higher education, formative feedback is more normally provided *after* the coursework has been submitted along with the grade achieved. Gibbs and Dunbar-Goddet (2009) studied three universities and found that formative assessment was only widely offered during the assessment writing process at an Oxbridge university. In both the pre- and post-1992 universities sampled, formative feedback was more normally provided after the assessment was completed. Moreover, Gibbs and Simpson (2004) argue that, due to the massification of higher education, the use of formative feedback is declining across the sector.

The practice of giving feedback only after the work is complete means that it can only be dialogic if the student possesses the skills and motivation to apply it to the next piece of work. It also contrasts sharply with the widespread post-16 practice of feedback *during* the assignment. This would not matter if the differences were widely recognized. However, Weaver (2006) found that three-quarters of students had received no advice about how to use feedback prior to entering higher education. If students are to use feedback to help them learn, either the feedback model needs to be adapted, or the students need preparation in learning how to engage with it. Interestingly, Stephani (1998) found that many higher education staff assumed students already possessed the skills to use feedback upon arrival at university.

Students working with feedback

It is worth pausing here to consider the sort of strategies adopted by lecturers in trying to help students use feedback. Two of the authors engaged in an action research project in which a range of learning and teaching activities were developed, with the aim of helping first year students use feedback to improve their academic writing. They worked with a humanities programme with an established practice of supporting the transition of new students into higher education. The programme team had previously organized activities, such as essay planning exercises, student discussion and peer assessment of exemplar essays. It was agreed that the authors would develop a more comprehensive set of activities around a diagnostic essay submitted in the fourth week of the first term. This essay had previously been marked and feedback provided to the students within three weeks, in time to help them with their first formally assessed piece of writing. The programme team felt that, while the diagnostic assignment was valuable, students were not fully exploiting the opportunity it provided. In particular, students did not appear to be learning from feedback and were repeating the same mistakes in their first formal essay.

As students received the developmental feedback directly in their week seven seminars, it was agreed that the core of the activity would take place in the classroom. First, immediately after reading their feedback and mark, all students were invited to report their emotional response. They were presented with a grid of 40 words describing emotional states and asked to choose ten that most closely reflected their feelings upon receiving feedback. The words chosen were categorized by the project team as positive or negative, and passive or active. For example, words such as 'satisfied' and 'pleased' were felt to be positive-passive whereas words such as 'inspired' and 'enthusiastic' were positive-active. While this was in no way a precise measure, the team wanted to understand if emotional response to feedback influenced students' use of it.

After this initial activity was completed, different exercises were used in addition to the discussion of feedback that always took place in these seminars. In one group, students re-wrote the feedback comments in their own words and were given a resource with common feedback terms and links to further writing resources. In another, they also wrote an action plan based on the feedback, using a template. In a third, they re-wrote the feedback and made an action plan, discussing difficult terms with the tutor.

Following this, further activities were undertaken by the project team. The extent to which a common understanding of feedback was apparent in the tutor and student comments was assessed, and the language of the tutor comments was also explored. It was found that, on the whole, students' interpretations of tutor comments were quite accurate. Further, while lacking detail, the students' action plans looked plausible, containing commitments to wider research, more focus on the question, and a better use of evidence. These students appeared to know, broadly, what was needed to improve their writing. It was noted that, in re-writing tutor feedback, students largely ignored the positive comments, focusing instead on suggestions for improvement. Students also made value judgments where tutors had perhaps not intended them. For example, one student reported that 'interesting' meant 'not as good as good'.

An interesting finding was about students' reported emotional response to the feedback. Of the ten most commonly cited words, two were words the team considered to be positive-active, namely 'motivated' and 'optimistic', but the other eight were all positive-passive. The most popular word used was 'relieved'. This collective sigh of relief was not borne out for all in the next assignment, where the marks were worse for almost as many students as for those whose marks improved. The diagnostic assessment may not have prepared these students well.

Only those students with lower marks in the assessment reported any negative emotional responses. It appeared that the dividing line was at 53 per cent; no students achieving above this score reported any negative emotional responses. However, even when students used negative language, these were judged by the project team to be primarily passive in nature, 'disappointed' being the most common example.

Later, the 43 students who had made action plans were invited to report how they had used the feedback in subsequent assignments. Only four responded and of these only two had reviewed the feedback in preparation for the next assignment.

At the end of the year, students' grades in subsequent essay assignments were noted. No clear pattern emerged from the week seven classroom activities and resources. The classroom activities had apparently failed to make any impact on subsequent student performance. With hindsight, this might have been predicted; the intervention was very small in scope and restricted to one seminar in one module. The project team shared the findings with the programme team, but was able to offer little practical advice other than encouraging colleagues to be mindful of language and tone in feedback. However, the team remained puzzled by the fact that, although the students had apparently understood the feedback and some had made reasonable plans to develop their work, there was no apparent influence on subsequent performance. This apparent paradox contributed to a developing research interest in the students' experience of the transition between post-16 education and the first year at university.

The team devised a study to explore students' prior experiences of learning and their expectations about learning at university (Foster et al. 2010). In 2007, 100 undergraduates were interviewed during Welcome Week, the first week at university (Foster et al. 2008), which was followed by focus groups later in the year. A second round of 100 interviews was conducted at the start of the following academic year and questions have been used in the Welcome Week survey in subsequent years. Many aspects of studying were explored, including students' prior experience of feedback and expectations about feedback at university.

The early interviews suggested that feedback in post-16 education was primarily formative in nature, intended to improve the piece of work at hand. Many students explained that they could submit work more than once and many were expected to do so by their tutors: 'Every week you would show him what you had done so far and tell him what you wanted to do and he would set targets – every week for a whole year.' The qualitative responses that we received from some students revealed that this feedback could be substantial: 'We had to hand in 3 drafts for comment … sometimes the first draft was totally off so it was valuable.' It could also be highly directive; for example, students were told to 'add this in' or 'read this chapter', so there was a clear and immediate benefit to reading and responding to feedback. The subsequent focus groups indicated that some students were expecting this kind of feedback in higher education; for example, 'I wanted my tutorial leader to just correct and look at what I write; to write it down completely … and tell me the proper way to say things.'

The second round of interviews used a modified question set to further explore the apparent differences in feedback practice. Again, it was found that the majority of students (all except two) were used to handing in drafts for feedback at least once. Although the majority of students could only hand in their work 'once' or 'twice', ten students stated that they were able to hand in coursework for formative feedback an unlimited number of times, a process prevalent among students who had previously studied in both further education and sixth form colleges. This suggested that, for almost all the UK students entering university, formative feedback while writing assignments appeared to be the norm.

When asked 'Did you use feedback to improve subsequent pieces of work?' 27 of the 100 respondents stated that they had no experience of applying feedback to subsequent coursework. In most instances, this was because they had received no feedback with their final grade. However, it was apparent that some students chose not to use feedback in this way, even when it was available. For example, one student reported that 'It was all done – I didn't want to go into it any more.'

Sixty-seven students (a further six students who self-completed the survey did not answer this question) stated that they *had* used feedback for future assignments. A number provided instances of how they had used feedback that suggested they had developed strategies that would be valuable at university; for example, 'you learn your strengths and weaknesses and how you can improve', or 'experience from previous work helped me do later pieces better'. Some students also stated that their tutors' feedback was designed to help them better meet the criteria set by external examiners. However, many student responses were ambiguous about whether they were describing the next assignment or the next iteration of their current assignment. For example, one student explained that they had used feedback 'to redo a spreadsheet', probably referring to the next version of the current assignment. Another explained how 'if there was an area that lacked information, that became my target area'. Again this implies that they were making changes in response to formative feedback while writing an assignment, not using the feedback to develop approaches to subsequent work. It may be that some of this ambiguity arises from practices in post-16 education where students are able to resubmit assignments. For example, 47 per cent of students told the researchers that, even after a final grade had been given, they were able to resubmit a new version of the coursework in an attempt to improve grades. It is not difficult, therefore, to see how students might be unclear about how and when they are expected to use feedback.

It appears that, for most new university students, feedback is primarily a tool that they have used during the process of writing an assignment. Most students do appear to have some experience of using feedback to develop their overall academic practice. However, it appears that this is a secondary use of feedback. This ought not be a problem as long as students understand that feedback in higher education is framed differently and that they are required to engage with it in a different manner. Students were asked what they thought would be different about learning at university. Most students recognized that they would not be 'spoon-fed' and that they would be required to engage in 'independent learning'. However, in the first interviews, only one student of the 100 recognized that they would not receive formative feedback while writing an assignment (Foster *et al.* 2008).

Recommendations

Students enter higher education with a fundamentally different understanding about the role of feedback in assessment to that of their tutors. They are experienced at using feedback within the assessment process, but far less so using feedback offered at the end. In our case study, it appeared that the students understood how to learn from feedback, but as Handley and Williams (2011) found, they failed to turn understanding into action. We suspect that this is often the response from students to limited classroom interventions. It is unrealistic to expect that a single class within a first year module will greatly influence students' engagement with feedback, assessment and their studies. Nicol (2009) argues that, all too often, formative feedback is ineffectively used on first year programmes. It is therefore important that feedback is integrated into the normal academic discourse and students are provided opportunities to engage with it frequently. Furthermore, Sadler (1989) argues that learning to learn from feedback is a gradual process requiring multiple activities over a sustained period of time. The recommendations below are based on both premises and are framed around Sadler's three conditions for effective learning from feedback.

Understanding what is expected

If students only receive feedback later in the first year, after their first assessments, they risk not understanding the expectations of their course until very late in the academic year. One strategy, then, is the systematic use of exemplars from very early in the first year. Exploring exemplars can also provide an alternative to the traditional lecture as a means to discuss 'subject content'. Handley and Williams (2011) advocate using annotated exemplars, providing students with examples of first year work and explanations of how tutors responded to it. Most importantly, students should have the opportunity to discuss and debate the exemplars, an activity that Solomonides and Martin (2008) argue raises student engagement.

Meeting the standard

Students should receive feedback about their writing before the end of the first term and before they submit their first assessment. For large cohorts, one pragmatic approach is to use shorter pieces of writing. Tutors ought to provide feedback on lecture notes, short essay questions, class tests and other pieces of in-class writing. As this process is resource-intensive, it may be more beneficial to mark a sample and provide regular feedback at the start of each lecture, or ask students to mark their own, or one another's work. This would also mean that writing for assessment becomes an open part of course activity, rather than separate and private.

Closing the gap between expected and actual performance

This may be the hardest task of all, as modular degree structures often do not encourage students to reflect between assignments and especially not across modules. Hand and Bryson (2008) argue that the process of discussing feedback and forthcoming assignments aids engagement because it is one of the few opportunities a student has to talk one-to-one with a tutor, but often it is only the more engaged students who seek out these opportunities. Students can be aided in planning and preparation by activities such as keeping reflective journals or portfolios. However, as these are often framed as additional or optional activities, students can struggle to engage with them. This may mean, in the first year, assessing the process of reflection and planning.

Assessment and feedback can help students to engage with the learning process; at the very least, providing a focal point for students' attention. However, engagement is not an automatic outcome of the process. Higher education institutions need to develop strategies for helping students understand the differences between feedback usage in post-16 and higher education. Institutions then need to provide increased opportunities for students to actively read, debate and use feedback. If both conditions are met, more students will have the opportunity to become engaged, autonomous learners rather than dissatisfied consumers of feedback.

References

Argyris, C. and Schön, D. (1974) *Theory in Practice: Increasing Professional Effectiveness*, San Francisco: Jossey-Bass.

Bailey, R. (2009) 'Undergraduate students' perceptions of the role and utility of written assessment feedback', *Journal of Learning Development in Higher Education*, 1.

Available at: http://www.aldinhe.ac.uk/ojs/index.php?journal=jldhe&page=issue& op=view&path[]=8 (accessed 22 May 2011).

Black, P. and Wiliam, D. (1998) 'Assessment and classroom learning', *Assessment in Education*, 5(1): 7–74.

Bryson, C., Cooper, G. and Hardy, C. (2010) 'Reaching a common understanding of the meaning of student engagement', paper presented at the Society of Research into Higher Education Conference, Celtic Manor, Wales, 14–16 December 2010.

Carless, D. (2006) 'Differing perceptions in the feedback process', *Studies in Higher Education*, 31(2): 219–33.

Crisp, B. R. (2007) 'Is it worth the effort? How feedback influences students' subsequent submission of assessable work', *Assessment & Evaluation in Higher Education*, 32(5): 571–81.

Foster, E., Bell, R. and Salzano, S. (2008) '"What's a journal?" Research into the prior learning experiences of students entering higher education', in *Proceedings of the European First Year Experience Conference*, University of Wolverhampton, 7–9 May 2008.

Foster, E. and Brittain, M. (2010) *Flying Start End of Project Report: Shadowing at NTU*. Available at: http://www.hope.ac.uk/collaborativeprojects/flyingstart/case-studies/flying-start-the-case-studies (accessed 12 March 2011).

Foster, E., Lawther, S. and McNeil, J. (2010) 'Learning developers supporting early student transition', in P. Hartley, J. Hilsdon, C. Keenan, S. Sinfield and M. Verity (eds) *Learning Development in Higher Education*, Basingstoke: Palgrave Macmillan, pp. 79–90.

Gibbs, G. and Dunbar-Goddet, H. (2009) 'Characterising programme-level assessments that support student learning', *Assessment & Evaluation in Higher Education*, 34(4): 481–9.

Gibbs, G. and Simpson, C. (2004) 'Conditions under which assessment supports students learning', *Learning and Teaching in Higher Education*, 1: 3–31.

Hand, L. and Bryson, C. (eds) (2008) *Student Engagement: SEDA Special 22*, London: Staff and Educational Development Association.

Handley, K. and Williams, L. (2011) 'From copying to learning: using exemplars to engage students with assessment criteria and feedback', *Assessment & Evaluation in Higher Education*, 36(1): 95–108.

Hartney, E. (2007) 'Strategies for the management of lecturer stress in feedback tutorials', *Active Learning in Higher Education*, 8(1): 79–96.

Jessen, A. and Elander, J. (2009) 'Development and evaluation of an intervention to improve further education students' understanding of higher education assessment criteria: three studies', *Journal of Further and Higher Education*, 33(4): 359–80.

Juwah, C., Macfarlane-Dick, D., Matthew, B., Nicol, D., Ross, D. and Smith, B. (2004) *Enhancing Student Learning Through Effective Formative Feedback*, Higher Education Academy. Available at: http://www.heacademy.ac.uk/assets/documents/resources/resourcedatabase/id353_senlef_guide.pdf (accessed 22 May 2011).

Kolb, D. A. (1984) *Experiential Learning: Experience as the Source of Learning and Development*, Englewood Cliffs, NJ: Prentice-Hall.

Kuh, G., Cruce, T., Shoup, R., Kinzie, G. and Gonyea, R. (2008) 'Unmasking the effects of student engagement on first-year college grades and persistence', *The Journal of Higher Education*, 79(5): 540–63.

Leask, B. (2006) 'Plagiarism, cultural diversity and metaphor: implications for academic staff development', *Assessment & Evaluation in Higher Education*, 31(2): 183–99.

MacLellan, E. (2001) 'Assessment for learning: the differing perceptions of tutors and students', *Assessment & Evaluation in Higher Education*, 26(4): 307–18.

Mann, S. (2001) 'Alternative perspectives on the student experience: alienation and engagement', *Studies in Higher Education*, 26(1): 7–20.

McInnis, C. (2005) 'Reinventing student engagement and the learning community: strategic directions for policy, research and practice', keynote speech presented at the Higher Education Academy Conference, 29 June 2005.

National Audit Office (2002) *Improving Student Success in English Higher Education*, Norwich: The Stationery Office. Available at: http://www.nao.org.uk/publications/0102/improving_student_achievement.aspx (accessed 3 August 2011).

——(2007) *Staying the Course: The Retention of Students in Higher Education*, Norwich: The Stationery Office.

Nicol, D. (2009) 'Assessment for self-regulation: enhancing achievement in the first year using learning technologies', *Assessment & Evaluation in Higher Education*, 34(3): 335–53.

Prosser, M. and Trigwell, K. (1999) *Understanding Learning and Teaching*, Buckingham: Society for Research into Higher Education and Open University Press.

Race, P. (2006) *The Lecturer's Toolkit: A Practical Guide to Assessment, Learning and Teaching*, 3rd edn, Abingdon: Routledge.

Ramsden, P. (2003) *Learning to Teach in Higher Education*, 2nd edn, London: Routledge.

Sadler, D. R. (1989) 'Formative assessment and the design of instructional systems', *Instructional Science*, 18: 119–44.

Solomonides, I. and Martin, P. (2008) '"All this talk of engagement is making me itch": an investigation into conceptions of "engagement" held by students and tutors', in L. Hand and C. Bryson (eds) *Student Engagement: SEDA Special 22*, London: Staff and Educational Development Association, pp. 13–19.

Solomonides, I. and Swannell, M. (1996) 'Encouraging students: making the passive active at Nottingham Trent University', in G. Wisker and S. Brown (eds) *Enabling Student Learning: Systems and Strategies*, St Ives: Kogan Page, pp. 102–15.

Stephani, L. (1998) 'Assessment in partnership with learners', *Assessment & Evaluation in Higher Education*, 23(4): 339–50.

Stough, L. M. and Emmer, E. T. (1998) 'Teachers' emotions and test feedback', *Qualitative Studies in Education*, 11(2): 341–61.

Thomson, A. (2008) 'Why we can't turn our backs on the league-table generation', *Times Higher Education*, 10 January, pp. 26–31.

Weaver, M. (2006) 'Do students value feedback? Student perceptions of tutors' written responses', *Assessment & Evaluation in Higher Education*, 31(3): 379–94.

Willis, D. (1993) 'Academic involvement at university', *Higher Education*, 25(2): 133–50.

Yorke, M. (2003) 'Formative assessment in higher education: moves towards a theory and the enhancement of pedagogic practice', *Higher Education*, 45(4): 477–501.

CRITICAL FRIEND COMMENTARY

Ian Solomonides

Student engagement, the first year experience, and feedback are high on the perennial agendas of what is right, good and proper in university education around the world. And within these overarching concepts there are sub-domains of activity that seek to tease out cause and effect relative to the quality and quantity of learning. Graham Gibbs (2010) provides a comprehensive report of many input, process and output variables in *Dimensions of Quality*, while Trowler (2010) presents a review of the literature on engagement. Thereafter, there is a small but growing interest in emotion as an aspect of engagement and especially feedback (Rowe and Wood 2008). This is important for much of the work on engagement and feedback tends to focus on the cognitive at the expense of the affective and relational (see, for example, Solomonides, Reid and Petocz (in press) for discussion on this and other contemporary issues in student engagement).

In their chapter, Foster, McNeill and Lawther discuss the central role of diagnostic, formative and summative assessment and feedback in student learning and the features of these relative to transition into the first year of study and with student engagement more broadly. They promote the opportunities afforded by diagnostic and formative assessment and feedback, encouraging more emphasis – rightly in my opinion – being placed on the formative. Indeed, I am drawn to the idea of a 'fourth dimension' of *integrative* assessment where, as Crisp (2010: 9) points out:

> [J]udgements for these integrative tasks come from the teacher, the student or from peer review (or a combination of all three) ... the key characteristics for the integrative task are that its primary purpose is to influence students' approaches to future learning, and the reward mechanisms in place for students will reflect an analysis of approaches to learning, rather than the learning itself.

Variable modes of assessment and feedback are not completely absent in higher education. At my own university the assessment policy explicitly calls for three types of assessment with an early 'diagnostic' in every module and there are many other institutions with similar practices. However, as the authors point out, 'modular degree structures often do not encourage students to reflect between assignments and especially not across modules'. Rare, except perhaps in studio-based disciplines, is the integrative, tripartite, expositional kind of assessment that offers much for formative and summative evaluation, reflection and feedback. Moreover, this kind of activity is inherently engaging and may also afford more emotional involvement with learning (Reid and Solomonides 2007). With this in mind, many universities are seeking to introduce 'capstone' courses and projects (and with the affordances of Web 2.0 tools this means these do not have to be limited to a physical space). Capstone courses are one of the ten practices shown to have a net positive effect on measures of student engagement (Kuh 2008). If these types of courses are so effective, then perhaps we need to seriously consider including them at every year of study – especially the first year.

References

Crisp, G. T. (2010) 'Integrative assessment: reframing assessment practice for current and future learning', *Assessment & Evaluation in Higher Education*. Available at: http://dx.doi.org/10.1080/02602938.2010.494234 (accessed 3 August 2011).

Gibbs, G. (2010) *Dimensions of Quality*, York: The Higher Education Academy.

Kuh, G. D. (2008) *High Impact Practices: What They Are, Who Has Access to Them and Why They Matter*, Washington, DC: Association of American Colleges and Universities.

Reid, A. and Solomonides, I. (2007) 'Design students' experience of engagement and creativity', *Art Design and Communication in Higher Education*, 6(1): 25–39.

Rowe, A. D. and Wood, L. N. (2008) 'Student perceptions and preferences for feedback', *Asian Social Science*, 4(3): 78–88.

Solomonides, I., Reid, A. and Petocz, P. (eds) (in press) *Engaging with Learning in Higher Education*, Faringdon: Libri Publishing.

Trowler, V. (2010) *Student Engagement Literature Review*, York: Higher Education Academy.

Chapter 4

Helping them succeed

The staff–student relationship

Christine Broughan and David Grantham

Introduction

> They didn't even know my name …

These were the words of a first year student who left university after six weeks, feeling isolated, unsure and floundering in an unwelcoming environment. Unfortunately we probably all have similar stories to share. What then *is* our relationship with students? In a recent workshop we asked senior academics why they persisted in higher education. Many identified 'special relationships' with one or two key staff who inspired, motivated and showed a personal interest in their development as a learner. It is this relationship that we explore in our chapter using metaphors to conceptualize different relationship styles, their impact on assessment and feedback and ultimately on learning and success. We also reflect upon how this experience might be different for non-traditional students. We discuss the key tutor skills of a successful staff–student relationship that have a positive impact on assessment and feedback and conclude with our idea of a developmental personal tutorial that uses assessment feedback as its catalyst.

Metaphors

The Nuremberg Funnel

The Nuremberg Funnel metaphor dates from the seventeenth century and depicts a tutor holding a funnel over the head of a student and pouring in knowledge. The communication is simple and one-way; we have the knowledge and, suitably packaged, we deliver it to the student, to be unpacked and regurgitated at a later date in an assessment. We might refute this notion of learning in higher education yet often our antiquated systems reflect such a model; the ubiquitous lecture followed by an end-of-year exam is such an example. In this model, assessment is a means of measuring a student's success, against predefined specific goals. No relationship develops between tutor and student; there is no negotiation, meaning-making or conception of the process of learning which is based on repetition; if the student fails to learn, then the problem lies with them. There would be no need to accommodate different learning styles, have an understanding of the diverse range of students entering our classrooms, or develop different types of assessment. In this metaphor, learning is a low-context communication (Hall 1976), a commodity that can be bought and sold. Promoting higher forms of knowledge requires some level of personal investment surely?

Prison governor to inmates

> Too often staff-driven assessment encourages students to be dependent on the teacher or examiners to make decisions about what they know and they do not effectively learn to be able to do this for themselves.
>
> (Boud 1995: 39)

This metaphor also implies a low-context relationship with very clear power dynamics. Tutors continue to have the knowledge, but students must engage in our way of thinking in order to 'pass the assessment'. This metaphor draws heavily on a modernist perspective based on a single truth, or set of rules that are non-negotiable. This relationship discourages students from challenging dominant thinking; they assimilate it and provide evidence of its credibility through carefully defined assessment. This metaphor would discourage the relational, social and emotional aspect of learning.

In assessment terms, the tutor keeps students on the straight and narrow, encouraging conformity. The relationship is authoritarian and reflects Perry's (1970) single truth paradigm that suggests that learning is a simple process of assimilating the knowledge provided at appropriate points of assessment. A strict hierarchy is established with little room for negotiation of rules or processes. Assessment would be highly structured with no scope or credit for innovative or creative approaches. Like the Nuremberg Funnel model, this metaphor serves to inculcate the dominant culture (Bourdieu 1984). The learning environment is punitive, and plagiarism and its detection feature highly (most likely because the nature of the assessment encourages rote answers). Passing the assessment is the criterion by which students are judged to see if they are fit to join society, either on full release or, in the case of postgraduate studies, on probation.

You can imagine here a Eurocentric, highly westernized curriculum with little or no thought given to global or inclusive issues. Students from families and backgrounds who see higher education as a rite of passage will succeed as they understand the rules and often have some say in defining them, while those from a widening participation background are disadvantaged.

This type of metaphor applies in many Chinese institutions where it is difficult for students to develop a relationship with tutors, resulting in 60.6 per cent of students reporting that they would rather turn to their peers for support than a tutor (Xie *et al.* 2005, cited in Foster 2008). This metaphor creates an ideological dilemma in that it seeks to reduce the complexity of the relationship which is the very essence of deep learning and assessment types that will serve to deepen and reinforce these cultural defences. In such a power-charged learning environment, tutors appear to hold all the power as curriculum designers, deliverers and assessors, yet they often report feeling disempowered (not knowing the learning needs of their tutees, demands for standardization, quick turnaround of assessed work).

Students rarely feel able to raise power issues or issues of difference themselves without a framework to do this provided by the tutor. They do not want to be seen to 'rock the boat' or challenge the dominant culture unless they feel explicitly supported in this endeavour. Hackett and Marsland (1997) suggest that this relationship can result in a number of outcomes relating to assessment:

- *Secrecy*: the student does not disclose the impact of assessment. The tutor covertly restricts opportunities for discussion during tutorials.
- *Helplessness*: the tutor holds false expectations that the student should be able to cope. Views those who ask for help as weak and uncomplaining ones as coping well.
- *Entrapment and accommodation*: student sees the tutor as 'good' and therefore any failing must be on their part.
- *Delayed or unconvincing disclosure*: often difficulties with the course come to light at critical and delayed points, for example, a failed assignment. Characterized by behaviours such as volatility, anger, aggression, or by over-work.
- *Retraction*: difficulties that are communicated to others but met with scepticism, punishment, stigmatism or non-action can lead to retraction i.e. 'it's fine now'.

We suggest adding *mutual seduction* – students seek clues as to the nature of the assessment and tutors are happy to give them to those who can understand them, both believing that success is assured.

Assessment can act as a critical point to challenge the dissonance or discomfort in relation to power issues. And yet the difficulty for students is that they are expected to critically challenge the same context in which they are assessed. Assessment in this metaphor can act to disempower students and stifle the very nature of learning that higher education strives to create.

Carer to the needy

In this metaphor we identify the beginnings of a relational view of tutor–student interaction. Clear power dynamics persist and the relationship is infantile as the tutor accepts some caring responsibility. The students are viewed as weak and vulnerable and therefore need tutor control, which is exerted through carefully delivered bite-sized chunks of information. Assessment too would be designed for students to tread carefully; there would be no elements of surprise, nothing to stretch them. The atmosphere would be safe, nurturing but possibly over-powering and with no opportunity for the students to discover things for themselves: students are (s)mothered.

In this metaphor we see students as requiring looking after by a responsible adult. It also implies a somewhat closed institution in which students are pro-tected from the real world, and tutors can collude with and guide their students through the various assessment hoops designed by others. The metaphor does imply a relational aspect to learning and assessment as a social process. It also suggests that students will thrive in an environment they perceive as safe and one that allows them to tentatively explore new possibilities. The role of the tutor as the friendly parent to students who feel lost in the comparative anonymity of higher education can work to a point, but is often problematic when it comes to assessment as tutors become both guide and judge. Assessments would be very safe, we imagine; nothing too stretching, and carefully overseen. But under this regime, students are likely to feel unfulfilled, a far cry from Yorke and Longden's (2008) notion of the purpose of higher education as a mechanism to see how far we can stretch and be stretched. In Perry's (1970) terms, students would simply identify rights from wrongs. Regular phase tests would be the order of the day and would fit with a modernist reductionist view of the world.

This metaphor represents a significant step forward from that previously pre-sented and recognizes the relational and emotional aspects to learning. Damasio (1996: xv) asserts that 'certain aspects of the process of emotion and feelings are indispensable to rationality' and suggests that tutors who pay attention to the emotional dimension of the classroom experience are more likely to develop a state in their learners which is conducive to learning, with an increased likelihood of learners being engaged, motivated, ready to take risks in their learning and assessment, positive in their approach to learning, ready to collaborate, be creative and resilient. Harkin (1998) notes the most important determinants of student satisfaction with tutors were based on affective behaviours (listening, showing respect, sharing a joke). When the emotional environment is healthy, it leads to students who are more likely to take risks, explore, make connections and enquire. Mortiboys (2005) suggests that tutors should ask whether they are encouraging an emotional environment in which learners feel safe, trusting, challenged and motivated.

There is a danger, of course, that this kindly approach will cultivate a feeling of dependency and fail to encourage self-assessment of learning. Ideally we need to work towards an emotionally healthy relationship with students, which empowers and guides, yet develops them as autonomous and independent learners.

Parliamentary whip

In this metaphor the dynamics of the relationship begin to change and we see the tutor as the parliamentary whip trying to coerce or steer backbenchers. Their power is no longer a 'right' but something that they earn through gaining credibility. In some ways learning and assessment form a journey or a story to be told. The parliamentary whip becomes a storyteller, a social being who uses stories as a highly effective vehicle for fostering open-mindedness to new ideas in a safe environment (Denning 2001). Students and tutors develop a shared understanding and are able to communicate complex ideas in a non-threatening manner. However, a freer environment can be both liberating and frightening (Jaques 1990). Without any intervention by a third party, the student is likely to adopt a personal strategy which involves playing the system and assuming that accurate reproduction of knowledge is all that is necessary for survival; in our parliamentary whip terms, they will 'abstain'. The personal tutor has a vital role to play in developing the students' awareness of learning processes and in changing habits. And nothing will grab students' interest and effort so much as rewarding marks (Alvermann 2001). The sequence of learning and assessment, however, is far from smooth and uninterrupted.

This metaphor persuades students that they can be agents of their own learning (Woods *et al.* 2001) and that they can develop a critical awareness of how conventions of language (Milambiling 2001) and texts (Chambliss 2001; Hynd 2001) work to convey certain messages, which they can choose to take up, modify or resist (Alvermann *et al.* 1997). These choices point to the reciprocal nature of the instructional process and away from the misinformed notion that it is the tutor's responsibility to transmit knowledge and the student's job to absorb it (Alvermann 2001).

This metaphor challenges the hierarchy destabilizing the tutor–student binary and emphasizing interdependence. Assessment therefore becomes negotiable and personalized. In fact, assessment can be used as a tool to destabilize previously assumed power relations and a Modernist view of knowledge. An exemplar of this type of relationship and its impact on assessment could be found at the Lancaster University School of Independent Study which allowed students to negotiate a unit of study and the appropriate form of assessment. In order for the student to flourish in this type of relationship, it is necessary to build into the course and assessment a means of developing the skills needed to learn effectively within such a context.

Experienced navigator to explorers

> Every day some new fact comes to light – some new obstacle which threatens the gravest obstruction. I suppose this is the reason which makes the game so well worth playing.
>
> (Robert Falcon Scott, Polar explorer, 1868–1912)

This metaphor describes a very different type of relationship in which trust and respect are fundamental. The tutor's role is to guide the student and create an environment in which they feel confident to take on new challenges and test out new territories. The relationship develops over time, resulting in a form of communication where few words are required to express a great deal. This type of high context relationship (Hall 1976) is often seen when musicians are improvising and each knows intuitively how to respond to a particular move or development in the direction or trend of the music. The relationship leads to the development of students as 'junior members of the academy' (Elton 1996) and introduces them to the language game that higher education institutes play to protect the dominant culture (Wittgenstein 1953). This is particularly important for non-standard entry students where the language used might present itself as a barrier to learning and the tutor has a key role in helping the student navigate their way through higher education. As the relationship matures, the student becomes less reliant on the tutor explaining the rules of navigation and becomes one who intuitively knows how to apply their learning to the situation.

The tutor provides a space for learning that is relatively secure, but challenging, and a safe base for exploration. Diversity thrives as the student controls the learning environment, the direction of travel they choose, the pace, expedition equipment, and their team. As such, the learning experience can be as exciting and adventurous for the tutor too who is responsible for guiding and intervening when required. This metaphor requires mutual commitment, a shared understanding and good communications. The tutor needs to be attuned and supremely attentive to the environment while understanding the capabilities of their navigators. They need to know when to encourage exploration of unknown territory, be aware of the potential to grow academically, socially and emotionally, but also be wary of signs of fatigue or disillusionment.

In this metaphor there is no pre-defined trajectory to gaining knowledge, rather, it is a process of negotiation and incremental steps (Weick 1995). Goals are not predefined but the structure is one of coalition where the activities and outcomes are strongly influenced by environmental factors (Scott 1987). Learning becomes a voyage of discovery. Assessment in this metaphor would be focused on the process of learning rather than the outcome, highly individualized and potentially negotiated. Work would be assessed by asking: did the student use smart methods to gain the knowledge required or solve the problem? How did the student make sense of the material? Success will rely heavily on interpersonal skills, an understanding of the environment and a good base of skills upon which to draw. It is likely that students will develop many of the capabilities required for a graduate career.

The skills of the personal tutor

If we agree that the quality of the relationship between subject tutor and student is important, then it follows that the role of the personal tutor will be pivotal to the development of the student as a learner. There are a number of skills that a personal tutor can use to mentor the tutee to aid their intellectual and personal development. As a basis for some model of this kind of development, we have taken the work of Perry (1970) and Belenky, Clinchy, Goldberger and Tarule

(1997). This, in brief, charts the movement of the student from a view of 'x is either right or wrong and academics decide which' through a realization that there are a variety of legitimate opinions, to the importance of contextual relevance and the making of a personal commitment to a theme of study or action. For most tutors, this is reflected in the work they are hoping to see from their students and their approach to the learning process itself. We want to know that it is the personal work of the student that is presented and that it reveals a high degree of understanding, reasoned critique and sound judgement.

Many of the skills required to aid the developmental process are the stock qualities of a 'reflective practitioner' (Schön 1983), the thoughtful and professional tutor who is prepared to provide a context in which the student can grow both intellectually and personally. Assessed work provides excellent material with which to work with the student on these developmental aims. This approach to the personal tutorial aims beyond traditional feedback and seeks to examine where the student is located at a particular moment in time, in relation to the thinking processes involved and in what it reveals about how the student perceives learning and how their own values impact upon it.

Qualities required of the tutor during a tutorial are well documented (ibid.): careful and attentive listening, the intentional and creative use of silences, and the sharing of intellectual doubt. Above all, it is important that the tutor allows the student to make most of the running and not to turn tutorials into a minilecture. Those techniques that personal tutors and students may find most helpful are briefly explained below:

- *Reflecting back*: Repeating the student's words, or some of them, back to the tutee in order to prompt reflection or simply to signify that the words used are important.
- *Praise and reinforcement of confidence*: Student confidence can be very fragile and this is especially highlighted when the time for the returning of assessed work comes round. To give praise for achievement is a good way to begin feedback even if less praiseworthy comments are to follow.
- *Areas for development*: It is important that the tutor can recognize areas of the student's work where there is scope for improvement and can draw out from the tutee what needs to be done to enhance the quality of what is produced. Examples would be where the student has misunderstood a concept, draws unsupportable conclusions from the evidence, or where they have failed to identify the weaknesses in the arguments of others. Tutors should not only decide what the crucial 'threshold concepts' are in their own disciplines (Land and Meyer 2008), but also what their tutees are finding to be 'troublesome' concepts in the learning process itself. Sometimes called 'shift points', these crucial turning points need to be monitored and encouraged.
- *Student recognition of the nature of a barrier to development*: Rather than speculate on the nature of what it is that is preventing the student from moving forward, it is far more effective if the tutor can get the student to

identify the barrier(s) themselves. This can be done by reflecting back, challenging and sharing an understanding of the problem.

- *Restatement of a barrier to development:* It is one thing to recognize a barrier but it is quite another to do something about it. One technique that is often used is to get the student to restate the barrier, or for the tutor to give a reminder of it.
- *Challenges:* One of the most potentially developmental weapons in the armoury of the tutor is the challenge. Best done quietly and at the most appropriate time in a tutorial, it can take the form of reflecting back (see earlier), asking the student to repeat a statement or by direct challenge: 'Do you really think that?'; 'You are going to have to explain that to me again'; 'I wonder if you can see the flaw in what you have said.' Such direct questions could be written into an assessment as part of the feedback, then followed up at the personal tutorial.
- *Silences:* These are really powerful allies in the fight against intellectual and personal stagnation. Used strategically, silences can be uncomfortable, even disturbing, but can be the catalyst for much reflection. Best used after reflecting back, identification of barriers and challenges.
- *Acceptance of doubt:* Creating the conditions in which a student can admit to doubt in their approach to their work, even their approach to learning, is a high point in their development. Its antithesis is, of course, *denial* and this too is not an uncommon feature of tutor/tutee discourse. Admissions of doubt can be prompted by any of the tools designed to give rise to reflection.
- *Shared doubt:* If there is one way of moving a student on developmentally that stands out from the others, it is when the tutor can admit to similar doubts to those revealed by the students. Mutual reflection on issues such as the fragility of certain arguments, the difficulties inherent in critique and when learning becomes, as it often does, an emotional as well as an intellectual journey, can be pivotal to development.
- *Tutor's own development:* Before the practitioner can offer opportunities for student growth, it may be necessary for similar processes to be made available to tutors. As Derek Rowntree (1981) famously persuades us, before any educational development can have any hope of success, it should be preceded by staff development.

Personal tutors need to develop or advance the skills described earlier. A precondition of such development would be that the tutor should, without sentimentality, care about their students. How best to engage students in the discipline and how to work with colleagues on using the discipline and assessment strategies as tools for personal and intellectual growth, are the questions uppermost in the minds of such tutors. Assessments should be designed to include contentious issues so that the student has an opportunity to apply higher levels of learning, including evaluation and judgment. Students should be made aware of this through clear assessment guidelines and subsequent feedback should reflect the importance of these abilities. This approach to assessment may be familiar to many practitioners in higher education, yet keeping a more careful eye on student development than hitherto could be viewed as a natural development if we are to properly address the issue of how we are to prepare students for a 'super-complex' world where academic learning alone will not be enough for success (Barnett 2000).

The developmental tutorial

A fictional account of a personal tutorial where many of the tutor skills are demonstrated is provided below. In this account the student has had the same personal tutor throughout the three years of their undergraduate programme. This particular meeting focuses on the return of assessed coursework by the personal tutor who has an overview of work across the course. Personal tutorials are by diary appointment. The dialogue is annotated to provide signposts to the kind of developmental steps referred to earlier. These are shown in italics.

The knock on the door had half-surprised Lynn. Praveen was expected for a personal tutorial but it was five minutes to the agreed time. This was the third year of the student's programme and Lynn had seen Praveen from a raw first year to a more confident near-graduate.

'Come in – hello Praveen, how are things?'

'OK. … I think,' said the student.

'You think,' said the tutor *(Reflecting back)*

'Well, I have been worried about the last two courseworks. I need good marks if I'm going to get a 2.1.'

The tutor frowned, 'Still a bit driven by the marks then, Praveen?' *(Something of a challenge)*

'I guess so – but I always read the feedback now. My marks have improved since I have taken more of it on board.'

'Well, let's look at these two then,' said Lynn, 'There's good news and bad news. Good news is that both bear out what you say – your work has improved – so well done.' *(Praise and reinforcement of confidence)*

'However, they both also raise something we have talked about before – the lack of in-depth critique of the material, especially this second piece where it was clearly wanted.' *(Area for development)*

Praveen shrugged, 'I know, I know, I just can't seem to be able to find fault with what others say or write.'

The tutor smiled, 'Same old block, then?' *(Restatement of a barrier to development)*

'What do you mean?' responded Praveen. *(Denial)*

'Are you sure you don't know?' the tutor quietly said. *(Challenge)*

Praveen shifted uneasily, 'But we always learned to have respect for the academic writers – those better than ourselves.' *(Student's recognition of the nature of the barrier)*

'Better?' inquired Lynn. *(Reflecting back)*

There was a long silence. *(Tutor's acceptance of silences)*

'I mean, those who know more,' said Praveen, 'who have written books and things.'

'And does that makes them better then?' asked Lynn. *(Challenge)*

The student looked puzzled, 'I don't know.' *(Acceptance of doubt)*

'Neither do I,' responded Lynn, 'I have to find out.' *(A shared doubt)* 'So what can we do to be critical?'

Another silence ensued until the student said, 'I suppose we could check that the writers are being consistent with each other and are up to date.' *(Threshold concept)*

'Yes,' the tutor replied, 'and we could test whether what they say rings true or has a high or low degree of predictability – that it will hold true for at least some time and in a number of contexts.' *(Introduction of contextual relativism)*

'It's trickier than it looks,' said Praveen.

Conclusion

Any study of the developmental stages of personal growth will show that the student in the vignette above has still some distance to travel on the continuum. However, the tutor is attempting to encourage that growth made possible by a trusting relationship.

Some of these relationships may already exist but we suspect that they are not fully embedded in higher education where tensions exist. On the one hand, we are required to be canons of the establishment, holders of the nation's 'knowledge' where standards, conformity and standardization are key. Driven by metrics such as league tables, on the other hand, we are supposed to provide agile, dynamic learning environments operating at the edge of chaos (Welsh 2006), constantly pushing the boundaries of knowledge and understanding. The two suggest very different forms of assessment and yet the paradox of higher education structure is that while it offers us tools for our liberation, it simultaneously attempts to shape and dominate us.

This dichotomy has implications for our relationship with our students; are we the custodians of knowledge or merely the guides in a privileged position to assist students in their own personalized journey of discovery? In terms of learning as a relational and social process, our formal organizational structures and rules might appear distinctly juxtaposed. In our metaphors we have tried to show alternative possibilities for how tutors might relate to their students.

An enhanced relationship between tutor and student will enable students to identify their personal resources and aspirations, the demands and opportunities of the learning environment in which they are studying, ways in which they can enhance their own learning, the progress they are making towards achieving personal goals, and ways in which they can effectively plan for further progress. A learner who is able to engage in these processes will become more focused on personal achievement and will be able to utilize the facilities offered by the institution. Above all, perhaps, they will be better prepared for a rapidly changing environment and uncertain future.

References

Alvermann, D. E. (2001) 'Teaching as persuasion: the worthiness of the metaphor', *Theory into Practice*, 40(4): 278–83.

Alvermann, D. E., Commeyras, M., Young, J. P., Randall, S. and Hinson, D. (1997) 'Interrupting gendered discursive practices in classroom talk about texts: easy to think about, difficult to do', *Journal of Literacy Research*, 29: 73–104.

Barnett, R. (2000) *Realizing the University in an Age of Supercomplexity*, Buckingham: Open University Press.

Belenky, M. F., Clinchy, B. M., Goldberger, N. R. and Tarule, J. M. (1997) *Women's Ways of Knowing*, New York: Basic Books.

Boud, D. (1995) 'Assessment and learning: contradictory or complementary?', in P. Knight (ed.) *Assessment for Learning in Higher Education*, London: Kogan Page, pp. 35–48.

Bourdieu, P. (1984) *Distinction: A Social Critique of the Judgment of Taste*, Cambridge, MA: Harvard University Press.

Chambliss, M. J. (2001) 'Teaching as persuasion: a new metaphor for a new decade', *Theory into Practice*, 40(4): 255–64.

Damasio, A. (1996) *Descartes' Error: Emotion, Reason and the Human Brain*, London: Papermac.

Denning, S. (2001) *The Springboard: How Storytelling Ignites Action in Knowledge-Era Organizations*, Boston: Butterworth-Heinemann.

Elton, L. (1996) 'Strategies to enhance student motivation: a conceptual analysis', *Studies in Higher Education*, 21(1): 57–68.

Foster, M. (2008) *Enhancing the Experience of Chinese Students in UK Higher Education: Lessons from a Collaborative Project*, Birmingham: Staff and Educational Development Association.

Hackett, S. and Marsland, P. (1997) 'Perceptions of power: an exploration of the dynamics in the student–tutor-practice teacher relationship within child protection placements', *Social Work Education*, 16(2): 44–66.

Hall, E. T. (1976) *Beyond Culture*, New York: Anchor Press/Doubleday.

Harkin, J. (1998) 'Constructs used by vocational students in England to evaluate their teachers', *Journal of Vocational Education and Training*, 50(3): 339–53.

Hynd, C. (2001) 'Persuasion and its role in meeting educational goals', *Theory into Practice*, 40(4): 270–8.

Jaques, D. (1990) *Being a Personal Tutor*, Oxford: Oxford Brookes Education Methods Unit.

Land, R. and Meyer, J. H. F. (2008) *Threshold Concepts within the Disciplines*, Rotterdam: Sense Publishers.

Milambiling, J. (2001) 'Opening minds or changing them? Some observations on teaching introductory linguistics', Theory into Practice, 40(4): 249–54.

Mortiboys, A. (2005) *Teaching with Emotional Intelligence*, Abingdon: Routledge.

Perry, W. G. (1970) *Forms of Intellectual and Ethical Development in the College Years*, New York: Rinehart and Winston.

Rowntree, D. (1981) *Developing Courses for Students*, London: McGraw-Hill.

Schön, D. (1983) *The Reflective Practitioner*, London: Temple Smith.

Scott, W. R. (1987) *Organizations: Rational, Natural and Open Systems*, 2nd edn, Engelwood Cliffs, NJ: Prentice-Hall.

Weick, K. (1995) *Sensemaking in Organisations*, Thousand Oaks, CA: Sage.

Welsh, I. (2006) *Complexity and Social Movements: Multitudes at the Edge of Chaos, Protest at the Edge of Chaos*, Abingdon: Routledge.

Wittgenstein, L. (1953) *Philosophical Investigations*, Malden, MA: Blackwell.

Woods, B., Demerath, P. and Woolfolk Hoy, A. (2001) 'A rose by any other name: a cross-domain explication of the metaphor "teaching as persuasion"', *Theory into Practice*, 40(4): 228–34.

Yorke, M. and Longden, B. (2008) 'The first year experience of higher education in the UK'. Available at: http://www.heacademy.ac.uk/assets/York/documents/resources/publications/FYEFinalReport.pdf (accessed 9 December 2010).

CRITICAL FRIEND COMMENTARY

Steve Larkin

In this chapter, Broughan and Grantham dissect the pedagogical conundrum of how one should best teach and how students best learn. Or put another way, should the educational imperative be defined by successful teaching or by how students learn effectively? Clearly this has universal relevance as the international academy becomes globalized and fiscally competitive. By necessity, many teaching institutions now embed teaching and learning quality as a first order corporate goal so as to distinguish themselves in the student market and thereby establish an edge over their competitors.

Teaching and learning as both conceptual constructs and pedagogical practices are mutually constitutive; one cannot be understood without reference to the other. In deconstructing this dynamic through an analysis of the various social relations potentially manifested through the teacher–student binary, Broughan and Grantham draw attention to the power dimensions of these relationships and how these shape the quality of learning outcomes. Such relations are both determined and intersected by social categories of race, class and gender. Inevitably, considerations of epistemology, axiology and ontology must be confronted in order to uncover how such power indices influence and impact on the student experience and concomitant opportunities for success.

I have argued recently that for indigenous Australian students, who collectively experience poor access, retention and completion rates across most sectors of the education system compared to non-indigenous Australians, the higher education sector is not racially inclusive. In my view, this is in part attributable to a dominant racialized, neo-positivist epistemology which presupposes one reality that can be discovered and known while at the same time disregards alternative ways of knowing and understanding that reality. A hegemonic white epistemology permeates across all dimensions of a university so that the academic culture of the institution reflects the learning imperatives of this racial group while disregarding and marginalizing other alternative epistemologies and pedagogies.

The chapter offers insight as to how present inequalities might be overcome through a move towards a more inclusive, post-modernist view of learning and teaching in higher education. It suggests that the staff–student relationship is a key driver through which to achieve these aims. Notwithstanding, the staff–student relationship should constitute the terrain from which pedagogical transformation must be negotiated. The staff-dominant approaches depicted by Broughan and Grantham, where teaching and learning methodologies are defined unilaterally by staff, arguably achieve some level of knowledge acquisition by the student, but questions remain as to quantum and quality of the outcome(s). Signifiers of such relations are likely to be found in adverse rates of attrition and completion, student surveys and even grade point averages. I would argue this would be especially so for student cohorts constituted as 'Other' or more commonly referred to as 'equity groups'.

The inclusive approach advocated by Broughan and Grantham provides a compelling argument to rethink current hegemonic staff logics and practices that pervade the academy. The perpetuation of these rationales are complicit in maintaining racial and gender inequities largely by presupposing a homogeneity among students as to how they ought to be taught and how they should learn. Such ideas are not racially-neutral or gender-neutral and extend to notions of definitions and understandings as to intellectual capability. Yet at the same time, there exists a form of social contact between the teacher and the learner; the student delimits a form of personal power while simultaneously allowing a power of authority in the teacher in order to attain knowledge from the teacher. However, in applying the insights of Broughan and Grantham, such relations are to be re-negotiated so as to provide a mutually constructed set of relations between staff and students to better facilitate teaching and learning outcomes that ensure high attainment.

The Broughan–Grantham paradigm shift is predicated on newly constituted staff–student relations relying on respect, integrity and heterogeneity. Differentiation in learning styles, for example, can now be identified, embedded and applied in the staff–student relationship without the need to default to hierarchical power relations as well as the standard staff retreat to attributions of student deficit to explain attrition, non-completions and supposedly academic incapability. For these reasons alone, Broughan and Grantham's call for a reconfiguration of the staff–student relationship must be read and taken seriously for those of us dedicated to academic freedom and the production of knowledge in the academy. To not do so risks pedagogical stagnancy, epistemological paralysis, adverse homogeneity, and an academy defined by lethargy rather than dynamism. The legacy for our students as a consequence is best captured by a quotation generally, but inconclusively, attributed to Einstein: 'Everyone is a genius. But if you judge a fish by its ability to climb a tree, it will live its whole life believing it is stupid.'

Chapter 5

Evaluating assessment practices

The academic staff perspective

Frances Deepwell and Greg Benfield

Introduction

There is a problem with assessment. We know students report that they are least satisfied with this aspect of their higher education experience. We know the assessment load on staff is often greater than the time available for the task. We know that we do not assess adequately the more tacit understandings within disciplines (Lea and Street 1998; Jones 2009). We also know that there is a wealth of research evidence and guidance on what constitutes valid, reliable and fair assessment in higher education; and yet troublesome assessment practices continue. Poor assessment practices have an adverse effect on student satisfaction, and also on staff morale. In the widely cited words of David Boud: 'Students can, with difficulty, escape from the effects of poor teaching, they cannot (by definition if they want to graduate) escape the effects of poor assessment' (Boud 1995: 35). Bearing this in mind, therefore, we must ask ourselves, how is this still the case? The aim of this chapter, therefore, is to explore some academic staff perspectives to understand better why it appears to be so hard for university programmes to heed the good practice advice and evidence and change their practices in assessment.

The chapter opens with a brief overview of three relevant aspects of assessment and feedback from the literature. We will then evaluate three case study vignettes of assessment strategies used at programme level using a simple evaluative model. We conclude the chapter with a summary and recommendations for adopting programme-level, team-based approaches to assessment redesign.

Where assessment fits in the course design for students and staff

Studies of student expectations and experiences reinforce the significance of assessment in the way students approach their learning. Ramsden (1992: 187) wrote: 'from our students' point of view, assessment always defines the actual curriculum'. This is typified by student persistence in asking what will be assessed and how to gain marks. It is also reflected in the 'notably less positive' results in the United Kingdom National Student Survey for assessment and feedback as opposed to other aspects of their course (Williams and Kane 2008: 5). Anecdotally, when selecting their programme of study, many students look first at the mode of assessment. If they like exams, group projects, essay-type assignments or presentations, then they will look for modules that offer these modes of assessment.

For academic staff, however, a natural starting point in planning teaching traditionally has been a mirror image of this. What am I going to cover, and how?; and then thoughts turn to how the learning might be assessed. Additionally, assumptions about assessment are based on practice and custom within the departmental setting and are not open to challenge. As higher education is changing, however, these practices are no longer tenable. This is something we will return to later in the chapter but next let us look at a curriculum model that has sought to rebalance assessment in the equation.

Learning outcomes and their impact on peer and self-assessment

In the UK, curriculum development over the past 10–15 years has been dominated by the overwhelming influence of the two connecting ideas of learning outcomes and constructive alignment (Biggs and Tang 2007). Stating the intended learning outcomes upon completion of the course has been helpful in sharing understandings of what should be assessed among a wider team of colleagues. One of the further effects of such clear descriptions is that it has enabled a growth in self-assessment and peer assessment. By producing well-written learning outcomes, staff can work with students around a set of statements against which to judge the quality of coursework (Rust et al. 2005). It is no longer uncommon for staff to provide opportunities for self-assessment, with multiple choice quizzes, rubrics for essays, model answers and other reflective activities in advance of coursework deadlines, providing a high volume of formative feedback for the individual student.

Peer review and self-assessment have moved into the mainstream, and have become common components in undergraduate modules where they were once a niche innovation. For the purposes of this chapter, 'peer review' means students critically appraising each other's work, while the awarding of grades predominantly remains with the teacher. In a recent evaluation of assessment practices in one UK institution, many academic staff evaluated peer review positively (Price et al. 2011). It is seen as a means to develop employability skills, such as teamworking, self-critical awareness, evaluative and communication skills. So, from a staff perspective, the opportunities for students to engage with peers are beneficial; however, there is recognition that peer review is particularly difficult to enact in larger classes.

Feedback as a key element in the assessment process

Changing assessment practices is difficult and slow, and there are powerful systemic factors making some assessment practices surprisingly resistant to any change at all. Let us take feedback as an example. This features most prominently in students', lecturers' and especially institutional managers' anxieties about National Student Survey (NSS) scores in the UK. Feedback is 'the most important part of the assessment process' say Price, Handley, Millar and O'Donovan (2010: 277). Indeed, learning is unlikely to happen without information that can help to modify and improve future performance. But this is a particularly frustrating area for teachers, as we have repeatedly found in our educational development work with academic staff, and as Nicol (2010: 502) describes:

> A commonly expressed concern is that even though teachers spend considerable time carefully constructing feedback comments on assignments, these are often not collected by students and, when they are, students often do not seem to act on the feedback provided.

There is therefore a staff perception that feedback does not work (Weaver 2006) and/or that students do not act on it (Mutch 2003; Weaver 2006), and in many cases do not even bother to collect it. There are a host of possible explanations for this. Teachers perceive that students are preoccupied with marks, rather than qualitative feedback. In part, they are right; grades are important to students. But it is more complicated than that; students are interested in grades *and* how to improve them (Higgins *et al.* 2002). Teachers may conceive of feedback as being principally for justifying the grade (Price *et al.* 2010). They may be using implicit criteria, so that students find their feedback difficult to interpret (MacLellan 2001). Or the feedback is so carefully crafted by teachers that it may be unintelligible to students (Bloxham and Boyd 2007), or they may have insufficient working knowledge to be able to understand and act on it (Sadler 2010).

We have a variety of very clear and consistent models of good feedback practice to work from (see, for example, Gibbs and Simpson 2004; McDowell *et al.* 2005; Nicol and Macfarlane-Dick 2006).

But despite large-scale efforts to promote improvements to feedback (see, for example, Nicol and Macfarlane-Dick 2006; ASKe 2009, 2010), the research literature abounds with the ineffectiveness of assignment feedback (see, for example, Rust *et al.* 2005; Hounsell 2008; Burke 2009; Sadler 2010). Processes such as modularization and semesterization can result in the bunching of assessments near the end of a module. This tends to mitigate against feed forward practices to inform and improve subsequent pieces of work (Yorke 2001; Higgins *et al.* 2002; Irons 2008). By imposing tight time constraints on teachers producing feedback (Chanock 2000), the quality and timing of feedback can be compromised.

The vignettes

Let us now take a look at the first of our three vignettes, which concentrates particularly on efficient feedback mechanisms and peer review. We are evaluating them using the simple 'What? So What? Now What?' model of evaluation (Patton 2008). The presentation in the box is derived from interviews with each of the academic staff concerned. There is then a 'so what?' analysis of the issues raised and an indication of 'now what?'.

Vignette 1: Undergraduate and postgraduate Biosciences, Life Sciences School

Andrew took on a leadership role in learning and teaching around 10 years ago because of a deep personal interest in assessment and feedback. At the time, it was regular practice for students to be set coursework in week 1 for submission in week 10. Andrew realized then that more could be done to bring assessment into the learning experience of his students and has seen things change quite considerably since that time. His approach to introducing change has several interrelated elements but what unites them all has been his desire to change practices across the entire programme, and has evolved into a School-wide strategy on assessment.

For example, in response to external examiner comments that modules had unequal workloads, Andrew worked with the programme team to devise assessment weightings according to the average study time needed for each type of assessment, including exams. This is most visible in each module handbook where there is a page of 'Study Time Expectations and Coursework Weightings' setting out the contact time and expected private study time, and the associated assessment weighting.

Knowing that his colleagues felt increasingly overburdened with assessment, and that some were resistant to change, Andrew tackled one particularly significant issue, namely the feedback given to students. Over time, Andrew devised and piloted a set of feedback sheets for common assignments, such as scientific reports, essays and presentations. Colleagues could tick or strike out carefully worded, critical or positive statements as required, and then provide some specific free-text comments at the end. The latter point is an important outlet for colleagues to address students directly. They are used to taking great care in crafting the feedback to students, and while they complain that coursework is not collected, they do not want to lose that potential connection. The outcome of using these feedback sheets has been greatly improved speed of return, positive evaluations by students, and also consistency in the advice given to students, including reiterating the use of local resources such as the skills handbook.

The shape and use of these feedback sheets have developed in light of evaluations over the past few years, and they have become something now shared with students as they are preparing to submit their assignments. The sheets provide students with insights into common mistakes and remind them of the marking criteria, thus enabling them to make informed judgements about their own work. Peer review of other students' work is something that Andrew values highly in his courses, but less for the benefit in students receiving peer feedback and more because it gives them the chance to scrutinize someone else's work and develop their critical awareness to better judge their own output. To this end, Andrew has designed a reciprocal peer review process which is simple and rigorous. Students who have not presented draft assignments are not permitted to participate.

The next challenge was to encourage student engagement with the feedback given. The solution that Andrew has implemented provides motivation to engage. He oversaw the introduction of a requirement for each module to have at least one piece of assessed work where students are required to demonstrate how they have engaged with feedback received for an earlier assignment.

So what?

In the first vignette, we can see that Andrew has developed the use of statement banks for speed and consistency, and has provided strong motivation for students to engage in feedback by making it part of a future assignment. The peer review mechanisms he is using enables students to develop self-evaluative capacity as well as to benefit from the views of others on their work. In establishing the use of the feedback and peer review processes, Andrew has had to work hard to persuade his colleagues and remain vigilant to the possibly unexpected outcomes of his new approaches.

Andrew is in a leadership position within the programme team, but does not have line management responsibility and is working on a collegiate model of leadership. His solution is to provide well-structured forms, which closely guide his colleagues in providing what he considers to be appropriate feedback. The forms help to limit the lack of consistency in feedback given between the other lecturers who support his modules. While more experienced and long-standing colleagues have expressed their feelings that the forms constrain their freedom of expression, other colleagues welcome the simplicity of them. In most cases, the time required to give useful and readable feedback to students is cut substantially.

Now what?

Gradually several of Andrew's initiatives to improve assessment practice have cascaded into the learning experience. He has used the evidence of time savings and efficiency to change colleagues' practices. Through evaluations he has been able to demonstrate greater effectiveness of the feedback received, and used his experiences to develop a School-wide assessment strategy that is now having greater impact beyond his own programme areas.

We now hear from Emma, an experienced occupational health lecturer who has developed her assessment techniques within a community of practitioners responding to new technologies and new policy drivers.

Vignette 2: Undergraduate, Health and Social Care, Occupational Therapy

Emma has taught on the BSc Occupational Therapy (OT) programme for over ten years. She is the module leader for Anatomy and Physiology (year 1) and Professional Practice (year 3). Only rarely in her experience are conditions ripe for significant changes to assessment practices. These are a combination of institutional policy initiatives finding resonance with colleagues she respects, agreeable to the members of her teaching team and offering significant improvements in students' experience.

In the past two years Emma has sought to make the assessment more 'progressive', coherent and developmental, to shift the balance of assessment in her modules from summative to formative assessment. What have been the key drivers? The Oxford Brookes University Assessment Compact (Oxford Brookes University 2011) is the policy driver. It was designed to improve student engagement in assessment and feedback and to improve assessment standards.

But for Emma, 'It isn't policy alone that drives things.' Emma is a member of a variety of communities of practice (Lave 1993; Wenger 1998), both disciplinary ones and communities largely concerned with learning and teaching development. Her involvement in these stems in part from her completing the Postgraduate Certificate in Teaching in Higher Education. Emma is unlikely to respond in any but a formalistic way to initiatives that do not resonate within these communities. Thus, the Assessment Compact has been regularly discussed in several of Emma's professional communities.

The personalities, preferences and beliefs of members of the course team are also a critical ingredient of conditions for change. About six years ago, Emma introduced computer-aided assessment into her Anatomy and Physiology module. This intersected with a university strategy to enhance e-learning and her own desire to find better ways to promote deep learning and wider reading by her students. Critically, a new, young, staff member with an appetite to introduce fresh approaches, especially e-learning, joined her in her teaching of the module.

In Emma's experience, it can be easier to make changes to module assessment with a large teaching team than a small one. She said, 'It felt hard to change that year one assessment with just two of us on the team', because of the relatively greater level of investment by each party in the smaller team. Thus, disagreements over changes to assessment practice can frequently lead to inaction, or minor, compromise modifications only.

Finally, Emma points out that staff strongly feel they perform a balancing act between supporting students and structuring active learning, particularly formative tasks giving them feedback on their learning, and encouraging learner independence and self-reliance. As Emma puts it:

> In one breath we are saying we want students to be responsible, self-directed learners; in the next, we list their assessments, tell them this is a compulsory assessment, they must press their clicker in class and 'I won't press the button until I have 50 responses' ... You know, one moment we are being really directive about assessment and the next we're saying, 'Hey, learning is your responsibility.' So our students get really mixed messages.

So what?

In this second vignette, the shift from summative to formative assessment has challenged Emma and her colleagues. Interestingly, Emma adopted technology at a time when computer-aided assessment usage was on the increase. Now, however, her institution has other headline policies for her to respond to and she feels unsure of the value of these assessments. Also significant for her is consistency in the messages given sometimes tacitly to students, either to be more independent, autonomous learners or to be more passive, guided learners. These mixed messages are equally a paradox for Emma and her colleagues; it is often not clear where lies the boundary between providing good support and scaffolding learning, and creating learner dependence.

Now what?

Emma's primary task now is to find evidence that her efforts to improve students' performance with more formative assessment and opportunities for feed forward have made a difference. She is evaluating the changes she has made, but this takes time and effort and there is no guarantee that the results will be conclusive.

Our final vignette comes from our own teaching on initial professional development courses for lecturers. At our institution this is called the Postgraduate Certificate in Teaching in Higher Education.

Vignette 3: Postgraduate taught programme in higher education teaching

The authors have been involved in postgraduate certificate courses in teaching in higher education for many years. The current course is long established as internal, initial professional development for academic staff and associate lecturers. Five years ago, the course moved away from portfolio-based assessment to a collection of discrete assignments. This was a compromise made in response to pressure to reduce the assessment load on the course. The course is now approaching its five-yearly review, and this has prompted careful re-thinking about its assessment. We are recommending that assignments remain, because of the benefits they bring to the learners. Assignments are word-limited, phased across the year, allow for formative feedback on drafts and employ generic academic conventions. All of these features are significant items of good practice that we encourage our learners to cascade within their own teaching and assessment practices.

The assignments retain the reflective, work-based focus of the course, but provide greater clarity to learners. Tasks include using multiple sources to evaluate a lesson design you have delivered; writing a course review focusing on assessment practices; conducting an enquiry into a facet of teaching practice. Learners used to complain about the potential vastness of the portfolio – 'How many examples do I need to put in there? How long should the narrative be? How much evidence is enough?' These complaints no longer arise. On the other hand, as educators, we do question whether a set of assignments can actually interrogate practice as rigorously as a teaching portfolio might. Of benefit to learners and tutors, however, is that we allow for formative and early feedback on progress, which has proven invaluable since reflective writing is new to many of the learners on the course.

As a team, we have introduced specific assignment-focused activities into the taught sessions, some of which involve peer review, in line with the university strategy for enhancing assessment. Another notable development in recent years is online submission and draft feedback handled through the virtual learning environment. We have also developed methods for learners to provide peer-to-peer support in online groups and longer-term learning sets outside of the formal workshop sessions.

Our feedback processes have been praised by externals; we distinguish between feedback to justify the mark (set clearly against the criteria) and feedback to improve the work, and offer further professional development commentary too. One area that we have struggled with over the past five years is awarding percentage marks for the assignments. The teaching portfolio was a pass/fail grade but we were compelled to adopt a percentage tariff when we changed to using assignments. As a team, and conscious of the literature on marks obscuring the usefulness of feedback, we had misgivings about fine-grain distinctions between percentage points – what makes this assignment a 62 per cent or a 63 per cent, or why not a 64 per cent? Our decision was therefore to limit our marks to high or low within each band of fail, pass, merit or distinction.

So what?

Leaving behind a portfolio assessment, with its demand for an extensive reflective commentary supported by assorted evidence, coupled with increased opportunities to develop assignments through participation in peer-supported learning activities, has markedly improved the student assessment experience on the course. Reflection on practice is securely embedded but the assignments allow for a broader set of literacy practices. They also more readily invite our learners, new academic staff, to engage in behaviours that Macfarlane and Gourlay (2009: 458) call for, namely 'to contest existing orthodoxies about teaching, rather than simply demonstrating that they have internalized the mantras presented to them'.

Now what?

The vignette captures the course at the end of a five-year cycle in which it has evolved gradually in response to evaluation by students and others. In the renewal process, the course team seeks to build on what is working with the programme and in particular to strengthen learner engagement and co-construction of the curriculum. The assignments remain largely work-based and tutor-led, but will incorporate structured peer review and formative feedback. With the revalidation, we are planning to switch to a broader band marking of fail, pass, merit or distinction.

What sense can we make from these perspectives on assessment?

The process of evaluating three short vignettes of assessment practice, from the academic staff perspective has helped us to identify several pointers in answer to our introductory question: why does it appear to be so hard for university programmes to heed the good practice advice and evidence and change their practices in assessment? For us, this is a central question, and one that affects how we conduct our own practice as educational developers. We now briefly consider what we have identified as the key factors to address this question.

Management of change

A natural moment for changing assessment comes when the course approaches periodic review or other major re-write. However, both institutional policy and working practices impact significantly at this point in assessment design and may mitigate against desired changes in assessment. Decisions on assessment design are, to a greater or lesser extent, shaped by the cultural expectations within the discipline, the quality frameworks and goals of the department, the institutional strategic direction and the national agenda. In respect of student satisfaction scores, one of Williams and Kane's (2008: 4) key recommendations is that 'effective change requires concerted action over many years'.

Time allocation

Institutional expectations of academic staff time is represented in workload models. These are constantly under review and many variations of schemes are in operation. Time allocation or workload planning may take into account the preparation and marking time associated with modules dependent on cohort size, and there may be additional hours for module leadership, or there may not. Regardless, these ideal models bear little resemblance to the marking experience of colleagues on the ground, the Scottish Enhancement workshops on assessment loads concur:

> The next time you sit down to mark 250 case studies, essays, laboratory reports or examination scripts, ask yourself one question. Can I do this differently, in a way which makes my assessment more efficient and more effective?
>
> (Hornby 2005: 27)

The chances are that, even if you do identify the need for change, few if any steps are taken to rationalize assessment in the normal run of a course because of the impact on other people's allotted time. Consequently, while individuals and small groups might be able to achieve some improvements in the efficiency and effectiveness of their practices, large-scale or radical changes to assessment are harder to achieve.

Adopting a team approach

Assessment improvement is achieved differently in each our vignettes, but what unites them is the team context. Lasting changes in assessment require the buy-in of all those involved in enhancing the student learning experience. In all circumstances, the assessment design needs to be robust and explicit, and understood in dialogue with a range of team members and students. By developing a shared understanding of assessment practices through dialogue, academic members of staff are also better placed to communicate the purpose, the process and the expected outcomes of the assessments to their students.

So, what does lead to changes in assessment practices? In many countries, and well established in the UK, new academics are offered an accredited course in learning and teaching, such as the Postgraduate Certificate in our vignette above. This form of initial professional development, often mandated by the institution, provides a good impetus for individual academic staff to consider alternative assessment strategies and to open up the scholarship of teaching, learning and assessment. However, this is not enough to effect lasting changes in assessment practices nor to combat the factors identified in the previous section. For this reason, we close this chapter with a recommendation on how this might be achieved, as alluded to in the previous paragraph, within a team context.

As educational developers, we have experienced tangible benefits in working on course design, including assessment design, at the programme level where members of staff can collaboratively engage with as many relevant stakeholders as possible (academic staff plus learning technologists, quality officers, subject librarians, course administrators, educational developers), rather than working individually at module or unit level with their usual subject-focused autonomy. The latter approach can lead to students experiencing assessment bunching, either too varied or too narrow a range of assessment types, over-assessment of some learning outcomes (and under-assessment of others) and lack of developmental coherence across their programme. A programme-level approach to enhancing assessment would start with an articulation of the merits of the current programme in order to open up discussion and practical work around what needs to change. The process has been found to be effective at engaging staff with alternative and better conceptions of assessment practices. An evaluation of the process found that this team approach 'can facilitate conceptual change about learning and teaching in some participants, sharing good and/or innovative practice, and foster productive networking with otherwise unfamiliar colleagues' (Dempster *et al.* forthcoming).

Indeed, recent moves in educational development favour change initiatives targeting departmental or programme level design, for all the reasons listed above. These task-focused workshops go under a number of guises; currently some examples are: CDIs (Course Design Intensives, Oxford Brookes University), CAMEL model (JISC InfoNET), Change Academy (Higher Education Academy), Carpe Diem (University of Leicester), Engaging Departments Institute (Association of American Colleges and Universities). Academic staff evaluations of such work-based development events are broadly positive and lasting changes in practice seem to emanate from them.

It is challenging to implement significant and sustainable improvements to assessment practices within the resource constraints and complexity of higher education. Programme-level, team-based approaches to assessment redesign offer fruitful opportunities for creatively addressing the challenge.

References

ASKe (2009) *Feedback at a Crossroads: Where Do We Go from Here?* Available at: http://www.brookes.ac.uk/aske/OsneyGrangeGroup/ (accessed 18 January 2011).
——(2010) *ASKe 1, 2, 3 Leaflets.* Available at: http://www.brookes.ac.uk/aske/Resources/ (accessed 18 January 2011).

Biggs, J. and Tang, C. (2007) *Teaching for Quality Learning at University*, 3rd edn, Maidenhead: Open University Press.

Bloxham, S. and Boyd, P. (2007) *Developing Effective Assessment in Higher Education: A Practical Guide*, Maidenhead: Open University Press.

Boud, D. (1995) 'Assessment and learning: contradictory or complementary?', in P. Knight (ed.) *Assessment for Learning in Higher Education*, London: Kogan Page, pp. 35–48.

Burke, D. (2009) 'Strategies for using feedback students bring to higher education', *Assessment & Evaluation in Higher Education*, 34(1): 41–50.

Chanock, K. (2000) 'Comments on essays: do students understand what tutors write?', *Teaching in Higher Education*, 5(1): 95–105.

Dempster, J., Benfield, G. and Francis, R. (forthcoming) 'An academic development model for fostering innovation and sharing in curriculum design', *Innovations in Education and Teaching International*, in press.

Gibbs, G. and Simpson, C. (2004) 'Conditions under which assessment supports students' learning', *Learning and Teaching in Higher Education*, 1: 3–31.

Higgins, R., Hartley, P. and Skelton, A. (2002) 'The conscientious consumer: reconsidering the role of assessment feedback in student learning', *Studies in Higher Education*, 27(1): 53.

Hornby, W. (2005) 'Dogs, stars, Rolls Royces and old double-decker buses: efficiency and effectiveness in assessment', in *Reflections on Assessment*, vol. 1, Scottish Enhancement Themes, 15–29. Available at: http://www.enhancementthemes.ac.uk/themes/Assessment/outcomes.asp (accessed 20 January 2011).

Hounsell, D. (2008) *The Trouble with Feedback: New Challenges, Emerging Strategies*. Available at: http://www.tla.ed.ac.uk/interchange/spring2008/hounsell2.htm (accessed 18 January 2011).

Irons, A. (2008) *Enhancing Learning through Formative Assessment and Feedback*. Abingdon: Routledge.

Jones, A. (2009) 'Generic attributes as espoused theory: the importance of context', *Higher Education*, 58: 175–91.

Lave, J. (1993) 'The practice of learning', in S. Chaiklin and J. Lave (eds) *Understanding Practice: Perspectives on Activity and Context*, Cambridge: Cambridge University Press, pp. 3–32.

Lea, M. R. and Street, B. V. (1998) 'Student writing in higher education: an academic literacies approach', *Studies in Higher Education*, 23(2): 157–72.

Macfarlane, B. and Gourlay, L. (2009) 'The reflection game: enacting the penitent self', *Teaching in Higher Education*, 14(4): 455–9.

MacLellan, E. (2001) 'Assessment for learning: the differing perceptions of tutors and students', *Assessment & Evaluation in Higher Education*, 26(4): 307–18.

McDowell, L., Sambell, K., Bazin, V., Penlington, R., Wakelin, D., Wickes, H. and Smailes, J. (2005) *Assessment for Learning: Current Practice Exemplars from the Centre for Excellence in Learning and Teaching*, Northumbria: University of Northumbria.

Mutch, A. (2003) 'Exploring the practice of feedback to students', *Active Learning in Higher Education*, 4(1): 24–38.

Nicol, D. J. (2010) 'From monologue to dialogue: improving written feedback processes in mass higher education', *Assessment & Evaluation in Higher Education*, 35(5): 501–17.

Nicol, D. J. and Macfarlane-Dick, D. (2006) 'Formative assessment and self-regulated learning: a model and seven principles of good feedback practice', *Studies in Higher Education*, 31(2): 199–218.

Oxford Brookes University (2011) *Aske/Brookes' Assessment Compact*. Available at: http://www.brookes.ac.uk/aske/BrookesACompact/ (accessed 5 August 2011).

Patton, M. (2008) *Utilization-Focused Evaluation*, Thousand Oaks, CA: Sage.

Price, M., Benfield, G., Rust, C. and Outer, B. (2011) *Assessment Compact Survey Interim Report*, Oxford: Oxford Brookes University.

Price, M., Handley, K., Millar, J. and O'Donovan, B. (2010) 'Feedback: all that effort, but what is the effect?', *Assessment & Evaluation in Higher Education*, 35 (3): 277–89.

Ramsden, P. (1992) *Learning to Teach in Higher Education*, London: Routledge.

Rust, C., O'Donovan, B. and Price, M. (2005) 'A social constructivist assessment process model: how the research literature shows us this could be best practice', *Assessment & Evaluation in Higher Education*, 30(3): 231–40.

Sadler, D. R. (2010) 'Beyond feedback: developing student capability in complex appraisal', *Assessment & Evaluation in Higher Education*, 35(5): 535–50.

Weaver, M. (2006) 'Do students value feedback? Student perceptions of tutors' written responses', *Assessment & Evaluation in Higher Education*, 31(3): 379–94.

Wenger, E. (1998) *Communities of Practice: Learning, Meaning, and Identity*, Cambridge: Cambridge University Press.

Williams, J. and Kane, D. (2008) *Exploring the National Student Survey Assessment and Feedback Issues*. Available at: http://www.heacademy.ac.uk/resources/detail/ourwork/nss/NSS_assessment_and_feedback_report (accessed 17 January 2011).

Yorke, M. (2001) 'Formative assessment and its relevance to retention', *Higher Education Research & Development*, 20(2): 115–26.

CRITICAL FRIEND COMMENTARY

Philip Watland

It was with great interest that I read this chapter as I too am interested in why it appears good practice advice and evidence on assessments do not change our assessment practices. I write my critical friend comments principally from a Canadian College perspective.

I agree with the suggestion in this chapter that assessment requirements influence students to focus on certain aspects of the course material, and the development of assessment typically occurs at the end of the course design process. In my work, while peer review is less common, other assessment types are used and are based on learning outcomes which directly impact on the depth and the type of assessment.

The key factors identified from an academic staff perspective were related to administrative concerns: timing, time allocation, and a team approach. I am advocating that these changes should be allied with the students' experience, for example, as noted in Vignette 3, where learners complained about the portfolio assessment which resulted in changes to the assessment practice.

I agree with the authors' recommendations for effecting lasting changes in assessment practices based on working in a team environment and institutional process. However, I suggest that considering changes to assessment practices based on the additional dimension of students' experience is essential, with more effort placed on the types of assessment and approaches to feedback that are valued by students.

Based on my own research, which focused on the students' experience of online tutor support, I suggest continued effort in researching the students' experience of assessment and feedback – in particular, not taking for granted that students are homogeneous, will react to various assessment and feedback strategies in a predictable fashion, and have shared or complementary conceptions of assessment. Simply put, teachers do not have access to how students experience assessments and feedback unless they make an effort to have such access, and this potentially will lead to opportunities to change our assessment practices that have a positive effect on student learning.

What this seems to point towards is the need to spend more effort improving and understanding our own practice. While workshops, conferences, webinars, community and peer learning are all typical of the professional development activities undertaken at our College, many are on subject area interests and not on the use of assessment and feedback as part of a holistic continuous approach to improving our own professional teaching practice.

Chapter 6

Assessment for learning

Liz McDowell

Introduction

Assessment is a significant factor in students' experiences of academic study and participation in higher education. Assessment influences students' experiences of engagement, and their engagement influences the ways in which they regard assessment. Trowler and Trowler (2010) identify two dimensions of engagement that are particularly relevant to assessment. One dimension is individual engagement with learning activities and subject matter, where assessment is significantly involved. The second is engagement through participation and development of identity. Mann (2001) argues that pedagogic practices, and especially assessment, need to be reconfigured to reduce student alienation and promote engagement.

Over the past 20 years or so there has been evidence of a shift in assessment culture (Birenbaum 1996). There is considerable ongoing pressure to move from 'traditional' views and practices of assessment, with an emphasis on testing and measurement, a shift from assessment *of* learning to 'Assessment *for* Learning' (AfL). Assessment *of* learning is assessment that has the purpose of identifying a student's level of performance, often summed up in the form of marks or grades. Assessment *for* Learning is intended to support and promote learning.

Assessment and learning

Long-standing research (e.g. Marton *et al.* 1997; Sambell and McDowell 1998) demonstrates that assessment has a significant impact on learning, often termed the 'backwash' effect (Biggs 1996). Many students use the assessment system as a key indicator of what it is they are supposed to learn and how they are required to demonstrate their learning.

A pedagogic tool deriving from this insight is the idea of 'constructive alignment' (Biggs and Tang 2007) where assessment, as part of an integrated teaching–learning–assessment system, is designed to send out signals that promote students' active engagement in appropriate learning. Constructive alignment has provided support to the diversification of assessment tasks so that they more accurately reflect desired learning goals and demonstrate face validity (see Brown and Knight 1994; Brown and Glasner 1999; Bryan and Clegg 2006).

Another key change in view of assessment is an increasing recognition of the active role of students. Assessment can be seen as a way of managing student behaviour but students act on the basis of their individual and collective *perceptions* of assessment requirements, interpreted in the context of their own positioning as a student. A common pedagogic response has been to place more emphasis on guidance and information to help students to understand the 'real' requirements of assessment and feedback on their performance. The use of feedback depends on the active engagement of students and, in a broad sense, self-assessment (Sadler 1989). Recent work also suggests that, rather than just giving and receiving feedback, engagement in dialogue is essential (Carless 2006).

AfL and student engagement

AfL varies in different contexts and encompasses a range of practices but is always based on the fundamental principle of using assessment to improve learning. AfL can therefore make a positive contribution to many of the challenges currently experienced in higher education. Engaging students actively in assessment can assist in student retention. It also gives the increasing diversity of students the best possible chances to reach their full capability.

The model of AfL presented here was developed by the National Centre for Excellence in AfL funded by the Higher Education Funding Council for England and is put into effect at Northumbria University (www.northumbria.ac.uk/ cetl_afl/). The model has been used to guide the development of assessment practices across a wide range of subjects by presenting a conceptual framework for a set of inter-linked practices. Extensive case study research has been undertaken to investigate the student response and the impacts on learning of AfL approaches. In this development we have been particularly aware of the resource constraints and the impact of large classes in many higher education contexts. This chapter goes beyond a statement of AfL principles to illustrate ways in which they can be implemented despite sometimes challenging circumstances. The key components of the AfL model are:

- authentic assessment
- balancing formative and summative assessment
- active and participatory learning
- feedback through dialogue
- feedback through participation
- development of student autonomy.

Authentic assessment

Authentic assessment is about making assessment tasks more 'realistic' and meaningful, ensuring that assessment is about important and valuable knowledge, skills and understanding. This is about the *nature of assessment tasks*, either summative or formative. Students experience many assessment tasks, such as exams and assignments, as nothing more than 'hoops to jump through'. They often say that assessment tasks bear no relationship to anything one would have to do in 'real life'. Perceptions of meaningless activity are significant factors in students' disengagement from their academic programmes (Sambell *et al.* 1997). This may be particularly problematic for students who are less well prepared for university study or who have a fragile sense of themselves as learners. It can, however, be equally experienced by high-achieving students.

Authentic assessment is based on meaningful tasks that can act as an effective hook to engage students more purposefully in their studies. Students' approaches to assessment tasks that appear to them to be 'meaningful' rather than 'meaningless' are of a very different quality. Authentic assessment may be based on tasks with an external 'real-life' basis, clearly indicating that what students are being required to demonstrate has some application beyond the classroom and the test. Other authentic assessment allows students to engage, at an appropriate level, in the normal practices of the academic discipline they are studying, participating in what has been termed the 'ways of thinking and practising' (McCune and Hounsell 2005). Another approach to authenticity is assessment which is designed to give students opportunities to link the assessed work to their own lives, interests or concerns. Finally, authentic assessment is often based on a process which would be regarded as more realistic: for example, the task may be carried out in a group, or students may have access to expertise and advice while completing the task. Even the change from a traditional closed book exam to an open book exam can make a difference. Some examples of how students' work can be made more authentic are as follows:

- *Authentic to the 'real world'*: Students in Sports Science were asked to write a leaflet for an individually chosen audience, such as teenagers or the elderly, with suggestions and guidance about taking part in exercise. This was accompanied by a commentary explaining how the student had based the leaflet on sound scientific research and the choices made in writing it. Writing for a 'real' audience led to many students engaging with theory and evidence in a more active way than with more conventional written assignments.
- *Authentic to the discipline*: Biology students were asked, in groups, to develop questions (or hypotheses) about factors affecting plant growth, and design an experiment to test a chosen hypothesis, gathering data over an extended period of time. Many of the students said that this was 'more like being a real scientist' and much better than the normal 'experiments' that they routinely carried out in practical classes.
- *Authentic processes*: Post-graduate students in product design were assessed by means of a group design project with a simulated client (a lecturer) who gave the initial brief then visited the group from time to time to review progress. Students found that views from the client often changed or the information

he gave was partial and sometimes not accurate. The final outcome was presented to the client and his colleagues by demonstration, a technical specification, and discussion. Students appreciated that the simulation made the process more like a 'real-world' experience than the normal precise brief that they were used to for projects. As such, it gave them more scope to use their own ideas and judgement.

Balancing formative and summative assessment

In recent years there has been an increasing awareness that the balance of assessment in universities is tipped towards summative assessment and that formative assessment is not used effectively (Knight and Yorke 2003). The balance between summative and formative assessment has both quantitative and qualitative aspects. The quantitative balance is related to the challenges of resources. Academic teachers find that there is no time for formative assessment activities, especially with large class sizes where traditional formative assessment methods such as setting and marking practice tasks would be very time-consuming. Students often say that much of the time that they spend in study is focused on the requirements of summative assessment. However, a large body of research in education has shown that formative assessment is one of the most powerful tools for improving learning (Black and Wiliam 1998). We therefore need to find time and resources for formative assessment.

The qualitative balance between formative and summative assessment relates to the experience of teachers and students. Do teachers feel that they are teaching genuine subject matter and related skills and understanding? Or do they feel that they are 'teaching to the test' driven by an emphasis on summative assessment? Are students mainly working to achieve what Dweck (2000) calls learning goals, that is, developing their understanding, knowledge and skills? Or are they mostly driven by performance goals, only willing to engage in what is specifically required to demonstrate performance for summative assessment – as many lecturers fear?

From a quantitative perspective, steps can be taken to ensure that students take part in formative assessment by combining it with required summative assessment. For example, students may be required to submit small 'formative' assignments which do not carry marks in themselves but must be submitted before the student is eligible to submit a final piece of work or sit an exam. To promote productive engagement rather than simply 'time on task', the qualities of student experience need to be considered. A focus on learning goals, with intrinsic motivation coming from the process of learning, personal development and the achievement of meaningful outcomes, can lead to positive student engagement with subject matter and also, potentially, contribute to the longer-term development of student identities as capable and knowledgeable learners. Examples of students performing tasks that shift the balance towards formative assessment are:

- *Shifting the quantitative balance towards formative assessment:* In an experimental science subject, the programme team decided to reduce the amount of summative assessment in the first year practical programme. The normal approach was that all weekly practical reports were submitted and marked with feedback but this did not seem to improve students' performance very much over the year. The new approach was that students still submitted weekly reports but these were selectively evaluated and not marked. For example, one week, students all received feedback on the 'methodology' section of the report; another week, the feedback was about reporting data. Each student received written feedback promptly and the aspect of the report for that week was also discussed in one of the lecture sessions with the whole student group. Students submitted two final reports for summative assessment where the whole report was considered. Overall much more student and staff time and effort went into formative assessment; in the former approach staff spent a lot of time on summative assessment, marking and writing feedback on students' submitted reports but it was less effective.
- *Shifting the qualitative balance towards formative assessment:* Art History students were asked to produce, individually, an online art exhibition (a set of web pages) for summative module assessment. This was a form of simulation of a real activity, made possible by the wealth of visual material available on the Internet. The normal seminars were replaced by weekly practical classes where students worked on their exhibitions and a lot of formative assessment went on with guidance from the lecturer and interaction with other students. Students' engagement throughout was about producing an exhibition that they could be proud of and overcoming problems in doing so. There was evidence of intrinsic motivation and a focus on learning goals rather than just getting the work done because it was required, solely focusing on the marks they would achieve.

Active and participatory learning

Most programmes intend that students should develop capabilities such as critical thinking, communication skills, use of evidence, and abilities to address novel problems or questions drawing on relevant subject knowledge. If summative assessment is designed to test the full range of goals, students need to practise appropriate kinds of activities, obtain and use feedback. However, it is not unusual to find that the first time students try something out in earnest it 'counts'. For example, students may be marked on giving an oral presentation when it is the first time they have given such a presentation during their programme. A further example is requiring students to submit for marking an analysis of statistical data when methods have been demonstrated but students have never actually carried out the analysis for themselves nor been given feedback on their approach. These kinds of situations arise particularly in programmes divided into modules, often with little time to spend on active tasks and feedback except as part of the summative module assessment.

Active and participatory methods prepare students for the ways in which they will be summatively assessed. This gives students a fair chance to present what they know and can do, without being 'caught out' by not having understood what is required or not realizing that their approach to a task is not correct or is not meeting the standards required. A fair system where they can demonstrate what they are capable of is important to students (Flint and Johnson 2011). If students see the system as unfair they are more likely to disengage from their learning, to focus on just getting by, or 'faking good' (Gibbs 2006: 26), appearing to meet assessment requirements by playing the system. An example of students being involved in practice and participation is as follows:

- *Practice and participation*: A Business Studies lecturer teaching Human Resources Management built in opportunities for students to practise the approaches that were important in the subject and were needed for the summative assessment (an open book exam) by replacing some of the lectures and seminars with structured activity. For instance, in one lecture, students worked in small groups to explain how they would address a given HRM problem using course notes and texts that they had been asked to bring along with them. One person in each group posted the group's answer on the VLE site for the module. This meant that students had an opportunity to practise a valuable skill, applying theory and ideas from the module to a professional problem. Working with fellow students and seeing other responses online meant that they could also see other ways of thinking and approaching a problem, in a context that would also help them understand exam requirements. The lecturer was also able to comment online and in the next lecture about the responses to the task and make suggestions for improvement.

Feedback through dialogue

Feedback in higher education is mainly viewed as teachers' comments on student work. Quality assurance approaches, with their tendency to emphasize standardization, consistency, precision and the justification of marks, often require routine feedback such as check lists. Conventional feedback approaches have their limitations. Students often perceive that the delay between completing the task and receiving feedback comment is too long. Students frequently have difficulty in understanding the feedback and applying any messages from it to future academic work. Many programmes are now delivered as a series of modules, which exacerbates these problems. By the time students receive feedback, they have moved on to new modules and find it difficult to transfer anything gleaned from feedback to this next set of modules. Piecemeal feedback by module can also be criticized for the focus on single assignments or exams rather than looking more broadly at students' performance and progress. Where feedback arrives with marks and justification of marks awarded, research has shown that it is difficult to get students to pay attention to qualitative feedback (Wiliam 2008).

Considering the limitations and difficulties surrounding 'normal' feedback, it is not surprising that many students do not appear to learn from feedback, may not read it and in many cases do not even collect the feedback or marked work as they are expected to do. Feedback is significantly improved if it is more dialogic with opportunities for students to check out their understanding of staff comments and with teachers having the opportunity to explain and extend their feedback.

It is possible to give students feedback in a timely manner which encourages them to consider and use the feedback, even within the constraints of current higher education. For example, students can be asked to produce preliminary work, such as an essay or report outline, and post it online for discussion, take a computer-delivered test with in-built feedback on topics related to the summative assessment, or give a short presentation (individually or in groups) to their lecture group or seminar class where tutor and peer feedback can be given. All of these activities make students' ideas available for feedback and discussion by the lecturer and in some cases others, at individual or group level. An example of feedback dialogue is as follows:

- *Feedback dialogue*: A lecturer in English gave students the opportunity to submit a draft essay in one of their modules which the lecturer would assess, giving detailed comments. Over 90 per cent of students submitted a draft and all were very interested in the comments and wanted to discuss them with the lecturer. She organized one of the taught sessions as a discussion of feedback on the draft essays, common problems, questions, and so on which reduced the one-to-one load. When final essays were submitted, the lecturer gave a mark and very minimal, if any, comments. The students had understood and agreed in advance that this would be the case so that the lecturer's workload was not increased unreasonably. Results showed that most students had paid attention to feedback. There was still a range of marks in the group but many students had improved their marks in comparison with their performance in other modules.

Feedback through participation

Teaching and learning methods within the lecture room or classroom, based on participation, can provide a feedback-rich environment where feedback comes from a range of sources and methods and does not depend solely on conventional lecturer-to-student feedback. A rich feedback environment is best developed by participatory approaches where students learn in collaboration with others. In this context, feedback comes from hearing what fellow students say and think and seeing how they approach tasks and at the same time gauging the response to one's own ideas and proposals. Most of this feedback can 'just happen' if the learning environment is set up appropriately.

Many practical classes are feedback-rich in this way. In laboratories, students often work on tasks in small groups and interact with other groups – especially where they want to compare results or have 'got stuck' and want to know how others are doing. Another example is the use of a simulated patient by health students. This is an interactive technologically advanced mannikin which gives immediate feedback in relation to the treatment given and can be used by individuals, groups and observers, sharing ideas and suggestion. Even a large lecture theatre can become more feedback-rich with the use of response systems which allow students to record their responses to questions and view a bar chart showing the overall responses of the class. This can form the basis of discussion and comparison among students.

Students find feedback in the classroom a very useful indication of how they are doing and whether they are on 'the right lines'. It is short-cycle feedback, specific and contextualized, which complements more formal tutor-written feedback. This kind of feedback is better at communicating tacit understandings and requirements which are difficult to explain through written feedback but are generally absorbed through participation and interaction with others. This raises awareness of how subject matter can be seen differently and increases the range of ideas available to each individual. It helps in the less tangible aspects of learning such as the purpose, nature and importance of the subject area and ways in which individuals can engage with it, building current and future identities. An example of classroom participation by students is as follows:

• *Classroom participation*: A lecturer in Cultural Studies designed a module based on active participation of students in lecture classes of about 60 students. He organized activities which led the students from expressing personal ideas about the topics addressed to the use of academic knowledge and discourse as the module progressed. One activity was the 'graffiti exercise' providing small groups of students with different film posters on and around which they were asked to write or draw. Students initially used their personal knowledge and ideas, and then used ideas drawn from non-academic texts such as film reviews and publicity, later adding perspectives from relevant scholarly texts. In each session there was an opportunity for students to talk about or display their ideas and understanding, to hear what colleagues had to say and receive comments from the lecturer individually, in small groups, to the whole class or afterwards online. The lecturer spent his time listening, commenting and guiding rather than presenting information.

Development of student autonomy

Students' abilities and dispositions to manage their own learning and to review, or self-assess, their own progress are regarded as key graduate attributes. These capabilities are important in the professional employment that students take up after graduation. Developing them significantly contributes to enabling higher education programmes to address the challenge of enhancing employability in their students. AfL approaches allow students to become informed participants in assessment, not just victims caught up in a system where they have little control.

One important aspect is that students should come to understand the performance requirements and quality standards in their discipline or professional field. This is relevant to all students, but especially important for some, such as international students, who may be adjusting to a very different context, and need help to do this quickly. A range of practices can help students to understand assessment requirements (O'Donovan *et al.* 2008). Students can be encouraged to work with the criteria used for judgement in their subject. An example of this would be students undertaking marking exercises on exemplar assignments. The aim is for students to understand the specific requirements and also become familiar with the processes of standing back and evaluating their own performance, giving feedback to others and using feedback and guidance from others, whether these are fellow students and lecturers or, in the working context, colleagues and managers. Students are in a much more powerful situation when they understand requirements and the evaluation process. This means that they can play an active role, rather than feeling disempowered by 'never knowing what the lecturers really want'.

Autonomy and a sense of ownership of one's own academic work are also key features of productive student engagement. A sense of ownership and a wish to tell other people often arise for undergraduate students when they do a final year dissertation or project, but this approach can be fostered in other ways and earlier stages. Choice, even within a set form of assignment, can enable students to link their academic work to their own knowledge, interest and experience, thus increasing authenticity and intrinsic motivation. Students often feel that what they produce in response to academic tasks is of no real importance. It may be 'questions that hundreds of students have done before' or 'showing' that they have put what they have read into their own words – but without *really* using their own words or having anything to say. Student who feel that they are in the position of 'author' with something to communicate will take more control and responsibility for their own output and gain satisfaction from doing so. Examples of developing student autonomy are given below:

- *Understanding assessment criteria*: Marketing students were given an assignment where they applied theories concerning 'customer identity' to a specific self-selected context. Some class time was spent in working with the learning outcomes of the module, including staff and students negotiating some re-wording to make the learning outcomes clearer. Students had the opportunity to propose a format in which they wanted to present their ideas for summative assessment as long as it would show that they had met the learning outcomes. Some chose to do a conventional report. Other proposals included: an oral presentation; a set of Web materials; a podcast; and a recorded online discussion involving a fellow student, a (volunteer) academic and a business contact of the student. These alternatives gave students more experience in self-direction.

- *Taking responsibility*: Computing and information systems students from a range of different disciplines collaborated in group work where they were each expected to use and contribute their own specialist knowledge and skills to complete the overall group task. Students found this a very positive experience because they became the 'expert' in their group on specific aspects of the task. Working with other students and being relied upon for specialist input was motivating and engaging.

Conclusion

Assessment for learning is an approach that addresses many of the challenges in contemporary higher education in a positive way. Assessment is often seen as something more like 'a necessary evil' than a positive force for learning. This suggests that although ideas about learning and teaching may have changed, assessment has not been successfully accommodated into new ways of thinking. University teachers recognize the active role of learners in constructing knowledge, the need to support a diverse range of learners and the wider range of attainments that society demands from graduates but, despite this shift, find it difficult to manage assessment. Student engagement in meaningful activity, as active learners, is at the heart of assessment for learning. Student attainment is supported by guidance, feedback, participation and dialogue. AfL promotes engagement through collaboration within programme learning communities to balance the competitive ethos that is often set up by traditional ways of conducting and thinking about assessment. This chapter has shown, through a range of examples, that AfL can be put into practice even in these current resource-constrained times.

References

Biggs, J. (1996) 'Assessing learning quality: reconciling institutional, staff and educational demands', *Assessment & Evaluation in Higher Education*, 21(1): 5–15.

Biggs, J. and Tang, C. (2007) *Teaching for Quality Learning at University*, 3rd edn, Maidenhead: Open University Press.

Birenbaum, M. (1996) 'Assessment 2000: towards a pluralistic approach to assessment', in M. Birenbaum and F. J. R. C. Dochy (eds) *Alternatives in Assessment of Achievements, Learning Processes and Prior Knowledge*, Boston: Kluwer, pp. 3–29.

Black, P. and Wiliam, D. (1998) 'Assessment and classroom learning', *Assessment in Education: Principles, Policy and Practice*, 5(1): 7–73.

Brown, S. and Glasner, A. (eds) (1999) *Assessment Matters in Higher Education*, Maidenhead: Open University Press.

Brown, S. and Knight, P. (1994) *Assessing Learners in Higher Education*, London: Kogan Page.

Bryan, C. and Clegg, K. (2006) *Innovative Assessment in Higher Education*, London: Routledge.

Carless, D. (2006) 'Differing perceptions in the feedback process', *Studies in Higher Education*, 31(2): 219–33.

Dweck, C. S. (2000) *Self Theories: Their Role in Motivation, Personality and Development*, Philadelphia, PA: Psychology Press.

Flint, N. R. A. and Johnson, B. (2011) *Towards Fairer University Assessment*, London: Routledge.

Gibbs, G. (2006) 'Why assessment is changing', in C. Bryan and K. Clegg (eds) *Innovative Assessment in Higher Education*, London: Routledge, pp. 11–22.

Knight, P. T. and Yorke, M. (2003) *Assessment, Learning and Employability*, Maidenhead: Open University Press.

Mann, S. J. (2001) 'Alternative perspectives on the student experience: alienation and engagement', *Studies in Higher Education*, 26(1): 7–19.

Marton, F., Hounsell, D. and Entwistle, N. (1997) *The Experience of Learning*, 2nd edn, Edinburgh: Scottish Academic Press.

McCune, V. and Hounsell, D. (2005) 'The ways of thinking and practising in three final year biology courses', *Higher Education*, 49(3): 255–89.

O'Donovan, B., Price, M. and Rust, C. (2008) 'Developing student understanding of assessment standards: a nested hierarchy of approaches', *Teaching in Higher Education*, 13(2): 205–17.

Sadler, R. (1989) 'Formative assessment and the design of instructional systems', *Instructional Science*, 18(2): 119–44.

Sambell, K. and McDowell, L. (1998) 'The construction of the hidden curriculum: messages and meanings in the assessment of student learning', *Assessment & Evaluation in Higher Education*, 23(4): 391–402.

Sambell, K., McDowell, L. and Brown, S. (1997) '"But is it fair?" An exploratory study of student perceptions of the consequential validity of assessment', *Studies in Educational Evaluation*, 23(4): 349–71.

Trowler, V. and Trowler, P. (2010) *Student Engagement Evidence Summary*, York: Higher Education Academy.

Wiliam, D. (2008) 'Balancing dilemmas; traditional theories and new applications', in A. Havnes and L. McDowell (eds) *Balancing Dilemmas in Assessment and Learning in Contemporary Education*, New York: Routledge, pp. 268–81.

CRITICAL FRIEND COMMENTARY

David Carless

The chapter by Liz McDowell addresses important issues at the interface of student engagement and assessment for learning. In the spirit of elaborating the relevance of the work for a globalized academy, this commentary touches on related developments in Australasia and Hong Kong.

In a steadily expanding higher education sector, the issue of student engagement is a highly pertinent one and has been the focus of recent large-scale data collection in Australasia. Adapted from an American instrument (see Kuh 2009), the Australasian survey of student engagement (AUSSE) gauges student behaviours and outcomes, and enables institutions to identify areas of good practice as well as those aspects in need of improvement (Coates 2010). It focuses on six engagement scales: academic challenge; active learning; student and staff interaction; enriching educational experiences; supportive learning environments; and work-integrated learning.

While providing a wealth of useful data, the extent to which any survey instrument such as the AUSSE can capture the complexities of student engagement is open to debate. In a recent critique, Hagel, Carr and Devlin (2011) point out that student engagement is a multi-faceted construct encompassing behavioural, emotional and cognitive elements, and that conceptions of engagement can range from deep flow experiences to involvement in a broad range of activities. Subtle distinctions also arise at the interface of engagement, alienation or compliance with the rules of the assessment game. However, large-scale surveys of student engagement are likely to remain a key feature of the documentation of the student experience. Of relevance to this volume may be comparisons of Australasian and US surveys, with those in the UK (see, for example, Little *et al.* 2009). Potentially illuminating would be further analyses of the interaction between student engagement and their experience of assessment.

I now turn to recent developments in Hong Kong where there is a shift from a three-year to a four-year undergraduate curriculum with students entering university one year earlier (after year 12 rather than year 13 of secondary school). Student engagement in relation to assessment for learning is a feature of current curriculum reforms at the University of Hong Kong. A new 'common core curriculum' aims to develop in students an interdisciplinary perspective on the complexities and interconnectedness of key significant contemporary issues (University of Hong Kong 2011). Diverse forms of assessment are used including, for example, posters, simulations, making short movies and analytic reflections on field trips.

The early experiences of this new curriculum in the 2010–11 academic year seem to be generally positive, although some tensions arise. Rich and diversified assessment tasks encourage productive student learning, but provide challenges in terms of the balance between summative and formative assessment. Tasks that do not count for marks risk being neglected by students. Worthwhile learning tasks then tend to be formally assessed which can lead to assessment overload and fragmentation if there are a number of low weighting assessment items not fully integrated into a coherent whole.

This common core curriculum also resonates with a number of themes addressed by McDowell, including authentic assessment, active participatory learning, and the development of student autonomy. In addition, the issue of dialogic feedback is at the forefront of research at the university (Carless *et al.* 2011), with an increasing recognition that feedback needs to be embedded within the curriculum, facilitated through integrated assessment tasks, and focused on the development of student self-evaluative capacities.

Student engagement lies at the heart of assessment for learning. In this brief commentary, I have provided a flavour of the globalized significance of the issues discussed in McDowell's chapter and in the volume as a whole.

References

Carless, D., Salter, D., Yang, M. and Lam, J. (2011) 'Developing sustainable feedback practices', *Studies in Higher Education*, 36(4): 395–407.

Coates, H. (2010) 'Development of the Australasian survey of student engagement (AUSSE)', *Higher Education*, 60(1): 1–17.

Hagel, P., Carr, R. and Devlin, M. (2011) 'Conceptualising and measuring student engagement through the Australasian Survey of Student Engagement (AUSSE): a critique', *Assessment & Evaluation in Higher Education*, in press.

Kuh, G.D. (2009) 'The national survey of student engagement: conceptual and empirical foundations', *New Directions for Institutional Research*, Spring(141): 5–20.

Little, B., Locke, W., Scesa, A. and Williams, R. (2009) *Report to HEFCE on Student Engagement*, London: Centre for Higher Education Research and Information.

University of Hong Kong (2011) *Common Core*. Available at: http://commoncore. hku.hk/ (accessed 12 May 2011).

Chapter 7

Finding their voice
Podcasts for teaching, learning and assessment

Graham Steventon

Introduction

In the wider context of technology-enhanced learning, the podcast, usually a digital audio recording in mp3 format or video in mp4 format, is a relatively simple device. It can be downloaded not only to a computer but also to an iPod or mobile phone, offering one of the most flexible means of communicating information of all the Web 2.0 technologies now available. Certainly, by tapping into the ubiquity of these devices, the podcast has become a means of making information accessible to the widest possible audience using a medium that fits within the comprehension of the majority of students, unlike many other technologies with which the familiarity of the so-called 'digital natives' of the 'net generation' is over-stated (Childs and Espinoza-Ramos 2008). While outside academia podcasts have become popular for delivering music, entertainment and news (Copley 2007), their educative potential is also increasingly being realized, catering especially for a more mobile generation of learners who need to learn on the move, often multi-tasking as they need to balance the conflicting demands of their course alongside the need to earn money (Walker 2009). However, much of the earlier research into podcast use in teaching and learning has been descriptive, focusing on the practical issues of application. It is only more recently that the pedagogic role of the podcast has begun to be critically evaluated.

The aim of this chapter is to explore the pedagogic potential of the podcast for teaching and learning, and particularly assessment, an area that has received little attention in the literature to date (although see Dale and Pymm 2009, on assessment; Cooper 2008; France and Ribchester 2008; Savin-Baden 2010, on assessment feedback). Drawing on my own experiences of using podcasts for assessment and the notions of 'consumption' and 'production' (Lim 2006, cited in Ralph *et al.* 2009: 17) as representative of conflicting pedagogies, I shall highlight how the podcast can be seen to symbolize the tensions between transmissive and transformative uses of technology. Its transmissive function represents the replication of the traditional role of teacher as definer of knowledge and the student as passive recipient, or consumer. Here, voice simply replaces text as an alternative medium through which this status quo is delivered enabling the student to fulfil extrinsic goals, such as revising for assessment. Its transformative potential, on the other hand, implies a change of paradigm which shifts the power base to the student as producer of knowledge and voice becomes the medium through which students can express themselves as reflective, creative beings, harnessing intrinsic motivations, such as the pleasure of learning and thrill of enlightenment (Hughes *et al.* 2009) and the opportunity to demonstrate it in the work on which they are judged.

The true transformative potential of technology and the podcast's contribution to it, however, continue to be challenged by wider agendas. First is the strategic level whereby governments seek to shape students into employable entities, a very different view of empowerment to that envisaged by educators such as Freire who see true empowerment as the development of agency in the learner so that they become aware of, and critical of, the structural forces that impact on them in order to achieve 'authentic freedom' (Crotty 1998: 156). Second is the level at which education becomes immersed in bureaucratic processes that are set up to respond to social trends, such as the commodification of education where institutions are reliant on income from students and in turn students expect results without jeopardy as a return on their investment. Third is the level at which the teacher sees her or himself as the appointed expert whose role it is to define the scope of the learning, prepare and deliver the appropriate material, and to test the student on their absorption of relevant knowledge. At this level the interests of traditional hierarchies of power are served and maintained. Technology's role is seen as a means of using new techniques to meet expectations of digitally aware students (Ipsos MORI 2007) but without compromising entrenched teaching principles. Such agendas belie the true potential of the podcast, particularly for students from non-traditional and marginalized backgrounds in higher education who are often penalized by assessment practices built on dominant pedagogies that centre on written text-based literacy (Mills 2010); in other words, assessments in which the capacity to think is predicated on the ability to write. These are retention issues that resonate strongly in the context of widening participation and this chapter concludes that assessment practices which allow and encourage students to express themselves through voice as well as text are more inclusive and more likely to embed the student in their learning in a meaningful way.

The podcast and the wider higher education context

Plenderleith and Adamson (2009) note the tensions between the political desire to realize the transformative powers of technology-enhanced teaching and learning and the policy emphasis on service provision and efficiency. This, they argue, emphasizes an economic rather than a pedagogic imperative in order to provide a return on investment in meeting the widening participation agenda, employability and the challenges of global competition. In the United Kingdom, despite the Conservative/Liberal Democrat Coalition's determination to cut costs leading to major changes in the delivery and funding of higher education, the widening participation agenda remains if only as rhetoric in the context of higher student fees and lifetime debts, whereas employability through selective funding of vocational courses is becoming a main driver of higher education provision in its many forms.

Technological capability and the capacity to participate fully in an increasingly digital society may certainly contribute towards satisfying the prerequisites of employability, and while young people born into a technological age are already technologically aware before they reach higher education, their engagement is mostly through social networking in ways that lack a critical or reflective dimension and the expectation is that higher education will fill that gap (Westerman and Barry 2009). However, higher education is also under pressure to change to become more effective and efficient in responding to the needs of students as well as employers by providing relevant courses (Reushle *et al.* 2009). These pressures create resource difficulties that are leading to shifts in delivery patterns over more variable time paths. For example, lifelong learning, distance learning and part-time study are trends in which 'presence and absence are becoming blurred' (Parson *et al.* 2008: 215) and learning becomes individualized and personalized (Cooper 2008).

Podcasts are well placed to respond to these demands in beneficial ways. They provide flexible delivery of teaching material in a very accessible form originally made possible through the development of portable audio devices such as the iPod and advances in mobile telephone technology, and the ubiquitous uptake of these devices has brought new delivery modes within reach of the majority of students (Dale and Pymm 2009). For example, teaching and learning material can be made available in audio form to supplement other forms of material such as lecture notes and Powerpoint slides and studies by Laing, Wooten and Irons (2006, cited in Cooper 2008) and Copley (2007) found these particularly useful to students as revision tools for assessments. Armellini, Salmon and Hawkridge (2009) emphasize the benefits of audio in certain types of course, such as languages, where the spoken word is an important part of the curriculum. Isolation and disconnectedness are commonly experienced by distance learning students leading to demotivation and high levels of attrition, and the use of voice in podcasts can help to humanize and personalize the learning experience embedding the student in the learning process, which in turn improves retention (Bolliger *et al.* 2010). Audio in teaching and learning also accesses different learning styles, particularly when used in conjunction with other approaches, thus catering for a diverse student audience (Parson *et al.* 2008; Walker 2009).

The danger in merely reacting to these wider pressures is that technology drives e-learning and simply becomes bolted on to curriculum delivery rather than driving pedagogy (Middleton 2010). It becomes a means of helping to satisfy the extrinsic requirements of the curriculum, that of the efficient delivery of teacher-produced knowledge for the consumption of the student (Ralph *et al.* 2009), and much of the evaluative work on podcast use to date has tended to focus on student uptake of the technology and reaction to it rather than deeper pedagogic concerns (Newton and Middleton 2009; Walker 2009; Middleton 2010). The emphasis is therefore transmissive rather than transformative and arguably to really engage with issues of retention, students need to become embedded in their learning through empowerment.

The limitations of traditional representations of knowledge

For education to be empowering, it needs to be liberating and that means freeing the student from the shackles of conventional ways of thinking about the world; in other words, to encourage learners to be aware of, and critical of, the very processes that shape their learning in particular ways. This is a process that Freire called 'conscientisation' (Crotty 1998: 148), literally, the awakening of con-sciousness through the release of the creative imagination. Crotty explains how Freire's work in building literacy skills with peasant groups in Brazil in the 1960s involved giving them a sense of agency in the context of entrenched, oppressive structural processes that shaped their lives; in short, making them aware of the very processes that limit their understanding by turning them into co-creators of their world rather than mere spectators of it. Reushle et al. (2009) argue that technology-enhanced learning has the power to be transformative in this way by promoting students' deeper reflection on, and understanding of, their work, thereby empowering them through their attachment of their learning to their own belief systems. It can also help challenge ingrained ways of thinking and acting by opening them up to new ideas. However, the transition from transmission to transformation has met with some opposition in higher education resulting in relatively little change compared with other arenas of life. This resistance has, in part, stemmed from the 'ivory tower' attitudes in traditional higher education reinforcing the privileged status quo, and the resistance to processes that challenge the established power relations in teaching, learning and assessment.

Deane and Borg (2011) highlight the importance placed on developing writ-ing skills in students, not only in order to fulfil the expectations of academic staff in assessments, but also those of prospective employers as a general indication of the capabilities of the student. Writing problems relate to both global and local issues; global issues are the extent to which a student lacks understanding of the material and disciplinary thinking, and local issues are presentational deficiencies, such as poor spelling, grammar and sentence structure, and lack of rigour in referencing. While it may be the global issues that signify understanding of the subject and would therefore be generic to any format of assessment, often students with good understanding of the subject are let down by poor written presentation of their work. However, this assumes a universal approach to literacy, which results in a diverse student population being shoe-horned into a particular paradigm that takes little or no account of their different backgrounds and experiences prior to coming into higher education. Mills (2010) argues that the link between literacy, cultural values and orientation, and the context-driven nature of that link, questions the whole idea of a universal view of literacy. The ideological nature of literacy and the power vested in pedagogy situate literacy practices in the context of wider social relations that establish socially and historically constituted patterns of marginalization and exclusion. Traditional forms of authoritative knowledge and expertise, as delivered through the reproduction of 'historically reified textual conventions' therefore often prejudice the opportunities for meaningful progression of traditionally marginalized students that make up the diverse student body in the widening participation agenda (ibid.: 256).

For some social groups, Mills argues, marginalization starts at home through attitudes to and practices of learning that ill prepare an individual for formal education and these relate to socio-economic as well as cultural factors, such as the availability of resources and the ways these are used. In a report that explored issues of attainment and progression in black and minority ethnic students at Coventry University, Broughan, Singh, Cullis and Lewis (2009) found that low entry tariffs were indicative of poor pre-university achievement, which tended to manifest in lower classification attainment, and in turn confirmed the low expectations of teaching staff. The report also highlighted the relationship between language skills and academic achievement and found that black and minority ethnic students often performed poorly in the structure and development of text, based on their command of language. Pedagogies based on textual representation of ideas are likely to be always self-limiting for students with poor writing ability or when writing in a non-native language, particularly when academics do not have the time, or do not feel it is their role, to help develop writing skills, especially with burgeoning student numbers, large class sizes and internationalized curricula. Thus, in order for higher education to be more inclusive, there is a need for pedagogies to take account of these cultural particularities by using nuances of communication that include for example, accent, dialect and other sub-cultural and peer group forms of language; in other words, pedagogies that embrace difference (Mills 2010).

It is not the aim of this argument to deny the value of text-based literacy for as Kress (2000b, cited in Mills 2010: 251) acknowledges, 'There is a shared recognition that reading and writing practices using words on paper-based text formats are necessary.' However, Kress goes on to suggest that these are 'not sufficient, for communicating across the multiple platforms of meaning-making in society' and this leads to the need to balance conventional textual approaches with literacies that are generally encountered outside the academic context. A multi-literacy approach to education incorporating the use of voice and other multi-modal means of expression as seen in popular culture and multi-media stories has a lot to offer teaching and learning (Parson *et al.* 2008; Mills 2010). This develops communicative skills of performance, creative interpretation, research and exploration, and the synthesis of complex information and theoretical concepts in relation to practice (Dale and Pymm 2009; Ralph *et al.* 2009) that are tested in text-based literacy.

Students as producers of knowledge

The problem of liberating pedagogies, of course, is that they are challenging for students and teachers, taking both out of their comfort zone. Teacher-centric pedagogies provide safe, comfortable learning environments in which knowledge is clearly defined and bounded, but may end up in superficial learning based on memory and rote (Brandes and Ginnis 1996). However, as Hughes *et al.* (2009: 37) note in their analysis of pleasure in learning, the market context of higher education presents students as customers/consumers, and educators are expected to promote the positive and downplay the negative experiences of learning; in other words, 'encourage pleasure (usually of various anodyne kinds) and discourage displeasure'. Hughes and her colleagues refer to this type of pleasure as 'plaisir', which is the easy-going and non-challenging aspect seen in classroom activities that are fun but not intellectually demanding, as opposed to 'jouissance', which accords with Freire's 'conscientisation' (Crotty 1998: 148) and is experienced when new horizons and perspectives open up, for example, when we see beyond the limits of our own way of thinking. In view of the increasing importance of national student surveys in steering curriculum delivery, it would be no surprise to see students demand, and institutions supply, paths of least resistance to attaining qualifications, although for some teachers in some institutions these wider issues may simply mask a lack of imagination and creativity in their teaching practice. Nevertheless, this is a far cry from the Freirian view of empowerment through education, and where the ongoing problem of retention and attrition for higher education institutions is concerned, serves little to meaningfully engage students in their learning.

By involving students in the production of knowledge they are more likely to be embedded in the teaching and learning process and develop cognitive abilities that deepen their learning, leading to a lifelong interest in learning, which improves motivation and therefore aids retention (Biggs 2003, cited in Cooper 2008). Furthermore, user-centred pedagogies based on these objectives are empowering both for students and teachers (Hall and Conboy 2009). This constructivist view sets out to align teaching and assessment and it is in both areas that use of voice, and access to voice, can heighten personal engagement and reflection (Newton and Middleton 2009), and the dialogic potential of podcasts opens up the possibilities of students moving across conceptual thresholds (Savin-Baden 2010).

With these principles in mind I embarked on using podcasts as part of an assessment for a third year criminology module at Coventry University in 2009 in which students were asked to explore the relationship between crime and dystopia. With the intention of breaking down the hierarchical distancing of traditional teacher–student relationships (Hughes *et al.* 2009), a student-centred approach was adopted and workshops were run collaboratively with students as active participants in the teaching and learning process, defining and producing knowledge rather than being passive recipients. A wide brief was given asking the students to analyze a novel and a film drawn from the dystopian genre to provide a critical theoretical and philosophical analysis of how aspects of the human condition are expressed in broader societal processes of crime, control, order and disorder and the consequences arising from these inter-relationships. It was left to the students to choose their sources and justify their choices.

In order to access different learning styles and not penalize particular students, the assessment took the form of a patchwork text analysis made up of three parts: (1) an analysis of the key conceptual issues drawn from both sources and synthesized into a concept map; (2) a podcast in which students discussed how they had arrived at their conceptual framework from the stories of the two sources; and, finally, (3) a short written conclusion in which they reflected on their understanding of the relationship between crime and dystopia. While the module was not formally evaluated beyond the standard university module evaluation, there were some outcomes that deserve scrutiny. The emphasis in the assessment was the same as with any written assessment: to develop a reasoned argument; synthesize relevant information; exercise critical judgement; and communicate effectively and fluently (Ralph *et al.* 2009). However, the different components of assessment, each with its own presentational requirements, meant that every student had an opportunity to find part of the process that enabled them to succeed, with the result that all 112 students on the module passed. Moreover, with the compensatory nature of the individual components, students who notably produced poor written work and were consistently low achievers demonstrably performed at a higher overall standard and this was reflected in a raised level of confidence and satisfaction recorded in the evaluation. What was particularly interesting was the response of students to the podcast, how initial resistance gave way to appreciation of a different approach:

> I really enjoyed this coursework … a lot of people made a fuss about it being difficult but I just thought it made a nice change. I enjoyed the podcast and the concept map a lot as they were different to what I was used to. Academically it seemed more challenging as it wasn't anything I had done before, but I found this appropriate for final year work.
>
> (White female student)

> I thought at first the coursework seemed like a daunting task … [but] … it all seemed to fall in place and this is where I gained my understanding. I feel that this work is something that is hard to be taught and rather is something that you learn more from actually doing. I found it surprisingly enjoyable to ·complete, never having done a podcast before, and I was ecstatic with the mark I got for the concept map after all the effort I had put into it. [The coursework] provided a different challenge, rather than the monotonous completion of essays … it was refreshing to have something new and different to do, and I feel I am leaving university a better person for it. .
>
> (White male student)

The introduction of a new approach at third year was particularly daunting for many students because of not knowing what was expected of them and the fear that not being able to rise to the challenge might have a direct impact on classification, and this suggests the need to build innovative approaches to delivery and assessment into courses from the beginning to change perceptions that teaching and learning are always teacher-led:

> It would have perhaps been less stressful had we done something similar beforehand, because most of the other coursework was from a different perspective (particularly for me doing a psychology joint – it was mostly reports, etc.). However, I enjoyed the challenge and thought having something new to do was refreshing.
>
> (White female student)

What was perhaps most striking about the podcast element of the coursework was the enthusiasm that radiated from the audio recordings, where the affective dimension of learning (Hughes *et al.* 2009) was expressed not just in what was said but the way it was said through intonation and self-projection, a sense of performance (Goffman 1969) that is difficult to put across in writing particularly for students who at the best of times find written expression a challenge. Overall, the chance to express themselves in different ways led some students to reappraise the way they learn, drawing together a range of cognitive abilities ranging from reflection to concise thinking:

> On reflection, I preferred the podcast to any written assignment I've ever done! The concept of a podcast provides alternative methods of expression, rather than the standard essay. I think a variety of ways for students to present work should be encouraged, for someone like myself it was appealing as my assignments so far had only ever been essays. I was encouraged to think more about this idea of conceptual analysis and apply it, knowing I had the ability to play it back. I think listening to something is a good way to reflect on what you've done and then if needs be, correct or further develop ideas. Although it is also possible to develop ideas via essays, I thought that the podcast encourages you to choose your words carefully and also removes the tendency to waffle or include irrelevant statements. Every sentence said needed to serve a purpose. I don't consider a podcast to be a short cut as it took as much time as an essay to research and gather ideas.
>
> (Black female student)

Conclusion

There is no doubt that podcasts are a useful and versatile tool in the armoury of e-learning technology in higher education. In a climate of increasingly flexible modes of delivery in which student–teacher interactions are distanced, where the virtual replaces face-to-face contact, they can bring voice to humanize the process. In their simplest form as a raw recording, they are easy to create, and, in more complex forms, they are easy to edit using freely available software downloaded from the internet, and involve relatively little cost. There are excellent guides that provide instruction on all aspects of podcasting, ranging from the technical (such as use of editing software) to the legal (such as copyright restrictions) for leisure and business use (see, for example, Holtz and Hobson 2007) and education (see, for example, Salmon et al. 2008; Salmon and Edirisingha 2008).

Pedagogically podcasts offer exciting possibilities for creative learning by allowing students to be the producers of media rather than end users, which taps into the cultural development of young people who have become active participants rather than passive observers of the various media they encounter in their social lives (Luckin et al. 2008). Advances in technology make this not only possible, but necessary if higher education is to keep pace with the changing demands of the wider world. The role of higher education is to turn out not only knowledgeable and skilled students, but also students with the capacity to think critically and reflectively, and podcasts have far more to offer in this respect than the evaluative focus on delivery of teaching and learning matter in the literature would suggest. As Biggs and Tang (2007) have argued, an interested, enquiring student is more likely to be embedded in their learning and it is the teacher's duty to whet their appetite to learn and desire to explore knowledge as the key to lifelong learning. It is also the duty of the teacher and institution to ensure that teaching, learning and assessment are inclusive and equitable and this becomes more imperative in a context of widening participation where the student intake is diverse, if students who are already culturally marginalized are to be retained and nurtured. To achieve all these objectives requires imaginative and creative curriculum design and delivery based on a student-centred pedagogic philosophy underpinning courses. However, with creativity comes risk, and the fear of failure is likely to stifle creative thinking as much as lack of imagination, despite the fact that risk can be managed through proper reflective evaluation.

Certainly in the future, with the student as consumer and where the power of the collective voice dictates the direction of teaching, learning and assessment, it is conceivable that the move to flexible teaching and learning will be mirrored by a move to flexible assessment. In this vision, it would be up to the student to decide how best to play to their strengths in meeting the assessment brief by selecting the format of their choosing, whether text or audio, or a combination of the two, and this would go some way to combating marginalization, facilitating engagement and aiding retention.

References

Armellini, A., Salmon, G. and Hawkridge, D. (2009) 'The Carpe Diem journey: designing for learning transformation', in T. Mayes, D. Morrison, H. Mellar,

P. Bullen and M. Oliver (eds) *Transforming Higher Education Through Technology Enhanced Learning*, York: Higher Education Academy, pp. 135–48.

Biggs, J. B. and Tang, C. (2007) *Teaching for Quality Learning at University: What the Student Does*, Maidenhead: SRHE and Open University Press.

Bolliger, D. U., Supanakorn, S. and Boggs, C. (2010) 'Impact of podcasting on student motivation in the online learning environment', *Computers in Education*, 55: 714–22.

Brandes, D. and Ginnis, P. (1996) *Student-centred Learning*, Cheltenham: Nelson Thornes.

Broughan, C., Singh, G., Cullis, T. and Lewis, S. (2009) *Exploring the Issue of Differentials in Degree Attainment and Progression of BME Students*, Report commissioned by Professor Donald Pennington, Coventry: Coventry University.

Childs, M. and Espinoza-Ramos, R. M. (2008) 'Students blending learner user preferences: matching student choices to institutional provision', in V. Hodgson, C. Jones, T. Kargidis, D. McConnell, S. Retalis, D. Stamatis and M. Zenios (eds) *Proceedings of the Sixth International Conference on Networked Learning*, 5–6 May 2008, Halkidiki, Greece, pp. 492–9.

Cooper, S. (2008) 'Delivering student feedback in higher education: the role of podcasting', *Journal of Music, Technology and Education*, 1(2–3): 153–62.

Copley, J. (2007) 'Audio and video podcasts of lectures for campus-based students: production and evaluation of student use', *Innovations in Education and Teaching International*, 44(4): 387–99.

Crotty, M. (1998) *The Foundations of Social Research: Meaning and Perspective in the Research Process*, London: Sage.

Dale, C. and Pymm, J. M. (2009) 'Podagogy: the iPod as a learning technology', *Active Learning in Higher Education*, 10: 84–96.

Deane, M. and Borg, E. (2011) 'Measuring the outcomes of individualised writing instruction: a multilayered approach to capturing changes in students' texts', *Teaching in Higher Education*, 16: 319–31.

France, D. and Ribchester, C. (2008) 'Podcasts and feedback', in G. Salmon and P. Edirisingha (eds) *Podcasting for Learning in Universities*, Maidenhead: Open University Press, pp. 70–9.

Goffman, E. (1969) *The Presentation of Self in Everyday Life*, Harmondsworth: Penguin.

Hall, R. and Conboy, H. (2009) 'Scoping the connections between emergent technologies and pedagogies for learner empowerment', in T. Mayes, D. Morrison, H. Mellar, P. Bullen and M. Oliver (eds) *Transforming Higher Education Through Technology Enhanced Learning*, York: Higher Education Academy, pp. 220–34.

Holtz, S. and Hobson, N. (2007) *How to Do Everything with Podcasting*, New York: McGraw-Hill.

Hughes, C., Perrier, M. and Kramer, A. (2009) 'Plaisir, jouissance and other forms of pleasure: exploring the intellectual development of the student', in the iPED Research Network (ed.) *Academic Futures: Inquiries into Higher Education and Pedagogy*, Newcastle-upon-Tyne: Cambridge Scholars Publishing, pp. 28–40.

Ipsos MORI (2007) *Student Expectations Study: Key Findings from Online Research and Discussion Evenings Held in June 2007 for the Joint Information Systems Committee*, July 2007. Available at: http://www.jisc.ac.uk/publications/research/2007/studentexpectations.aspx# downloads (accessed 27 June 2011).

Luckin, R., Logan, K., Clark, W., Graber, R., Oliver, M. and Mee, A. (2008) *Learners' Use of Web 2.0 Technologies in and out of School in Key Stages 3 and 4*, BECTA (July 2008).

Middleton, D. (2010) 'Putting the learning into e-learning', *European Political Science*, 9: 5–12.

Mills, K. A. (2010) 'A review of the "Digital Turn" in the New Literacy Studies', *Review of Educational Research*, 80: 246–71.

Newton, J. and Middleton, A. (2009) 'Podcasting for pedagogic purposes: the journey so far and some lessons learned', in T. Mayes, D. Morrison, H. Mellar, P. Bullen and M. Oliver (eds) *Transforming Higher Education Through Technology Enhanced Learning*, York: Higher Education Academy, pp. 235–48.

Parson, V., Reddy, P., Wood, J. and Senior, C. (2008) 'Educating an *iPod* generation: undergraduate attitudes, experiences and understanding of vodcast and podcast use', *Learning, Media and Technology*, 34(3): 215–28.

Plenderleith, J. and Adamson, V. (2009) 'The policy landscape of transformation', in T. Mayes, D. Morrison, H. Mellar, P. Bullen and M. Oliver (eds) *Transforming Higher Education Through Technology Enhanced Learning*, York: Higher Education Academy, pp. 6–18.

Ralph, J., Head, N. and Lightfoot, S. (2009) 'Pol-casting: the use of podcasting in the teaching and learning of politics and international relations', *European Political Science*, 9: 13–24.

Reushle, S., McDonald, J. and Postle, G. (2009) 'Transformation through technology-enhanced learning in Australian higher education', in T. Mayes, D. Morrison, H. Mellar, P. Bullen and M. Oliver (eds) *Transforming Higher Education Through Technology Enhanced Learning*, York: Higher Education Academy, pp. 58–71.

Salmon, G. and Edirisingha, P. (eds) (2008) *Podcasting for Learning in Universities*, Maidenhead: Open University Press.

Salmon, G., Edirisingha, P., Mobbs, M., Mobbs, R. and Dennett, C. (2008) *How to Create Podcasts for Education*, Maidenhead: Open University Press.

Savin-Baden, M. (2010) 'The sound of feedback in higher education', *Learning, Media and Technology*, 35(1): 53–64.

Walker, A. (2009) 'Confessions of a reluctant podcaster', in the iPED Research Network (ed.) *Academic Futures: Inquiries into Higher Education and Pedagogy*, Newcastle-upon-Tyne: Cambridge Scholars Publishing, pp. 209–22.

Westerman, S. and Barry, W. (2009) 'Mind the gap: staff empowerment through digital literacy', in T. Mayes, D. Morrison, H. Mellar, P. Bullen and M. Oliver (eds) *Transforming Higher Education Through Technology Enhanced Learning*, York: Higher Education Academy, pp. 122–34.

CRITICAL FRIEND COMMENTARY

Palitha Edirisingha

Improving teaching and learning has been a long-standing concern in higher education (see, for instance, Laurillard 2002; Biggs 2003; Entwistle 2009). However, pedagogical goals have always been subject to, and are increasingly dictated by, the broader policy context, and it can be argued that the tensions inherent in processes of massification, widening participation, and more latterly commodification, increasingly dictate pedagogic futures rather than the other way round. This chapter engages with these debates at different levels. First is the efficiency and effectiveness of the technology making the production, distribution and use of learning material readily available and easily accessible to both teacher and learner. Second is the potential for podcasts to meet the conflicting demands of higher education in a transformative way by freeing students of the shackles of conventional ways of thinking and means of expression. Steventon draws an important distinction between 'production', where students become creators of teaching and learning materials, and 'consumption' where they are simply the passive recipients of it. These are recurring themes in the literature reflecting Sfard (1998) and Collis and Moonen (2002), who refer to 'contribution-orien-ted' and 'participation-oriented' activities, the former of which have the greatest scope for embedding students in their learning through the generation of ideas and content.

The question is: to what extent can podcasts really offer a fundamentally different approach to teaching and learning? Certainly the competencies of digital technologies and the scope of internet delivery have improved exponentially in an incredibly short time span and there are no signs of this progress abating in the near future. The emerging academic and policy literature (e.g. Conole and Ale-vizou 2010; Sharpe *et al.* 2010) discusses the implications of a 'net generation' of students as 'digital natives' on university degree courses, although it is not only the students who need to be technologically aware and capable, but teachers too and this chapter highlights how traditional attitudes and practices embedded in conventional pedagogies are more likely to limit the use of technologies such as the podcast than the technology itself.

The important message here is that there is a deep-rooted, complex relationship between pedagogy and socio-economic and political culture in which technology is playing an increasingly significant role. As Ellis and Goodyear (2010: 1) point out, universities have many pivotal roles in society serving as 'hubs of innovation', contributing to societal development by attracting and developing talent, and creating new knowledge to fuel the economy, to name but a few. They are crucial assets in regional, national and, in a globalized world, international contexts. However, notwithstanding their economic contribution, they have the broader task of enhancing opportunities for all students irrespective of their diverse social and economic backgrounds and abilities, as well as improving curricula, teaching and assessment methods to suit the needs of the twenty-first century in an inclusive way. As rightly highlighted in this chapter, universities are having to fulfil all these demands against a backdrop of declining public funding for higher education. With a thorough analysis and understanding of the shifting sands of contemporary higher education, new information and communication technologies can provide a surprisingly important contribution in addressing some of the problems that universities face. Podcasts offer one of the simplest means of meeting some of the pedagogic challenges.

References

Biggs, J. (2003) *Teaching for Quality Learning at University*, 2nd edn, Maidenhead: Open University Press.

Collis, B. and Moonen, J. (2002) *Flexible Learning in a Digital World: Experiences and Expectations*, London: Routledge.

Conole, G. and Alevizou, P. (2010) *A Literature Review of the Use of Web 2.0 Tools in Higher Education: A Report Commissioned by the Higher Education Academy*, August 2010. Available at: http://www.heacademy.ac.uk/assets/EvidenceNet/Conole_Alevizou_2010.pdf (accessed 23 April 2011).

Ellis, R. A. and Goodyear, P. (2010) *Students' Experiences of E-Learning in Higher Education*, London: Routledge.

Entwistle, N. (2009) *Teaching for Understanding at University*, New York: Palgrave Macmillan.

Laurillard, D. (2002) *Rethinking University Teaching: A Conversational Framework for the Effective Use of Technologies*, London: Routledge.

Sfard, A. (1998) 'On two metaphors of learning and the dangers of choosing just one', *Educational Researcher*, 27(2): 4–13.

Sharpe, R., Beetham, H., and de Freitas, S. (eds) (2010) *Rethinking Learning for a Digital Age: How Learners are Shaping Their Own Experiences*, London: Routledge.

Chapter 8

Student peer mentoring for engagement and retention

Challenges in community building and assessment

Heather Conboy and Richard Hall

Introduction

There is growing interest in student peer mentoring as a way to enable new students to tackle the perceived cultural, academic and social boundaries associated
with the first year of study in higher education. Based on a case study of a student
mentoring scheme in a UK university, this chapter discusses the role of student
mentors in supporting new student understanding and engagement with diagnostic and formative assessment. In particular, it considers the communicative
potential of web-based technologies in transcending boundaries between 'formal'
and 'informal' learning opportunities. One of the main findings is that mentors
perceived their positioning in a semi-institutional role as having greater impact on
the nature of their communicative relationship with mentees than any technol-
ogy-related factors. The authors describe the lessons learned and follow-up action
research that ensued.

Context

New students face a constellation of challenges upon entering higher education
(HE) including adapting to cultural and academic expectations, alongside fitting
in socially with new peers (Yorke and Longden 2008; Joint Information System
Committee 2009). During this period of transition, students need to be encouraged to become independent thinkers who take responsibility for their own
learning and development. In terms of retention, Yorke and Longden (2008)
noted the negative impact on students of a perceived lack of contact with their
tutors. From this perspective of disconnect, peer mentoring offers the potential to
extend and enrich the process of academic tutoring, especially when tied to
diagnostic and formative assessment as a mechanism for personalized meaning-
making (Boud *et al.* 2001; Green 2007) and agency (Falchikov 2007; Carr
2008). This is because mentoring is generally aimed at encouraging first year
students to engage by taking the advice of more experienced peers, thereby providing inroads into the subtleties of institutional and academic culture and
promoting social links to enable more independent learning (Green 2007).

The mentors' role equates to a scaffold for new students in breaking through transitional barriers and reaching a personal 'turning point' or transformation, in which the learner becomes conscious of their engagement with their learning (Palmer *et al.* 2009). Over time, such scaffolding may fade as the agency and autonomy of the individual learner grow (Falchikov 2007). As Palmer *et al.* (2009) point out, management structures in the form of support services have little chance of reaching across the 'liminal space' of 'betweenness' that some students experience in their real or perceived exclusion from the academic or social. This need is amplified by the cultural nuances of internationalization and higher education's engagement with diverse cohorts of learners, each with their own perspectives. Here it is concrete engagements with the realities of the academic and social life-worlds of the novice student that matter in extending her/his autonomous work (Sambell *et al.* 2006).

Assessment is a core way in which the academic life-world of the student is made concrete or realized. Gibbs (2006) notes how assessment frames learning behaviour, and from this stems a view of how the novice learner needs to engage in meaningful conversations, in order to situate themselves in the processes of assessment-for-learning and assessment of learning (Kvale 2007). Conversations are a central way in which the complexities of assessment and the interpretation of its outcomes can be internalized by students (Joint Information System Committee 2010), in order that they can realize their place in the academic community (Earl and Katz 2008). Such self-realization can be framed institutionally by personal tutoring or study skills and allied support services, but more intriguingly has the power to be student-produced through peer mentoring (Joint Information System Committee 2009). The process of mentoring enables students to interact in a less formal way, and because mentors 'have no official assessment function and are well placed to solicit much higher disclosure of difficulties by mentees', they can potentially add value to the institutional support strategies by revealing issues that other institutionalized strategies cannot (Topping *et al.* 1998: 46). Thus, while novice students may have problems in deciphering assessment practices (Carr 2008), mentoring offers possibilities to learn from the experience of others through more informal processes and modelling (Sambell *et al.* 2006).

There is a growing recognition of the role of technologies in facilitating communication and the development of online communities with new students both prior to their entry into university (e.g. Cook and Rushton 2009) and in curriculum integration (Nichol 2006). This has a deeper impact, given the growing student preference for home-working and using personal technologies for self-regulation of their learning (Ramanau *et al.* 2008). A framework of technologies, including both institutional and non-institutional Web 2.0 tools, is crucial in connecting students' informal and formal learning and their agency (Hall 2009; Joint Information System Committee 2010). Anagnostopoulou and Parmar (2008) recommend that educators create opportunities to associate social and academic activities, at the same time respecting those who participate in different ways, for example, by lurking. With specific reference to student mentees, Page and Hanna (2008) found that students strongly favoured an online forum for peer communication.

Recent research on transitions (Manchester Metropolitan University 2007; University of Ulster 2008; Currant and Keenan 2009) evaluates the student-led development of online conversational spaces beyond the formal use of 'institutionally' provided technologies for communication that supports the development of critical literacy and engagement with assessment (Cotil Project 2009). Studies have focused upon the opportunities these tools offer for the development of connectivist approaches to learning (Anderson 2007; Siemens 2009) and the development of inclusive learning spaces that enable students to personalize their learning outcomes (Attwell and Costa 2009). This aligns with Siemens' (2009) view of personal development as a process of making meaning through socialization, interaction and collaboration, as well as with social and constructivist learning theories (Bandura 1977; Vygotsky 1978; Driscoll 1994), which highlight the importance of structured opportunities for developing mastery in new learning situations (Manchester Metropolitan University 2007). However, the *Learning Literacies in the Digital Age* report (Joint Information System Committee 2010) argued that for learners beginning their journey in higher education, there is a potential clash of formal academic and informal, web-based knowledge cultures that is revealed by the assessment process. Thus, conversations that support the novice student's awareness of how technologies can connect their informal/formal learning and assessment are crucial (Sharpe and Benfield 2005; Trinder *et al.* 2008; Joint Information System Committee 2009).

To engage students in their informal learning, we need to understand more effectively how specific social practices affect the negotiation of boundaries that emerge between different aspects of a student's learning experience, and hence how and what boundaries may impact upon engagement with the assessment processes. According to Giroux (2005), boundaries are personal binaries and dichotomies which can frame new epistemologies in order to question meaning and education, particularly in an information-rich world. For Giroux (ibid.: 2), 'Thinking in terms of borders allows one to critically engage the struggle over those territories, spaces, and contact zones where power operates to either expand or to shrink the distance and connectedness among individuals, groups, and places.'

A critical element, therefore, is whether and how boundaries such as formal/ informal and personal/institutional can be bridged, in order that the student's self-actualization is supported. Against this complex backdrop of transitions and emerging apprenticeship, of critical literacy and social learning, of the use of educational and personal technologies, and of the problematic nature of making sense of assessment (Kvale 2007), we need to look beyond the formal use of 'institutionally' provided technologies to learn from the experiences of mentors in their development of strategies for a student-produced higher education.

Mentoring case study context

This case study focuses on mentor perspectives on their efforts to engage new students in peer-led communities; it complements an evaluation of the same scheme in which first year student mentees reported overall satisfaction with the scheme, even though few students had actually met their mentors outside of formal arrangements.

The scheme discussed here was co-ordinated centrally and involved considerable awareness-raising and training of mentors, to engage new students as 'buddies' rather than apprentices. Its main aim was to offer opportunities for new students to develop a more proactive approach towards managing assessment and the allied development of critical literacy (Falchikov 2007; Joint Information System Committee 2009). The mentors had some possibilities for face-to-face contact with mentees through arrangements with their subject tutors, but most opportunities occurred through dedicated activities with academic guidance personnel; mentors also sought to run online communities alongside these activities. Suggested topics of conversation included discussing experiences of starting university, selecting a course, preparing for assessments, interpreting and building on feedback, recommending contacts for other academic work, as well as social venues and events. Volunteers from years two and three (levels five and six) were, individually or with another mentor, assigned to a group of first year students of the same discipline, with a focus on supporting their transition into higher education. Initially this involved 24 mentors and 130 first year students from Education Studies and Media Studies. Hence, as a pilot without any pre-planned technologies for collaboration and contact, researchers were able to liaise with mentors to explore and define the potential for online communication among students. A baseline survey showed that each of the mentors considered themselves to be conversant with web-based technologies and the majority felt themselves to be good 'online social networkers'. Students were given guidance, but ultimately decided which technologies to use for communication. Staff took care to support rather than lead, including over the recommendation of which technologies to deploy.

Mentors were asked to keep logs of student communication which identified: approximate times of communication; the rationale for the use of specific technologies; and any perceived benefits and disadvantages. The researchers attended a large number of mentor–mentee meetings, in order to facilitate an understanding of student perspectives within this context. Twenty students provided verbal feedback in meetings and focus groups and 13 'logs' of communication were received from mentors. The research was aimed at a better understanding of the following questions:

1 What strategies were deployed by students in the use of technologies for personal, social and academic purposes, including assessment?
2 What were the student experiences of using these technologies?
3 What types of conversations were facilitated by technologies?

This case study is reported in two phases. The first phase focuses on a pilot mentoring scheme within a Humanities Faculty and sets out to understand how web-based tools might form part of the communication strategies between mentors and mentees. The second phase reports on ongoing action research aimed at enhancement of the scheme, to support the self-actualization of mentees and their engagement in institutional assessment processes through more focused links with academic support.

Summary of findings

Initially, mentors asked to have an area for communication set up on the virtual learning environment (VLE), which they felt would act as a hub or central area for peer contact. One student commented that this was 'a positive sign of [our] legitimate role within the institution'. Students were also encouraged to use any other technologies they thought appropriate, and to this end they were offered induction workshops emphasizing a range of social media possibilities and support as needed.

Mentors were almost unanimous in saying they 'left it to the mentees' to select the technology to be used. However, their own preferences, along with considerations about which methods they thought mentees would be more likely to engage with, were clearly central factors in the suggestions they put forward. One mentor highlighted that, 'I offered many choices but the mentees felt more comfortable using (face-to-face, student email and VLE).' The mentor noted that 'only email was really used by this group'.

As time progressed, it became apparent that the VLE community area was not being used by mentees, although a quarter of the students did log-in. Despite introductory welcomes and offers of support from mentors on discussion forums and blogs, few mentees responded in the form of posting messages to the group. Although originally framed as an area for all peers, mentees suggested that information about the scheme should be posted there to attract and encourage more activity. For this reason they thought that tutors should have access to this area. Despite this, none of the tutors used it, preferring it to be student-focused. Thus technology use appeared to migrate from the VLE to other technologies, principally Facebook.

The 'institution', technologies and peer communication

A comparative thematic analysis identified two main attitudes among mentors: (1) those who favoured institutional technologies, in particular the VLE; and (2) those who preferred non-institutional communication tools like Facebook. The terms institutional and non-institutional are used for convenience, although interestingly these terms were rarely used by the mentors.

A mentor argued that, 'We looked into this [VLE] method and thought it was a great idea but because our Facebook group had been successful we decided to stick with one community to communicate.' The same student noted the impact of personal factors on mentee-engagement: 'Nobody wants to be first to write on the discussion board ... unfortunately the first years were either reluctant to use this or did not want to advertise their problems or may have had difficulty using this page.' Extrinsic motivations need to balance aspirations against cultures and personal fears that exist in the use of non-institutional tools. However, in sensitizing students to the demands of assessment in higher education, the mentors need to develop their role in order to be accessible particularly when needed in the early stages (Falchikov 2007).

Half of the mentor groups initially favoured using the VLE, citing its familiarity, its standing as 'legitimate' activity, and for its administrative convenience and potential for creating a student community. However, some mentors expressed their concern that mentees might think of 'institutional tools as too formal' and not engage there in talking about diagnostic or formative activities. They did not feel that they could be as chatty and informal, which perhaps indicated a reluctance to talk critically about the curriculum or the institution within the VLE. These mentors had clear reservations about using the VLE, mainly because they felt that their mentees would not use it. Several reasons for this notion were suggested. One mentor noted that, 'I did not use the [VLE] community as I felt it was quite impersonal and felt too formal.'. Another mentor projected that, 'It was a good idea, [but] I access Blackboard maybe only once a week and did so even less as a first year so didn't feel it would be the best way to contact mentees.' The same mentor team noted that communication with students depended on their continual prompting, rather than the mentees' needs: 'There has been one student [who] has consistently stayed in contact and others have dipped in and out when they need.' A second mentor in this group 'found that the mentees were not interested in using the VLE. Maybe, it would be useful to give them training on how to access it and use it to their advantage.' A third wondered about external stimuli: 'I think first year students should be encouraged to check their email and Blackboard accounts more often, as I know this was something I didn't realize the importance of upon beginning university.' This strategic engagement by mentees, linked to the pressure points of assessment was a clear frustration for mentors (Gibbs 2006).

Half of the mentor groups used Facebook, which was perceived to be a better alternative because of its currency with students and its more informal appeal. One mentor remarked that, 'Most people are on Facebook – that's where people hang out, so it's worth trying that.' Another added that, 'It [Facebook] is the best because most people have Facebook and it makes it less formal and more informal.' Interestingly, several students reasoned that they selected Facebook as 'it was important that the mentees did not feel intimidated by the scheme'. Even so, there appeared to be no greater engagement from mentees than with the VLE. Those mentors using Facebook invited first years to join their groups, and although all joined, mentors reported that they did not fully participate in meaningful discussions about socializing, learning or assessment. One mentor stated that, 'We felt we would get a better response by setting up an informal Facebook group than by using student email. However as time went by without contact we resorted to any methods available.' In summary, despite the efforts of mentors to stimulate and engage first years in conversation, by using a range of strategies such as posting personal stories and top tips on their experience of learning, and although first year students joined online groups, mentors felt there should have been greater engagement in the form of conversation.

Converting 'push' to engagement

Most mentors felt they were in a position of having to contact mentees to 'push' their services and to encourage input around learning and assessment. A number perceived that the lack of first year student responses was due to a lack of interest, an inability to formulate useful academic questions and queries, a lack of recognition of the role that mentees could play, or, as one student put it, because 'they were being lazy'. There was also an element of mentor desperation in not receiving responses from mentees, with several commenting that, 'The fact nobody turned up to meetings or even answered our messages and stuff was a little disheartening.' Mentors generally believed that the mentees did not take full advantage of opportunities to discuss assessment, and this was perceived to be the failure of the mentees to appreciate the good advice they would receive. It was a rejection of opportunities to learn independently. Mentors also felt that the scheme and the benefits that were available should be more widely disseminated and impressed upon students, especially ahead of key assessment points.

However, mentors recognized that mentees clearly responded and engaged at specific times of the year, such as when assignments were due and when mentors attended face-to-face classes to offer help. One mentor noted:

[I] had contact with three of my mentees who were very comfortable asking for advice and enquiring about information. One in particular was happy to keep in contact and see me as a valuable asset. I have offered my services about every two weeks via email and met up with mentees when required. Mentees only contacted me when they had a problem or were unsure, most of the correspondence came when assignments were due or when they had to choose modules.

One of his peers felt some frustration:

It's been hard to get the first years to actually make use of us, but they seem to be more collaborative lately and we've had a few chats with them about academic issues such as assignments and also some student life-related issues. Facebook and email have been very useful but only right after meeting with the students face to face.

These mentors recommended that face-to-face meetings, although infrequent throughout the year, provide crucial scaffolding and prompts for first year students. One mentor reflected that, 'the only thing that seems to be missing is the mentees getting more involved'. For a separate mentor, it was important to overcome fear through personal ownership: 'We should be left to make our own communication through email, social networking sites and phone calls/texts. I believe this makes the scheme more personal and less "scary" as it does not feel so affiliated with the university.'

Another mentor argued that while mentees might prefer anonymity in raising areas of concern, social networks and social modelling of practices were central to encourage engagement. For this mentor, the tool was not a barrier to involvement in the process: 'To be honest, there have been minimal results using my own form of communication, so [Facebook] may not be the best method, although I do find it easier for myself.' Another mentor disagreed:

> I don't think there's any need to be anonymous and I believe the private mentor-group of mentees Blackboard areas that are already set up are enough. We can always arrange our own communication separately so it's good that we have the chance to use the Blackboard community if the mentees want to.

On the overall use of technologies, there are interesting parallels with the study by Page and Hanna (2008) which found that mentees appeared to be satisfied with the overall scheme although few mentees actually contacted their mentor, preferring to communicate 'via email, texts and phone calls'. Only one student said they would like a dedicated physical space. It also points to the fact that where learning and assessment issues arose, mentees required quick answers rather than prolonged meetings. This was more about just-in-time support and acting as a broker between new students and the university than developing social relationships and community building.

Discussion and recommendations

It is important to note that, in general, students, both mentors and mentees, commented favourably on the overall experience and on the support they had been given. Mentors unanimously supported the delivery of technology-induction sessions and felt that this should be extended to mentees. Clearly, the main benefit for mentors was in social engagement and affective learning. One stated that, 'It has been very rewarding for me, knowing that I have eased other people's fears with regard to all aspects of the course.' He went on to emphasize the need for communication with mentees that was 'enjoyable and informative'. For a second mentor engaging with the process of mentoring and acting in an advisory role around assessment was 'very interesting and challenging'.

In terms of the boundaries between 'institutional' or 'non-institutional' tools, a complex context existed. Mentors felt appreciated as stakeholders in an institutional scheme, as evidenced in the reasons they gave for wanting to become a mentor: 'giving something back to the Faculty'. Yet many were very aware that a perception of being linked to the 'institution' might deter mentees from participating in the scheme and hinder communication. This impacted on their selection of technologies, with many mentors purposefully deciding to communicate with mentees using 'non-institutional' tools such as Facebook. Students clearly welcomed the possibility to use a range of methods of communication. This also connected into a just-in-time approach to the management of assessment.

The main technologies that were used and that facilitated mentee follow-up activity were texts and email, and these framed face-to-face interactions. Within this framework, mentors continually felt in a position of having to 'push' their services and expertise. Enforced use of the VLE may be problematic, as suggested by Page and Hanna (2008). Hammond, Bithell, Jones and Bidgood (2010: 202) also found that 'goals may be driven by the institution/tutor and consequently students may not be prepared or willing to learn with their peers'. Thus, a compulsory approach may run the risk of turning mentees into passive rather than (pro-)active participants.

The initial challenge identified by mentors and mentees, and staff, was that crucial opportunities may have been missed because of the unavoidable but relatively late start-up in week two. This was countered by early recruitment and training of new mentors and a Facebook group, which new students were encouraged to use prior to their registration. One sign of satisfaction with the training and experience was that five of the previous year's mentors decided to stay on as mentors, and three of the original mentees also took up the opportunity to become mentors in the following year. Hopefully, this will continue and contribute to the fostering and growing 'ethos' of mentoring (Treston 1999). Furthermore, a network of support around mentors helps 'link success to ownership' as well as 'constant improvement and adaptation' (ibid.: 236).

An academic guidance tutor took on the role of co-ordinator, which had the effect of enhanced links between this area and the mentor role and enabled a wider range of 'authentic' activities to be included for first year students, particularly before assessments, which mentors identified as a 'hot spot' for mentoring activity. The formalization of mentor log-books for recording activity is now linked to a volunteering certificate, awarded by the student union, offering mentors opportunities not only for personal development but also accreditation 'beyond the attainment of their degree' (UniversitiesUK and GuildHE 2007: 5). Finally, mentoring to support assessment practices has been shared through workshops at an institutional level.

As a result of an ethos of student production of peer mentoring, there are signs of community-building around the mentor group. This is in contrast to communication between mentors and their mentee groups, which continue to be principally, though not only, characterized by one-to-one contact. In particular, there has been increased sharing of experience and practice between mentors, and increased online communication between mentors and the faculty network. Mentors also value their involvement in extended faculty networks, while at the same time being content that online communicative networks have initially been set up on their behalf as a kind of 'proxy agency' (Bandura 2000: 14).

In summary, the pilot suggested that mentees need earlier training about the scheme and available technologies, tied to induction and the curriculum. Mentors require extended discussion on issues encountered in creating and maintaining online communities. This enables students to take ownership of the scheme (Treston 1999) in authentic contexts. Students should be supported in the development of online spaces for communication, with the freedom to select their own tools. Personal technologies provide possibilities for serendipitous peer interaction and keep mentors within the radar of new students. However, one challenge is in using the appropriate tone for promotion and awareness-raising of the scheme. Student expectations are influenced by how they perceive the balance between institutional involvement and a buddy scheme.

Conclusion

In their attempts to create a community of learners, mentors reported some tensions between the use of institutional and non-institutional technologies (Joint Information System Committee 2009). However, mentors' evaluations of the level of new student interest seemed to be based on the number of posts to discussion areas, neglecting the possibility of engagement by reading and following postings by mentors, as suggested by Anagnostopoulou and Parmar (2008). New students did participate in discussion, yet not at the level expected by mentors. Those who did contact mentors also spoke positively of their experience. This also suggests that those involved in the scheme should reflect on their expectations about what mentees' observable engagement might entail and any unspoken reasons for apparent low participation.

Evaluating the outcomes of such informal peer communication is notoriously difficult, particularly given the context-bound nature of many schemes (Hammond et al. 2010). It is clear that the impact of any mentoring scheme will depend on how it is presented and promoted to students and whether it is compulsory or voluntary, again changing the social dynamics and rendering the choice of technologies secondary to the development of meaningful social relationships. From the faculty perspective, the mentoring scheme did appear to add a new dimension to the student experience and an enhancement of existing structures by the involvement of mentors in special events. However, as Ashwin (2003: 171) warns, interventions such as mentoring 'should never be a panacea for poorly designed courses and assessment systems', nor should they distract focus from any areas that are genuinely in need of improvement, such as curriculum design or feedback practices (Gorard et al. 2006). Ongoing dialogue and liaison between faculty, mentors and mentees are essential to reap the rewards of the mentoring process, and to enable students to make the most of opportunities, and for staff to iterate their curricula.

References

Anagnostopoulou, K. and Parmar, D. (2008) *Practical Guide: Bringing Together e-learning and Student Retention*, Middlesex University and University of Ulster. Available at: http://mancons2.middlesex.wikispaces.net/file/view/Practical+Guide+%28Anagnostopoulou+%26+Parmar%2C+2008%29.pdf (accessed 28 June 2011).

Anderson, P. (2007) *What is Web 2.0? Ideas, Technologies and Implications for Education*, UK Joint Information Systems Committee. Available at: http://www.jisc.ac.uk/media/documents/techwatch/tsw0701.pdf (accessed 28 June 2011).

Ashwin, P. (2003) 'Peer support: relations between the context, process and outcomes for the students who are supported', *Instructional Science*, 31(3): 159–73.

Attwell, G. and Costa, C. (2009) *Integrating Personal Learning and Working Environments*, Bristol: Futurelab. Available at: http://www.beyondcurrenthorizons.org.uk/wp-content/uploads/ch4_attwell_graham_integratingworkandpersonallearning20090116.pdf (accessed 28 June 2011).

Bandura, A. (1977) *Social Learning Theory*, New York: General Learning Press.

——(2000) 'Exercise of human agency through collective efficacy', *Current Directions in Psychological Science*, 9: 75–8.

Boud, D., Cohen, R. and Sampson, J. (2001) 'Peer learning in higher education: learning from and with each other', *Adult Education Quarterly*, 53(1): 65–6.

Carr, M. (2008) 'Can assessment unlock and open the doors to resourcefulness and agency?', in S. Swaffield (ed.) *Unlocking Assessment: Understanding for Reflection and Application*, London: Routledge, pp. 57–72.

Cook, T. and Rushton, B. S. (2009) *How to Recruit and Retain Higher Education Students*, Abingdon: Routledge.

Cotil Project (2009) *Connecting Transitions and Independent Learning: An Evaluation of Read/Write Web Approaches (CoTIL)*, Sheffield: De Montfort University, Higher Education Academy/Evidencenet. Available at: http://bit.ly/gHHhDi (accessed 28 June 2011).

Currant, C. and Keenan, C. (2009) 'evaluating systematic transition to higher education', *Brookes eJournal of Learning and Teaching*, 2(4). Available at: http:/ http://bejlt.brookes.ac.uk/article/evaluating_systematic_transition_to_higher_education/ (accessed 31 July 2011).

Driscoll, M. P. (1994) *Psychology of Learning for Instruction*, Boston: Allyn and Bacon.

Earl, I. and Katz, S. (2008) 'Getting to the core of learning: using assessment for self-monitoring and self-regulation', in S. Swaffield (ed.) *Unlocking Assessment: Understanding for Reflection and Application*, London: Routledge, pp. 90–104.

Falchikov, N. (2007) 'The place of peers in learning and assessment', in D. Boud and N. Falchikov (eds) *Rethinking Assessment in Higher Education*, London: Routledge, pp. 128–43.

Gibbs, G. (2006) 'How assessment frames student learning', in C. Bryan and K. Clegg (eds) *Innovative Assessment in Higher Education*, London: Routledge, pp. 23–36.

Giroux, H. A. (2005) *Border Crossings: Cultural Workers and the Politics of Education*, 2nd edn, Abingdon: Routledge.

Gorard, S., Smith, E., May, H., Thomas, L., Adnett, N. and Slack, K. (2006) *Review of Widening Participation Research: Addressing the Barriers to Participation in Higher Education*, Higher Education Funding Council for England. Available at: http://www.hefce.ac.uk/pubs/rdreports/2006/rd13_06/ (accessed 28 June 2011).

Green, A. (2007) 'Peer assisted learning and the educative: how informal learning processes empower first year students to engage with formal curricula', paper presented at 4th LDHEN Symposium: 'How do students engage with learning?', 12 April 2007, Bournemouth University.

Hall, R. (2009) 'Towards a fusion of formal and informal learning environments: the impact of the read/write web', *Electronic Journal of eLearning*, 7(1): 29–40.

Hammond, J. A., Bithell, C. P., Jones, L. and Bidgood, P. (2010) 'A first year experience of student-directed peer-assisted learning', *Active Learning*, 11(3): 201–12.

Joint Information System Committee (2009) *Thriving in the 21st Century: Learning Literacies for the Digital Age*. Available at: http://elearning.jiscinvolve.org/2009/06/11/thriving-in-the-21st-century-learning-literacies-for-the-digital-age/ (accessed 28 June 2011).

——(2010) *Study of How UK, FE and HE Institutions Are Supporting Effective Learners in a Digital Age*, SLiDA. Available at: http://www.jisc.ac.uk/whatwedo/programmes/elearning/slida.aspx (accessed 28 June 2011).

Kvale, S. (2007) 'Contradictions of assessment for learning in institutions of higher learning', in D. Boud and N. Falchikov (eds) *Rethinking Assessment in Higher Education*, London: Routledge, pp. 57–71.

Manchester Metropolitan University (2007) *The Shock Absorber Project*. Available at: http://www.shockabsorber.mmu.ac.uk/ (accessed 28 June 2011).

Nichol, D. (2006) 'Increasing success in first year courses: assessment redesign, self-regulation and learning technologies', in L. Markauskaite, P. Goodyear and P. Reimann (eds) Proceedings of the 23rd Annual Conference of the Australasian Society for Computers in Learning in Tertiary Education: Whose Learning? Whose Technology?, Sydney: Sydney University Press. Available at: http://www.ascilite.org.au/conferences/sydney06/papers.html (accessed 28 June 2011).

Page, D. and Hanna, D. (2008) 'Peer mentoring: the students' perspective', *Psychology Learning and Teaching*, 7(2): 34–7.

Palmer, M., O'Kane, P. and Owens, M. (2009) 'Betwixt spaces: student accounts of turning point experiences in the first-year transition', *Studies in Higher Education*, 34(1): 37–54.

Prensky, M. (2001) 'Digital natives, digital immigrants', *On the Horizon*, 9(5): 1–6.

Ramanau, R., Sharpe, R. and Benfield, G. (2008) 'Exploring patterns of student learning technology use in their relationship to self-regulation and perceptions of learning community', paper presented at Sixth International Networked Learning Conference, Halkidiki, Greece. Available at: http://www.networkedlearningconference.org.uk/past/nlc2008/abstracts/Ramanau.htm (accessed 28 June 2011).

Sambell, K., McDowell, L. and Sambell, A. (2006) 'Supporting diverse students: developing learner autonomy via assessment', in C. Bryan and K. Clegg (eds), *Innovative Assessment in Higher Education*, London: Routledge, pp. 158–68.

Sharpe, R. and Benfield, G. (2005) 'The student experience of e-learning in higher education: a review of the literature', *Brookes eJournal of Learning and Teaching*, 1(3): 1–9.

Siemens, G. (2009) *elearnspace: everything elearning.* Available at: http://www.elearnspace.org/ (accessed 28 June 2011).

Topping, K. J., McCowan, P. and McCrae, J. (1998) 'Peer mentoring of students in social work education', *Social Work Education*, 17(1): 45–56.

Treston, H. (1999) 'Peer mentoring: making a difference at James Cook University, Cairns – it's moments like these you need mentors', *Innovations in Education and Teaching International*, 36(3): 236–43.

Trinder, K., Guiller, J., Margaryan, A., Littlejohn, A. and Nicol, D. (2008) *Learning from Digital Natives: Bridging Formal and Informal Learning*, a report for the Higher Education Academy, Glasgow Caledonian University. Available at: http://www.academy.gcal.ac.uk/ldn/ (accessed 28 June 2011).

UniversitiesUK and GuildHE (2007) *Beyond the Honours Degree Classification: The Burgess Group Final Report*, London: UniversitiesUK and GuildHE.

University of Ulster (2008) *Student Transition and Retention (STAR) Project.* Available at: http://www.ulster.ac.uk/star/index.htm (accessed 28 June 2011).

Vygotsky, L. S. (1978) *Mind and Society: The Development of Higher Psychological Processes*, Cambridge, MA: Harvard University Press.

Yorke, M. and Longden, B. (2008) *The First-Year Experience of Higher Education in the UK (Phase 2)*, York: Higher Education Academy. Available at: http://www.heacademy.ac.uk/assets/York/documents/resources/publications/FYEFinalReport.pdf (accessed 28 June 2011).

CRITICAL FRIEND COMMENTARY

Martin Oliver

This chapter tackles a perennial problem: how to help people who go to university stay the course. This has been the focus for research for a long time (see, for instance, Tinto 1993), and it is well established that retention requires a supporting social and intellectual community as well as a commitment to more obvious 'support' such as student welfare services.

A recent wave of literature has suggested a new problem, however: that young people's exposure to technology means that they are now fundamentally different to previous generations in terms of the way they relate to one another, understand the world or learn (e.g. Tapscott 1998; Prensky 2001). On the basis of these claims, higher education has been challenged to change the way it works, to adapt its practices to fit the patterns of technology use of this new generation of users. These claims continue to be made, even though careful reviews have found that there is no convincing evidence of generational differences, and that these calls for radical change might be better understood as a kind of 'moral panic' than reasoned or evidence-based policy making.

Nonetheless, technology can be used in important ways to help improve students' experience of higher education. Lefever and Currant's (2010) review of literature on this topic demonstrates how technology can help students settle in, socialize, and develop the skills they need to participate fully in their studies. This chapter by Conboy and Hall builds on such work by exploring how one particular initiative played out in terms of students' engagement and experience. It provides evidence about what students at De Montfort University actually wanted from a support service, both in terms of patterns of contact and uses of technology. It shows how even well-informed assumptions about what students might want may be mistaken, and how the success of schemes needs to be judged in terms of participants' experiences rather than presuppositions about volumes of use or blunt metrics such as contact time. Here, for example, institutionally-branded spaces failed to draw in new students, who preferred to make contact at times and in ways that felt comfortable to them. But this comfort did not mean that they fell back in some clichéd way to a reliance on Facebook or Twitter; instead, they developed some kind of compromise in the private-yet-affiliated use of institutional emails.

This reveals a different kind of account about student participation: not an input/output model of numbers entering and leaving prematurely, but a story of the process through which individuals managed to engage. This case study shows how important it is, if we want to make a difference to students' engagement and retention, to understand those liminal, in-between moments that bring private lives and study into contact.

References

Lefever, R. and Currant, B. (2010) *How Can Technology Be Used to Improve the Learner Experience at Points of Transition?* Bradford: University of Bradford. Available at: http://technologyenhancedlearning.net/files/2010/04/ELESIGli teraturereviewFINAL240210.pdf (accessed 18 July 2011).

Prensky, M. (2001) 'Digital natives, digital immigrants', *On the Horizon*, 9(5): 1–6.

Tapscott, D. (1998) *Growing up Digital: The Rise of the Net Generation*, New York: McGraw-Hill.

Tinto, V. (1993) *Leaving College: Rethinking the Causes and Cures of Student Attrition*, Chicago: University of Chicago Press.

Chapter 9

The impact of assessment and feedback processes on student engagement in a research methods module

Steve Jewell

Introduction

It should come as no surprise that students in higher education rate assessment and feedback processes as the least satisfactory aspect of their experiences (Higher Education Funding Council for England 2010) – the development of effective and efficient assessment and feedback practices is one of the biggest challenges facing teachers in higher education. The challenge is intellectually, linguistically and emotionally demanding and requires a major investment in time. This chapter will relate how a three-stage assessment and feedback process, designed to engage students in the process, has been successfully implemented over a three-year period. The three sequential stages were: (1) early pre-emptive feedback from the tutor to students to give students confidence that they are on the right track; (2) formative processes in which students are engaged in the assessment of the work of peers and their own work; and (3) summative assessment and feedback from the tutor. Students have expressed a high level of satisfaction with the process, and the pass rate has significantly improved over the period of this study. The implementation of these processes and achieving a quick turnaround of feedback were only possible through the use of online technology – a paper-based system would be too labour-intensive, take too long and be cumbersome.

Review of the literature on assessment and feedback processes

The Stage 1 pre-emptive formative processes are designed to give students early assurance and importantly to correct any misunderstanding of the task which, unless rectified, could lead to the final work being poor (Carless 2007). Within the literature there is limited discussion on this type of assessment and feedback presumably because most of it is done informally through 1:1 discussions and emails – see Carless (2007) for a review of studies on Stage 1 processes.

Why are Stage 2 processes important? If teachers find the assessment and feedback process challenging, then what chance for students? Indeed, studies have shown that most students entering higher education do not possess the skills to get the most out of feedback (Weaver 2006; Burke 2009). Stage

2 processes provide a way of students engaging in and building an understanding of the assessment and feedback process. Rather than the feedback being a one-way transmission from teacher to student, a dialogue is opened between teacher and student and between students (Nicol 2010). Sadler (2010) argues that students need a working understanding of three concepts: (1) the exact nature of the work required; (2) the characteristics of a work of good quality; and (3) the interpretation of assessment criteria (particularly abstract ones). The predominant Stage 2 processes reported as being used have been peer assessment and self-assessment. In a study by Falchikov (2005), 88 per cent of the students stated that the peer feedback had been used to improve their final submission. The potential advantages of peer assessment are considerable (Sadler 2009; Nicol 2010), the main ones being: the feedback can be of a different but complementary nature to that given by the teacher; it puts the student in the role of the assessor; and it exposes students to good and poor work from other students tackling the same work. The challenges with the use of peer assessment include students being uncomfortable with their skills at assessing their peers, and that the peer feedback may conflict with that of the teacher.

Why is self-assessment potentially of value? To be successful, organizations need employees with up-to-date knowledge and skills and good self-awareness. One potentially effective way of assessing this knowledge and skills on an ongoing basis is through self-assessment. Unfortunately, most people have difficulty in accurately assessing themselves (Sitzmann et al. 2010). These authors sought to clarify the construct validity of self-assessments of knowledge in education and workplace training through a meta-analysis of 166 separate studies involving over 40,000 learners across a number of disciplines. They found that self-assessment appeared to be more useful as an indicator of how learners felt about a training intervention (affective outcomes) rather than how much they had learnt (cognitive outcomes). In studies specifically with higher education students, Cassidy (2007) and Lew, Alwis and Schmidt (2010) found that the student-estimated and tutor marks were only weakly correlated. Both studies agreed, however, that the more able students are more accurate at self-assessment than the less able students. What can be done to improve the correlation between self-assessment and cognitive learning? One approach might be to increase the efforts to develop self-assessment skills in students in higher education so that this valuable skill can be transferred into their future profession. Boud and Falchikov (2006) argue that students who can accurately self-assess are effective learners; they have a realistic sense of their own strengths and weaknesses; and they can use this knowledge to become independent and lifelong learners. Like peer assessment, self-assessment offers the potential of increased student engagement, the development of critical thinking skills and the opportunity for improving work prior to submission. Nevertheless, although there have been positive responses from students to self-assessment (Andrade and Du 2007), there have also been concerns. Cassidy (2007) believes that students may be reluctant to participate if they see self-assessment as a means of alleviating assessment pressures for tutors or if they believe they lack the necessary skills. Lew *et al.* (2010) studied students' belief about the benefits of self-assessment on their learning and found there were two distinct groups of students: those who believed in the usefulness of self-assessment and those who did not.

The majority of studies have been on Stage 3 summative processes with two different lines of focus observed by Nicol (2010). One line has focused on students' perceptions of written feedback (Weaver 2006; Lizzio and Wilson 2008; Poulos and Mahony 2008; Rae and Cochrane 2008; Smith 2008; Walker 2009). In a study on the effectiveness of assessment and feedback from the students' perspective, Poulos and Mahony (2008) found that the students expressed strong preferences for: transparent and consistent practices; clear criterion referencing to a grade and marks; early feedback; and induction on feedback and assessment practices. In another study (Lizzio and Wilson 2008), the three dimensions of effective assessment were found to be: developmental, encouraging, and fair feedback. Of the three dimensions, developmental feedback was the most strongly associated with students' evaluations of effective feedback. This developmental feedback needs to seek a balance between 'assignment specific' on the current work and 'feed forward' for use in future work. The key issues under the second dimension, 'encouraging', were recognizing effort, acknowledging achievements, providing constructive criticism and giving hope. In terms of the third dimension, students see justice as encompassing fairness and equity. Nesbit and Burton (2006) also found justice to be important to students. Within Stage 3 processes, the use of criterion-referencing systems (also known as rubrics and grading forms) has become popular. However, in recent times the use of grading forms has been contested. Sadler (2009) criticizes their use on two counts: that, in terms of validity and reliability, their theoretical foundations are not as strong as is supposed; and that students need to be able to appreciate the holistic quality of pieces of work rather than having an over-reliance on rubrics. Reddy and Andrade (2010) have been critical of the clarity of language used in rubrics as ambiguity works against an accurate or consistent interpretation of the grading form by students and teacher. Finally, empirical evidence from a Swedish study (Dahlgren *et al.* 2009) indicates that in grading schemes the assessment tasks can put the focus on the reproduction rather than the synthesis of knowledge. This can have a deleterious effect on student learning.

The other line of study on Stage 3 processes has focused on engaging students in assessment and feedback processes (Nicol and Macfarlane-Dick 2006; Boud 2007; O'Donovan *et al.* 2008). There is strong support for students playing a proactive role in assessment and feedback, from both teachers and students themselves (National Union of Students 2008). How can it be possible for students to make sense of feedback unless students are initiated into the explicit and tacit knowledge of assessment and feedback processes? While teachers will often carefully induct students into the Stage 3 summative process, this is insufficient. Students need to be become active agents (Nicol 2010) through engaging in Stage 2 formative processes – the best way of learning is through doing.

The students and the coursework

The students in this study were postgraduate business students studying for a master's programme in general management, international business, marketing, finance, international tourism, and sport management at a UK university. The findings are from 600 students taught during the period 2008–10. The average age of the students was 26 (with over 80 per cent of the students below 30) and the gender split was 65:35 in favour of males. The students came from 46 different countries with the top countries of origin being India (29 per cent), Nigeria (23 per cent), China (10 per cent) and the UK (7 per cent). These four countries represented 68 per cent of the students. The students were required to produce a research proposal for a subsequent dissertation. I was responsible for teaching research methods to the students over a period of 14 weeks and for marking their research proposals. In one sense a research proposal is complex – it involves among other skills those of decision-making, information literacy, objective setting, and planning. However, its structure is generic, normally including sections such as an introduction, a preliminary literature review, a set of research objectives, research methodology and methods, ethical considerations and a timetable for the dissertation. The main purpose of the research proposal was for the student to convince me that sound foundations had been laid for their dissertation.

Development of the assessment and feedback processes

Systems are best designed holistically and here I was fortunate. Prior to the period of this study, the summative assessment and feedback process inherited was a simple pass/fail, accompanied by comments against five qualitative statements. At the start of this study the university decreed that all coursework must carry a mark and that the pass mark was to be 40 per cent. This was seen as a golden opportunity for a complete re-design of the assessment and feedback processes on the module. The first decision made was that the processes were to make the maximum use of the digital features in the institution's virtual learning environment (VLE), with the caveat that students would still have the opportunities for 1:1 discussions with the author. Given the multi-faceted assessment and feedback processes to be designed and the large student numbers (between 130–200 per cohort), the use of online technology was essential. This online system did not change the pedagogy of the process. It simply made it possible, reducing the sum of the tutor, student and administrative labour by a factor of at least five. Why in this technological age are students expected to come into the university to queue to hand in a hard copy of their work at a reception desk and then to return at some later date to queue to collect the feedback? Are we to be surprised that some students do not collect their feedback?

Systems are best designed with the end in mind – what would be the nature of the summative assessment and feedback? The major decision was whether or not to use a grading form – student preferences for a grading form were weighed against the critisisms of grading forms (Sadler 2009; Dahlgren *et al.* 2009; Reddy and Andrade 2010). A further decision required was which Stage 2 processes were to be used. Large student numbers meant that self-assessment was the only way of achieving individual formative feedback with peer assessment being reserved for whole-class activities. It was decided to develop a common grading form for both summative, peer and self-assessment and to be wary of potential deficiencies (since the students were novice assessors, a holistic assessment process using a series of qualitative statements was thought to be too conceptually demanding for the students). The structure of the research proposal lent itself to the use of the grading form; however, it was recognized that a grading form might not be suitable for certain types of essay where a holistic process may be more appropriate. The grading form for summative assessment and feedback was accompanied by digital annotations on the student script with the student accessing both from within the VLE.

The precursor to designing the grading form was a research proposal template. This gave students a framework for their proposal with a clear indication of the key sections of the proposal, and what each should contain with an indicative word count. Each section was then broken down into assessment criteria and marks were allocated to each assessment criterion to a total of 100 – this was done through consultation with other colleagues who taught research methods. In terms of constructive alignment, the assessment criteria and their weightings clearly spelt out to students the areas where the main marks were to be awarded and thus the important areas to address in writing a convincing research proposal – the literature review, research objectives and data collection strategy. The first version of the grading form was then developed, comprising a matrix of 17 assessment criteria and five levels of achievement against each criterion. The grading form was built as a learning objective within the VLE. Initially the author piloted the grading form solely for summative assessment to see if there were any technical problems: these were minor and easily rectified, and the anecdotal feedback from students on the process was positive. For future cohorts of students the grading form was used for peer assessment, self-assessment and summative assessment.

The use of the grading form was complemented with three other forms of assessment – all formative. A successful dissertation is based on a wise choice of a focused topic. After four weeks the students submitted their topic choice through the VLE. These were digitally graded as green (good choice), amber (needs more focus) or red (inappropriate topic) with digital comments if appropriate, and the feedback given through the VLE within days. If necessary, students could meet me to discuss their grade – regular weekly surgery hours were held. Once an appropriate choice of topic has been made, the next three keys to a successful dissertation are an up-to-date literature review, clear objectives and a robust data collection strategy. In the second option, after ten weeks the students could post a research proposal outline in the VLE. This asked for the details of two recent sources on the topic area, the research objectives, and their data collection strategy. These were colour-graded in an analogous way as for the topic, with the feedback once again being given within days through the VLE. It was intended that a green achieved at this stage would almost guarantee that the final research proposal would be a pass. Students could again meet with the author if necessary to discuss how their grade could be upgraded to a green. The final option was the facility for students to self-assess a draft for plagiarism through a Turnitin submission link within the VLE. This facility was important given that the concept of originality and paraphrasing is new to many international students.

The assessment and feedback processes developed were evaluated through an online survey. The students were asked to respond to a combination of general statements from the National Students Survey (Higher Education Funding Council for England 2010) and those specific to the processes developed in this study.

Discussion on the use of the process

Stage 1 pre-emptive formative processes

Over 85 per cent of students took advantage of the formative feedback on their research proposal and research proposal outline. In another illustration of how complex assessment can be to students, I had to articulate several times for several students the difference between these formative assessment processes and the summative one, and that any grades for the formative assessments did not count towards the final summative mark. When the students in the last group of the study were asked if they found these processes helpful, 95 per cent replied positively (the sum of strongly agree and agree on a 5-point Likert scale). Almost all students took advantage of the option to check their draft research proposal for plagiarism. Over the course of the study, plagiarism dropped from a level of 16 to 3 per cent.

Use of the grading form

In terms of the grading form, rather than simply presenting it to the students, a series of learning activities were eventually devised to allow the students and me to incrementally develop the grading form. In terms of peer assessment, the students were given a previously submitted mediocre research proposal to read and assess against the grading form. The research proposal was then marked jointly by the students and me using the grading form in the next class. I then used poetic licence to improve the research proposal and the joint marking was repeated in the following class. Students and I agreed that a mediocre piece of work (45–50 per cent) had been raised to distinction level (around 70 per cent). A number of exemplars of high quality proposals using a range of approaches were posted within the VLE. Students were encouraged to self-assess their research proposal using the grading form during the development of their research proposal. For example, if their final estimated mark was within plus or minus 2 per cent of mine, then they would gain a bonus of five marks.

Students were overwhelmingly positive about the use of the grading form:

> Great! The grading form known in advance gave me the opportunity to know what it is expected of me.
>
> The grading form was extremely useful. It helped me to include all the necessary components of the research proposal giving importance to components that were allocated high credits and made my research proposal a good one.

A number of students came to discuss their grading form. Encouragingly a significant number of students who had passed came to discuss their grading form – in the past it had been predominantly failed students who had come to do so. The student and I found it easier to have a constructive dialogue as to how the mark had been reached. It was also easier to explain to failed students what they needed to do to upgrade their work to a pass. One comment about the grading form gave concern:

> Knowing exactly what was expected of us was essentially giving away free marks. All you needed to do was follow the form, and you would get a good mark. It's not rocket science.

It suggests that a grading form may result in a strategic approach to learning at the expense of a deep one (Dahlgren *et al.* 2009). A number of students said that some of the performance level descriptors could be made easier to understand, confirming that clarity in language is a challenging aspect of grading form design (Reddy and Andrade 2010). These limitations are recognized but any assessment system will have its limitations.

As a result of the constant dialogue on the grading form, the students contributed in several ways to its improvement and use, and a couple of examples are given below. First, students gave suggestions on how a number of assessment criteria could be rephrased to be less ambiguous and clearer. In the second example, a student came up with the excellent idea of giving after each criterion on the grading form the location of where the criterion was covered within the teaching materials.

How good are students at self-assessment?

Some 457 students (72 per cent of the population) chose to self-assess and the relationship between the student's estimated mark and my mark, and the line of equivalence, is shown in Figure 9.1.

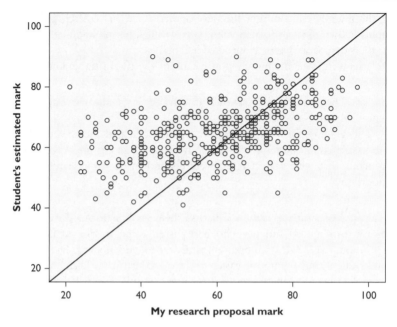

Figure 9.1 Plot of student's estimated marks against tutor's marks

Three things are clear. First, the students' accuracy of self-assessment was weak in agreement with other studies (Cassidy 2007; Lew *et al.* 2010). Second, in general, students had a tendency to over-estimate their performance (there are more circles above than below the line). Third, the less able students tended to over-estimate (circles towards the left-hand side of the graph) and the more able students (those marked by the author at over 70 per cent) to under-estimate. Orsmond, Merry and Reiling (1997) have also observed the second and third points in a previous study.

At one stage in the study, a minor survey of the cohort was conducted to find how students came to their estimated mark – I had some intelligence that not all students were using the grading form to estimate their mark. Of the students who had passed the module, 92 per cent had used the grading form to self-assess. However, the author was surprised, perhaps naively, to find that 80 per cent of the failed students had not used the grading form – they had based their estimate on a gut feeling, on how much effort they had put in, or that they had always received high marks at their previous educational institution. They had decided to base their judgement on affective rather than cognitive factors. Reasons for not using the grading form included forgetting, running out of time or not realizing the potential benefit of using the grading form. Less able students over-estimating their performance is of a major concern as several students who failed believed that they would pass – in subsequent discussions with these students, they did indeed express surprise that they had failed. If these students had used the grading form for their self-assessment, then perhaps they might have made more effort to ensure a pass. One lesson is clear – there is a need to impress on students the value of the grading form for self-assessment.

Why had the most able students under-estimated their performance? Perhaps they were simply being modest. An alternative explanation is that the use of a grading form stretched the range of assessment marks that was used. The spread of my marks was 18–96 per cent whereas many assessment processes confine marks to range between, say, 25–85 per cent, only using 60 per cent of the scale. Perhaps as a result of prior experiences of such assessment processes the more able students had downgraded their expectations. As one student said: 'My tip for other students would be to have the courage of your convictions. I actually scored my own proposal close to the actual mark awarded but "downgraded" my own score because it felt high.'

How did student attributes such as gender and nationality affect the accuracy of self-assessment?

Since the performance of a student is the result of a number of complex and intervening variables, the data collected does not lend itself to detailed statistical analysis. However, some general observations can be made of the effect of student attributes on the distribution of student-estimated marks to my marks. The effect of student attributes on average marks is also worthy of comment. The two attributes examined were gender and country of origin (age was not examined because of the similarity of ages in this group of students). There was no discernible gender difference in the distribution of students' versus my marks with both genders showing a similar pattern of less able students over-estimating and more able students under-estimating. There was, however, a significant difference between my marks for females and males (61.9 and 57.7 per cent respectively, $p < .01$). Are females more conscientious towards their studies than males? How did the four groups of different nationalities (Indian, Nigerian, Chinese and British) compare in their estimation of marks? All students, regardless of their country of origin, exhibited the trend of low performing students over-estimating and high performing students under-estimating. Nigerian and Indian students would appear to have a greater tendency to over-estimate than British and Chinese students. At the present time the author can only conjecture at the reasons for this. The average author's mark for the top four nationalities of student origin were:

British 66.9 per cent ($\sigma = 17.0$)
Nigerian 62.5 per cent ($\sigma = 14.8$)
Indian 55.0 per cent ($\sigma = 17.0$)
Chinese 54.1 per cent ($\sigma = 16.0$)

Table 9.1 Module questionnaire for the assessment and feedback responses

Statement	(%)
The criteria used in assessment were clear in advance	95
Assessment arrangements and marking have been fair	88
Feedback on my work has been prompt	92
I have received detailed comments on my work	91
Feedback on my work has helped clarified things I did not understand	81
The feedback will help me to improve my dissertation	90

Notes: The percentages are the sum of strongly agree and agree to the statement on a 5-point Likert scale.
N = 96.

An analysis of variance showed that Indian and Chinese students under-performed compared to British and Nigerian students ($p < .001$). This under-performance is believed to be due to a combination of the need to adjust to the Western participative educational style and a lesser proficiency in English. Although Nigerian students come from a didactic teaching background, their command of English is generally excellent.

Finally, it can be seen in Table 9.1 that students canvassed towards the end of the study (2010 students) were highly positive about the three-stage assessment and feedback processes developed.

These responses compare favourably with the data from the NSS (Higher Education Funding Council for England 2010) that shows that more than 30 per cent of students are not satisfied with current assessment and feedback processes. During the period of study the pass rate increased from 70 to 85 per cent.

Conclusion

It is proposed that for assessment and feedback processes to be effective and engage students in shaping their learning experience, they should follow three stages: (1) early pre-emptive formative feedback from the tutor; (2) formative processes in which students are actively involved; and (3) a final summative assessment into which the students have been collaboratively inducted. With large student numbers, this can only be achieved electronically. The turnaround time required for formative feedback to students was a few days with the more detailed summative feedback requiring ten days. Helping students to develop not only the knowledge of their subject, but also the understanding of the assessment processes within their discipline, offers a potential way of achieving a quantum rather than incremental change in improvement as to how students feel about assessment and feedback. More research is required on developing students' skills at peer and self-assessment. It is recognized that more effort is required to sell the benefits of these processes to the less able students. Different tasks will require different forms of assessment and ideally there should be a holistic design for introducing students to different assessment regimes across the modules in their programme.

References

Andrade, H. and Du, Y. (2007) 'Student responses to criteria-referenced self-assessment', *Assessment & Evaluation in Higher Education*, 32(2): 159–81.

Boud, D. (2007) 'Reframing assessment as if learning were important', in D. Boud and N. Falchikov (eds) *Rethinking Assessment in Higher Education: Learning for the Longer Term*, London: Routledge, pp. 14–28.

Boud, D. and Falchikov, N. (2006) 'Aligning assessment with long-term learning', *Assessment & Evaluation in Higher Education*, 31(4): 399–413.

Burke, D. (2009) 'Strategies for using feedback students bring to higher education', *Assessment & Evaluation in Higher Education*, 34(1): 41–50.

Carless, D. (2007) 'Conceptualizing pre-emptive formative assessment', *Assessment in Education: Principles, Policy & Practice*, 14(2): 171–84.

Cassidy, S. (2007) 'Assessing "inexperienced" students' ability to self-assess: exploring links with learning style and academic personal control', *Assessment & Evaluation in Higher Education*, 32(3): 313–30.

Dahlgren, L. O., Fejes, F., Abrabdt-Dahlgren, M. and Trowald, N. (2009) 'Grading systems, features of assessment and students' approaches to learning', *Teaching in Higher Education*, 14(2): 185–94.

Falchikov, N. (2005) *Improving Assessment through Student Involvement*, London: RoutledgeFalmer.

Higher Education Funding Council for England (2010) *2008 and 2009 National Student Survey Results for Students England*. Available at: http://www.hefce.ac. uk/news/hefce/2009/nss.htm (accessed 14 April 2010).

Lew, M. D. N., Alwis, W. A. M. and Schmidt, H. G. (2010) 'Accuracy of students' self-assessment and their beliefs about its utility', *Assessment & Evaluation in Higher Education*, 35(2): 135.

Lizzio, A. and Wilson, K. (2008) 'Feedback on assessment: students' perceptions of quality and effectiveness', *Assessment & Evaluation in Higher Education*, 33(3): 263–75.

Nesbit, P. L. and Burton, S. (2006) 'Student justice perceptions following assignment feedback', *Assessment & Evaluation in Higher Education*, 31(6): 655–70.

National Union of Students (2008) *NUS Student Experience Report*. Available at: http://www.nus.org.uk/PageFiles/4017/NUS_StudentExperienceReport.pdf (accessed 20 January 2011).

Nicol, D. (2010) 'From monologue to dialogue: improving written feedback processes in higher education', *Assessment & Evaluation in Higher Education*, 35(5): 535–50.

Nicol, D. J. and Macfarlane-Dick, D. (2006) 'Formative assessment and self-regulated learning: a model and seven principles of good feedback practice', *Studies in Higher Education*, 31(2): 199–218.

O'Donovan, B., Price, M. and Rust, C. (2008) 'Developing student understanding of assessment standards: a nested hierarchy of approaches', *Teaching in Higher Education*, 13(2): 205–17.

Orsmond, P., Merry, S. and Reiling, K. (1997) 'Students' and tutors' perception of a good essay', *Research in Education*, 58: 81–84.

Poulos, A. and Mahony, M. J. (2008) 'Effectiveness of feedback: the students' perspective', *Assessment & Evaluation in Higher Education*, 33(2): 143–54.

Rae, A. M. and Cochrane, D. K. (2008) 'Listening to students: how to make written assessment feedback useful', *Active Learning in Higher Education*, 9(3): 217–30.

Reddy, Y. M. and Andrade, H. (2010) 'A review of rubric use in higher education', *Assessment & Evaluation in Higher Education*, 35(4): 435–48.

Sadler, D. R. (2009) 'Indeterminacy in the use of preset criteria for assessment and grading', *Assessment & Evaluation in Higher Education*, 34(2): 159–79.

——(2010) 'Beyond feedback: developing student capability in complex appraisal', *Assessment & Evaluation in Higher Education*, 35(5): 535–50.

Sitzmann, T., Ely, K., Brown, K. G. and Bauer, K. N. (2010) 'Self-assessment of knowledge: a cognitive learning or affective measure?', *Academy of Management Learning and Education*, 9(2): 169–91.

Smith, L. J. (2008) 'Grading written projects: what approaches do students find most helpful?', *Journal of Education for Business*, July/August: 325–30.

Walker, M. (2009) 'An investigation into written comments on assignments: do students find them usable?', *Assessment & Evaluation in Higher Education*, 34(1): 67–78.

Weaver, M. (2006) 'Do students value feedback? Student perceptions of tutors' written responses', *Assessment & Evaluation in Higher Education*, 31(3): 379–94.

CRITICAL FRIEND COMMENTARY

David Sadler

Over recent decades several large-scale movements have taken place in teaching, learning and assessment. These include the shift from so-called teacher-centred teaching to the facilitation of student-centred learning, the introduction of self- and peer assessment and feedback, challenges to the idea of teachers as the sole authorities for grading decisions, and the use of online digital media. However, these changes have been partial – widely embraced in some countries, still virtually unheard of in others. In some contexts, uptake has been variable, depending on the discipline, field or profession. The chapter by Jewell provides a detailed account of actual experience with the two assessment-related aspects of the wider movements, and provides an important illustration of the applicability of the general principles to a particular field, namely, research methods, which many would regard as fairly cut and dried. The principles actually apply whenever qualitative judgements are made about the quality of student responses to assessment tasks, regardless of the field.

In assessment, the shift in mind-set for the student had been as dramatic as it has been for academics. Specifically, it represents a shift from having one's work assessed by the teacher (or tutor, graduate assistant or other marker) alone – the authority aspect – and, if feedback is provided, from primarily the sending and decoding of feedback to student engagement in appraisal processes with the student being a constructor of feedback. Participation in these introduces and smoothes student transition into the role of insider. Evaluative processes also provide a learning environment in which students can develop the art of perceiving, with detachment and objectivity, works of the same kind that they themselves are striving to produce. The benefit probably comes about mainly because appraising and constructing feedback requires closely focused attention to the characteristics of the work being appraised, with consequential development of student perception and sensitivity. In Jewell's approach, this was greatly facilitated by the use of online delivery technology.

As a student develops competence at peer assessment, it becomes a relatively small step to being able to monitor the emerging quality of their own productions and processes while their works are under construction. Ultimately, this is when it matters. Of course many learners will initially misjudge quality in the early stages. It would be surprising if that were not the case. But that is precisely the capacity that is under development. After graduation, when students move on to more advanced studies or into employment, being able to produce works of consistently high quality will form a valuable part of their personal professional repertoires.

Another shift in practice not mentioned so far in this commentary is from a make-everything-count marking economy to one that involves a stage which is purely formative. In contexts where such a step would be seen as taking unacceptable risks (the students might effectively opt out, or interpret it as patently unfair), students are pushed towards valuing learning for its own sake or for its later instrumental pay-off. In so doing, it promotes student acceptance of personal responsibility for learning. The process itself has potentially high gains for learning but imposes no penalties for any initial lack of sophistication, preliminary misunderstanding due to unfamiliarity with complex concepts, or attempts at experimentation during the early portions of the learning path. Work submitted and marked but not for credit might well differ from the students' previous experience, but how could it be construed as unfair?

A final potential stage, which was not part of the approach reported in Jewell's chapter, would be to throw the agenda wide open by having no preset criteria at all. This could pave the way for students to realize that high quality works can often be constructed in quite different ways. The respective rationales for judgements would make use of different criteria for different works. Embedded within the rationales would be the criteria that are salient for each particular judgement and work. This phenomenon reflects the existence of a larger pool of potential criteria, which is the same pool from which academic assessors, regardless of the level of consultation with their students, draw the criteria they traditionally identify.

Chapter 10

Digital storytelling as an alternative assessment

Martin Jenkins and Phil Gravestock

Introduction

This chapter sets out to evaluate the use of digital storytelling – the combination of narrative and digital media – as an alternative form of assessment. Drawing on underpinning pedagogies of storytelling, reflection and identity, this chapter will discuss the value of digital storytelling as a means of developing twenty-first-century literacies, student voice, reflective practice and how it challenges traditional read/write practices. The chapter concludes by considering the issues it raises as an alternative form of assessment.

What is digital storytelling?

Digital storytelling emerged as a technique in the 1990s, based on the work of Joe Lambert and Dana Atchley (Lambert 2009), and was added to through projects such as the BBC Capture Wales initiative (Meadows and Kidd 2009). These initiatives reflect the increasing access to easy forms of digital audio and image capture (McLellan 2006). A 'typical' digital story, in this original form, will be created by a single author, will last for 2 or 3 minutes and will consist of no more than 15 still images with a narrative of 250–300 words (Gravestock and Jenkins 2009; Hartley and McWilliam 2009; Jenkins and Gravestock 2009). These parameters are based on what is called the 'Center for Digital Storytelling' tradition (Hartley and McWilliam 2009), an approach which became widely used in community projects and in therapeutic disciplines.

Continued technological developments, especially the rise in Web 2.0 technologies, have encouraged the evolution of digital storytelling. As a consequence, new forms of use have emerged, meaning that clearly defining what a digital story is has become increasingly more difficult. Ohler (2008) recognizes this and uses the broader description 'new media narrative', although he acknowledges that the term 'digital storytelling' is more recognizable. Through Web 2.0 technologies new social forms of digital storytelling are emerging which allow greater interaction in the creation of stories, meaning they can evolve through time. This could be said to be re-engaging digital storytelling with elements of the storytelling tradition and its iterative and social nature.

Hartley and McWilliam (2009: 4–5) argue that at this moment in time digital storytelling provides a pivotal term that can be used to represent: an emergent *form*, combining the personal narrative and documentary; a new media *practice*, combining individual tuition with new publishing devices; an activist/community *movement*, combining experts with consumer-led activity; and a *textual system*, challenging the traditional view of the producer/consumer model and new forms of literacy.

Underpinning pedagogies

Digital storytelling can be seen as an adaptation of the storytelling tradition which has existed for more than 6,000 years (Abrahamson 1998). In whatever context they are used educationally, the process of developing and telling a story engages students in cognitive strategies. Story construction demands judgement in respect of the information required and the format of the story (Robinson and Hawpe 1986). Stories can be created as personal narratives, stories to inform, or as critical analyses. Meadows (2003) identifies digital storytelling as a social practice, and the act of storytelling is seen as a uniquely human experience (McDrury and Alterio 2003). Stories can be used to convey information, or perhaps to motivate colleagues or friends, but many stories are used to help give meaning to individuals' own particular experiences and to demonstrate their own understanding of the world (Nygren and Blom 2001; Miley 2009; Jamissen and Skou 2010; Moon 2010). In this respect, the sharing of stories is an important element (Orech 2008) and it is by sharing our stories that we can obtain a deeper insight into their meaning.

Benmayor (2008) identifies digital storytelling as a social pedagogy, approaching learning as a collaborative process. There are multiple opportunities for collaboration within the digital storytelling process, since story development is a self-reflexive and recursive process (ibid.), with the story being refined through the telling and re-telling of ideas. Through this interactive, iterative process, learning is reinforced through the synthesis of ideas and the multiple opportunities to gather feedback from both peers and tutors.

Creating digital stories enables students to use their own voice as well as providing a process to represent their ideas. Oppermann (2008) found that students recognized the importance of voice in presenting an argument and that this supports the development of students' own sense of agency. Freire (1970) identifies the value of a critical pedagogy in empowering learners, which he views as critical for social change and social justice. Learner empowerment requires the development of the learners' voice and identity, recognizing the affective as well as the cognitive domains of learning. Helping students to develop their own identity is a social process; our concept of identity is dialogical and so narrative can play an important part in its construction. It is recognized that digital storytelling encourages emotional engagement with the task (Oppermann 2008), which is indicative of its widespread use in community-based projects, and can be considered as a way of linking the cognitive and the affective domains. This is particularly so when students participate in activities that engage them with social and cultural issues (Benmayor 2008; Oppermann 2008) and through presentation of their own personal stories. Reflection on critical incidents, such as those from an industrial placement, is one such example of how students can use digital stories to present their own stories (Jenkins and Lonsdale 2008; Moon 2010). Reflections on critical points combine the affective and cognitive domains with an emphasis on the personal voice; they are not just reports on past events but have a role in helping the individual clarify their own self-concept.

Reflection is an important part of the learning process (Kolb 1984) and it is increasingly recognized that reflection is a social process (Boud 2010). The development of stories provides a space for contemplation, but active reflection for learning is enhanced through the sharing with others. This view of reflection has been an increasing feature in the caring professions (Bradbury et al. 2010) and links with research into professional learning which argues that the traditional academic separation between 'knowing what' and 'knowing how' is false, as knowledge is context-dependent (Schön 1983; Eraut 1994, 2009). Eraut (1994) reinforces this by arguing that for an idea to have value, it must be used, which reinforces the view that for a story to be a story, it must be shared.

Schön (1983) and Eraut (1994) recognized that some knowledge is implicit (i.e. tacit knowledge), which is difficult to share. Schön (1983) has highlighted the importance of experience over knowledge and of the value of reflective practice in accessing this tacit knowledge. Telling stories is one mechanism that can help achieve this. Storytelling has been identified as an important process in helping to develop communities of practice, not to achieve shared knowledge but to help develop a common framework which can lead to a shared interpretation (Brown and Duguid 2002). Each individual's learning from a story will be unique, as it emerges from a combination of the story (the external experience) and their own previous learning (internal experiences) (Moon 2010); however, stories help to provide common points of reference, which in organizational or community settings can be important in helping to develop and bind communities.

The Kolb experiential learning cycle (Kolb 1984) highlights that reflection on experience is fundamental to making learning apparent, although this is recognized as being challenging (McDrury and Alterio 2003). Learning is an iterative process, and digital storytelling can make this explicit (Leon 2008). Coventry (2008: 168) observes that 'digital storytelling encapsulates the important pedagogical principles of restatement and translation that are central to helping students engage with difficult material'. This communication of understanding with others allows a different perspective to be introduced and new questions to be asked, acknowledging reflection as a social process which can potentially prompt further thoughts. Oppermann (2008) sees the 'regurgitation' of practice, making learning explicit in different forms and contexts to others, as a means of evidencing learning. The process of constructing a story, which needs to be conveyed to others, forces the teller to move from actor to observer, a process that in the context of Kolb's experiential learning cycle is helping the learner move from 'concrete experience' to 'abstract conceptualization' (McDonnell *et al.* 2004).

Storytelling is then an approach that can be used to facilitate learners' reflection on their own experience and making this explicit to others; that is to say that it is a socio-constructivist pedagogy. McDrury and Alterio's (2003) *Model of Reflective Learning through Storytelling* and Moon's (1999) *Map of Learning* are useful models to help analyze how learning is being achieved through storytelling. They both have been used as frameworks for assessing the use of digital stories, in particular where used for reflection (Jenkins and Lonsdale 2008; Sanders 2009).

The process of creating the digital story – including identifying the story, producing the script, selecting and collecting the images and producing the final product itself – provides students with 'a strong foundation in 21st Century literacy' (Robin 2008: 224). Robin sees the act of creating a digital story as drawing upon a range of literacies, such as: *digital literacy* and the ability to communicate, discuss issues, gather information and be able to seek help in a digital world; *global literacy*, having a global perspective in information gathering and interpretation; *technology literacy*, to be able to use technology effectively for learning and improving performance and productivity; *visual literacy*, to be able to communicate, including the production of, visual images; and *information literacy*, to be able to locate, evaluate and synthesize information. This range of literacies, which necessitates students using their senses in a variety of different ways, has led to some authors referring to the creation of digital stories as a multimodal process (e.g. Jamissen and Skou 2010; Nilsson 2010). Freire (1970) sees the development of literacies as an important part of the learning process, as a means of enabling criticality and so ensuring learner emancipation; literacies having at least equality with subject knowledge. Emancipation, according to Freire, comes through participatory development. The nature of digital storytelling, including the social and iterative nature of story development, and the emphasis on personal voice in the sharing of stories, does make it a naturally active and participatory approach. In this sense, it does present an alternative form of assessment.

Digital storytelling as an assessment activity

Drivers for change

Recent national developments in the UK have renewed interest in the development of employability skills, mainly in response to a variety of government agendas (e.g. Higher Education Funding Council for England 2010). The multimodal nature of digital story creation, and the development of different literacies, offer one way in which these employability skills can be practised, developed, implemented and demonstrated. Reflecting upon the meaning of particular critical incidents, and articulating the learning and achievements which have resulted from these, are valuable skills that will support students during interviews and in the workplace. Eraut (2009) discusses the nature of situated learning (i.e. learning which takes place within a particular context, such as in education or in the workplace), and the fact that the meaning an individual places on the learning experience will be shaped by the context in which this learning takes place. Rather than focusing on competences, Eraut introduces the idea of learning trajectories. Learning trajectories are professional development pathways which can be used as a method of tracking performance. An individual assessment point (either formative or summative) will only provide a view of one trajectory at a particular point in time. In order to view and consider a learner's trajectories overall requires consideration of several windows which will provide a more holistic picture of the learner and their capabilities. Eraut recognizes that media artefacts, such as digital storytelling, may provide an approach which allows a holistic view of learning during these assessment points, particularly in helping to capture, and so share, tacit learning.

In addition to supporting the development of employability skills, digital storytelling may also address issues arising from the widening participation agenda; for example, there are issues of retention to consider when using assessment activities that solely rely on the ability to write in order to demonstrate knowledge and learning. With an increasingly diverse range of students in higher education – for example, in terms of age, ethnicity, nationality, disability, etc. (Grace and Gravestock 2009) – it is worth considering whether digital storytelling could be used as a form of assessment which will be of benefit to a broad group of students by allowing them to demonstrate that they have met the required intended learning outcomes. Anecdotal evidence from the University of Gloucestershire suggests that some students view digital stories as 'no text' or 'low text' assignments, possibly owing to the fact that this form of assessment does not require any form of written submission. A lack of written submission may benefit some disabled students and students who are not studying in their first language, and who may not always be able to express themselves fully through written assessment tasks. Hellawell (2007) describes a case study undertaken for the Joint Information Systems Committee (JISC) TechDis service using digital narratives and video journals with a student with dyslexia, where it was noted that the use of the digital media technique captured far more information than the student would have been able to record in a written format.

Another case study, presented in Gravestock and Jenkins (2009), describes the use of digital storytelling with students in their first year in higher education. In this case, digital storytelling was used to support and develop students' presentation skills prior to giving a live presentation in front of their peers. The important aspect of this development is the fact that the students who created the digital story became part of the audience when the story was presented to the group, and were therefore able to participate in the evaluation and critique of their own presentation. One of the groups contained a student with cerebral palsy and an international student. Both students benefitted from the fact that they were able to re-record parts of the narrative. The critique was able to focus on the content of the digital story 'presentation' and how this content was communicated to the audience, for example, whether the narrative made sense and the choice of images enhanced the narrative. This case study also highlights the benefit of sharing stories with others, and the subsequent development of stories based on the feedback received from peers or from self-reflection. As Jamissen and Skou (2010: 189) note, 'Stories are developed in interaction between the owner of the experience and his or her peers through listening and feedback over several iterations.' Although in this particular case study there was no requirement to redevelop the digital story following peer and tutor feedback, this technique has been used successfully in other higher education settings; for example, Davies (2008) describes the use of a computerized process for self-assessment and for-mative peer assessment of digital stories, and the subsequent re-development of some stories to incorporate the comments prior to final submission of the story for summative assessment purposes. This demonstrates the strong potential of digital storytelling as a formative assessment process, and as a method of organizing and re-organizing thoughts and reflections upon the meanings of particular activities and experiences.

Challenging traditional forms of assessment

In higher education the linguistic form is still the dominant paradigm (Oppermann 2008) and students can become accustomed to traditional forms of teaching, learning and assessment and internalize processes for coping with them; however, this reliance fails to recognize variations in how students learn. Digital storytelling forces both staff and students out of traditional written approaches to assessment and promotes new opportunities to capture learning. The multimedia nature of the digital story means that students are being asked to communicate their mes-sage in different forms: word, image and audio. Coventry (2008: 206) observes that 'as students move between traditional writing assignments and multimedia narratives, they are communicating across familiar and unfamiliar languages'. This means that students have to continually 'recreate' their understanding in different ways which leads to a reinforcement of the learning. Digital stories provide stu-dents with the opportunity to discuss personal issues in a way which they may not do so readily through a 'traditional' essay or report. The different 'languages' also mean that the process is slowed down, as the normal routine of the planning and writing an essay cannot be relied upon (Leon 2008). This can lead to more considered reflection on, and a deeper engagement with, the topic of the story. One of the outcomes of this process is that the strategies for creating and composing a coherent narrative become explicit to the student, and can be implemented during the development and completion of other written assignments or reports (Oppermann 2008). Jamissen and Skou (2010) discuss the difference between writing a 'traditional' essay or report and creating a digital story. They note that while a report or essay will tend to consider how things *are*, a story focuses more on what things *mean* and how this meaning can be understood and interpreted. This distinction is useful when considering whether the use of digital storytelling is an appropriate assessment technique in addressing the intended learning outcomes for a course.

Technological considerations

Digital storytelling can be seen as a deceptively simple technology. As a consequence, it would be easy for digital storytelling to be introduced without consideration of an appropriate learning design or how the digital storytelling process will be supported and assessed. Beetham, McGill and Littlejohn (2009) found that students are likely to welcome the use of technologies that they are familiar with and which are accessible; however, while engagement with a wide range of media is now a norm, rather than the realm of specialist areas, research indicates that students lack criticality and effective strategies for using technology in their learning (Beetham *et al.* 2009). It is therefore important that assumptions are not made about the level of students' digital literacy and the ability of students to apply this technological knowledge to approaches such as digital storytelling. It is recommended that staff should first create their own digital story to understand what is involved, and to provide an insight into what support is required.

Is digital storytelling a process or product?

Central to the use of digital stories is the debate about product versus process. Where the story is a vehicle for 'making learning explicit' to assessors, there is a risk that the actual manifestation of the story can fall by the wayside. There is an argument that seeing the final product as only a means to an end – for example, assessment – will lead to a diminishment of the potential of the story to affect its audience beyond the assessors. This debate can be seen to reflect potential tensions resulting from an expanding use of digital storytelling that is starting to operate outside the strict boundaries of the original 'Center for Digital Storytelling' approach; however, the growth in digital storytelling has resulted in part from the accessibility of the stories and the fact that they can be easily shared, reviewed and reflected upon. It is clear that there is a need for a baseline in terms of technical quality, as stories that are badly produced are unlikely to become effective pedagogic resources for others. This baseline will vary depending on how the digital stories are being used and who is producing them, and it is important to consider such factors when evaluating or assessing digital stories. Given that digital stories can be used in a wide range of applications, the criteria for assessment will vary considerably between applications. In response to this challenge, assessment frameworks have been developed that staff can use to assess digital stories (see, for example, Jenkins and Lonsdale 2008; Sanders 2009). These frameworks, which provide ideas for assessment criteria (e.g. project planning, creativity, academic understanding, organization, pacing), have value in supporting staff in the assessment of digital stories, although they are not intended to provide a list of comprehensive areas to consider. As with any assessment task, when assessing digital stories it is important to consider what the purpose of the assessment is and to ensure that the criteria match this purpose; however, there may be some additional aspects that need to be considered which relate to the use of the technology, such as use of voice or appropriate use of images to support the story. The frameworks provide a list from which criteria can be selected, depending on the purpose of the assessment.

Conclusion

This chapter has outlined the principles underpinning the development of digital storytelling and has outlined the application of digital storytelling as a form of assessment. It is not proposed that digital storytelling offers a conceptually different form of assessment, simply that it should be considered as an alternative form of assessment. The benefits of using digital storytelling as an assessment are that it supports: learners in reflecting upon their experiences; the development of multiple literacies, such as digital, visual, oral and written; students for whom 'traditional' written forms of assessment tasks may not provide the opportunity to demonstrate fully their achievements and learning. In relation to this latter point, digital storytelling has been shown to support some disabled students (e.g. students with dyslexia) and students for whom English is not their first language (e.g. international students) in meeting the intended learning outcomes of a course. The perception by some students that digital storytelling is a 'no text' or 'low text' form of assessment belies the fact that it involves the use of multiple literacies and cognitive strategies such as selecting, rejecting, ordering and structuring of both words and images. The use of digital storytelling may therefore not only be addressing a widening access issue, but may also support the retention of any students who have difficulty expressing themselves through standard written assessment formats.

The flexibility of the digital storytelling format means that it can be applied to a range of assessment tasks, depending upon the desired outcome. Some specific examples of how digital stories are used in different disciplines are presented in Jenkins and Gravestock (2009), but overall the use of digital stories can include: virtual tours (e.g. demonstrating specific architectural features of buildings); development of case studies; visual portfolios for use in critiques (e.g. art, landscape architecture); storytelling (e.g. in education, where the digital story can be re-used in subsequent years); reflection on critical incidents; demonstration of competence in particular skills (e.g. development of risk assessments); community-based projects; and alternatives to standard assessment activities such as presentations, reflective essays, illustrated journals, and group work.

One issue raised by the use of digital storytelling as an assessment activity relates to its use as a process or as a product. It is important to be clear about why digital storytelling is being used as an assessment activity and what it is assessing. As a *process*, digital storytelling can be an effective method of supporting students to reflect on aspects of their learning. The iterative process involved in the selection of words and images to create a digital story helps students to reflect on their experiences. Also, it is proposed that the ongoing act of sharing stories with others and then making changes on the basis of feedback from peers and tutors may be an effective method of formative feedback in the development of digital stories. As a *product*, digital stories can be used as a method of demonstrating technical expertise and competence in particular areas (e.g. narrative construction, appropriate combination of images and sound, editing, etc.), and may provide a student-generated resource which can be used with future teaching and learning activities (e.g. case studies in health work, as demonstrated by the Patient Voices Project (http://www.patient-voices.org/).

Some people may feel anxious about introducing digital storytelling as a form of assessment, particularly in terms of developing appropriate assessment criteria. Frameworks have been developed which provide prompts to consider when constructing assessment criteria. Depending upon the nature of the assessment activity, it may be appropriate to include some criteria which relate specifically to the digital nature of the product, but this is not always necessary. A strong recommendation would be for anyone thinking of using digital storytelling as an assessment activity to ensure that they have composed a digital story for themselves. This will allow for a greater appreciation of areas where students may need support during the development process.

References

Abrahamson, C. E. (1998) 'Storytelling as a pedagogical tool in higher education', *Education*, 118(3): 440–51.

Beetham, H., McGill, L. and Littlejohn, A. (2009) *Thriving in the 21st Century: Learning Literacies for the Digital Age (LLiDA project)*. Available at: http://www.academy.gcal.ac.uk/llida/LLiDAReportJune2009.pdf (accessed 17 September 2009).

Benmayor, R. (2008) 'Digital storytelling as a signature pedagogy for the new humanities', *Arts and Humanities in Higher Education*, 7(2): 188–204.

Boud, D. (2010) 'Relocating reflection in the context of practice', in H. Bradbury, N. Frost, S. Kilminster and M. Zukas (eds) *Beyond Reflective Practice: New Approaches to Professional Lifelong Learning*, London: Routledge, pp. 25–36.

Bradbury, H., Frost, N., Kilminster, S. and Zukas, M. (eds) (2010) *Beyond Reflective Practice: New Approaches to Professional Lifelong Learning*, London: Routledge.

Brown, J. S. and Duguid, P. (2002) *The Social Life of Information*, rev. edn, Boston: Harvard Business School Press.

Coventry, M. (2008) 'Engaging gender: student application of theory through digital storytelling', *Arts and Humanities in Higher Education*, 7(2): 205–19.

Davies, P. (2008) 'The computerized peer-assessment of digital storytelling in higher education', in *Proceedings of the 12th International CAA Conference: Research into e-assessment*, Loughborough University, UK.

Eraut, M. (1994) *Developing Professional Knowledge and Competence*, London: Falmer Press.

——(2009) 'Understanding complex performance through learning trajectories and mediating artefacts', paper presented at the *European Conference on Educational Research: Theory and Evidence in European Educational Research*, Vienna, 28–30 September.

Freire, P. (1970) *Cultural Action for Freedom*, Harmondsworth: Penguin Books.

Grace, S. and Gravestock, P. (2009) *Inclusion and Diversity: Meeting the Needs of All Students*, New York: Routledge.

Gravestock, P. and Jenkins, M. (2009) 'Digital storytelling and its pedagogical impact', in T. Mayes, D. Morrison, H. Mellar, P. Bullen and M. Oliver (eds) *Transforming Higher Education Through Technology Enhanced Learning*, York: Higher Education Academy, pp. 249–64.

Hartley, J. and McWilliam, K. (eds) (2009) *Story Circle: Digital Storytelling around the World*, Chichester: Wiley-Blackwell.

Hellawell, M. (2007) *The Production of Generative 'fly on the wall' Mini Documentaries Capturing a Physiotherapy Student's Personal Experience of their First Practice Placements*, JISC Techdis. Available at: http://www.jisctechdis.ac.uk/techdis/pages/detail/floating_pages/The_Production_Generative_Mini_Documentaries_Capturing_Physiotherapy_Students_Personal_Experience_First_Practice_Placements (accessed 6 February 2011).

Higher Education Funding Council for England (2010) *Circular Letter, Number 12/2010, Employability Statements*, 10 June 2010. Available at: http://www.hefce.ac.uk/pubs/circlets/2010/cl12_10/ (accessed 3 February 2011).

Jamissen, G. and Skou, G. (2010) 'Poetic reflection through digital storytelling: a methodology to foster professional health worker identity in students', *seminar.net: International Journal of Media, Technology and Lifelong Learning*, 6(2): 177–91. Available at: http://seminar.net/index.php/volume-6-issue-2-2010/152-poetic-reflection-through-digital-storytelling-a-methodology-to-foster-professional-health-worker-identity-in-students (accessed 3 February 2011).

Jenkins, M. and Gravestock, P. (2009) *Digital Storytelling Synthesis*, York: Higher Education Academy. Available at: http://digitalstorytellingsynthesis.pbworks.com/ (accessed 14 April 2011).

Jenkins, M. and Lonsdale, J. (2008) 'Podcasts and students' storytelling', in G. Salmon and P. Edirisingha (eds) *Podcasting for Learning in Universities*, Maidenhead: Open University Press, pp. 113–20.

Kolb, D. (1984) *Experiential Learning: Experience as the Source of Learning and Development*, Englewood Cliffs, NJ: Prentice Hall.

Lambert, J. (2009) 'Where it all started: the Center for Digital Storytelling in California', in J. Hartley and K. McWilliam (eds) *Story Circle: Digital Storytelling around the World*, Chichester: Wiley-Blackwell, pp. 79–90.

Leon, S. M. (2008) 'Slowing down, talking back, and moving forward: some reflections on digital storytelling in the humanities curriculum', *Arts and Humanities in Higher Education*, 7(2): 220–3.

McDonnell, J., Lloyd, P. and Valkenburg, R. C. (2004) 'Developing design expertise through the construction of video stories', *Design Studies*, 25(5): 509–25.

McDrury, J. and Alterio, M. (2003) *Learning through Storytelling in Higher Education: Using Reflection and Experience to Improve Learning*, London: Kogan Page.

McLellan, H. (2006) 'Digital storytelling in higher education', *Journal of Computing in Higher Education*, 19(1): 65–79.

Meadows, D. (2003) 'Digital storytelling: research-based practice in new media', *Visual Communication*, 2(2): 189–93.

Meadows, D. and Kidd, J. (2009) 'Capture Wales: the BBC digital storytelling project', in J. Hartley and K. McWilliam (eds) *Story Circle: Digital Storytelling around the World*, Chichester: Wiley-Blackwell, pp. 91–117.

Miley, F. (2009) 'The storytelling project: innovating to engage students in their learning', *Higher Education Research and Development*, 28(4): 357–69.

Moon, J. (1999) *Reflection in Learning and Professional Development*, London: Kogan Page.

——(2010) *Using Story in Higher Education and Professional Development*, Abingdon: Routledge.

Nilsson, M. (2010) 'Developing voice in digital storytelling through creativity, narrative and multimodality', *seminar.net: International Journal of Media, Technology and Lifelong Learning*, 6(2): 148–60. Available at: http://seminar.net/index.php/home/75-current-issue/154-developing-voice-in-digital-storytelling-through-creativity-narrative-and-multimodality (accessed 3 February 2011).

Nygren, L. and Blom, B. (2001) 'Analysis of short reflective narratives: a method for the study of knowledge in social workers' actions', *Qualitative Research*, 1: 369–84.

Ohler, J. (2008) *Digital Storytelling in the Classroom: New Media Pathways to Literacy, Learning and Creativity*, Thousand Oaks, CA: Corwin Press.

Oppermann, M. (2008) 'Digital storytelling and American Studies: critical trajectories from the emotional to the epistemological', *Arts and Humanities in Higher Education*, 7(2): 171–87.

Orech, J. (2008) Tips for Digital Storytelling, *Tech & Learning*. Available at: http://www.techlearning.com/article/8030 (accessed April 2009).

Robin, B. R. (2008) 'Digital storytelling: a powerful technology tool for the 21st century classroom', *Theory into Practice*, 47: 220–8.

Robinson, J. A. and Hawpe, L. (1986) 'Narrative thinking as a heuristic process', in T. R. Sarbin (ed.) *Narrative Psychology: The Storied Nature of Human Conduct*, Westport, CT: Praeger Publishing, pp. 111–25.

Sanders, J. (2009) *Reflect 2.0: Using Digital Storytelling to Develop Reflective Learning by the Use of the Next Generation Technologies and Practices*. Available at: http://www.jisc.ac.uk/publications/documents/reflectfinalreport.aspx (accessed 6 February 2011).

Schön, D. (1983) *The Reflective Practitioner: How Professionals Think in Action*, New York: Basic Books.

CRITICAL FRIEND COMMENTARY

Phil Davies

This chapter identifies digital storytelling as a possible key area for the future of assessment in various stages of education. The included emphasis towards 'multimodal' media within the production of a solution to an assessment problem fits in well with the expectations of our current students. Caution, however, must be shown in measuring the competence of our students in using media rather than the traditional written form of solution when creating the criteria for assessment. It must be clear to both assessor and assessed what is to be judged, for example, particular subject knowledge and understanding rather than the choice of a suitable image? In response to this, the issue of generating appropriate criteria and frameworks of assessment is identified as being key to the effectiveness of digital stories.

Concern may be expressed with regard to the use of media replacing traditional textual essay solutions as weakening the referencing and citations of research used by a student, often considered to be a measure of academic quality. It should be noted that, owing to the various use of conjoined media rather than the sequential textual process of an essay, the superimposing of supporting textual citations may be permitted at the same time as an image or voice-over is being performed. We are dealing with a method of presentation using digital stories that requires considerable alternative research and referencing skills.

The chapter notes that the inclusion of personalization and emotive response is encouraged by using digital storytelling among the methods used for assessment. This inclusion may offer a means of encapsulating the feelings of an individual in presenting a particular topic area; for example, it may be considered appropriate for the student to be able to use it as a means of performing 'technological role-play', by placing themselves in a position that requires them to assume the persona of another individual, hence having to assimilate that person's knowledge and experiences. Again, this produces the need for the assessor to be totally objective in their mapping of the outputs of the digital story directly to the criteria issued for the assessment. It should be noted, however, that although the measurement of emotion and reflection in a summative environment can be difficult, it is possible.

Digital storytelling, as the chapter highlights, is moving rapidly from simply being a means of 'reporting' to that of a tool that may be included in the assessment of students. Care must be taken in controlling this movement in order to maintain standards across various fields in the area of academic assessment; however, this should not be considered a reason to exclude digital stories from the assessment strategy, as it is clear that the resultant enhancement of student reflection and personalization in their solutions may well produce significant personal benefits.

Chapter 11

Interdisciplinary assessment

Clinton Golding and Chi Baik

The challenge of interdisciplinary learning and teaching

Interdisciplinary subjects focus on how to understand, navigate and employ multiple and often contrary ways of knowing. In these subjects, students learn how to integrate and synthesize different perspectives in order to advance understanding and solve problems that resist understanding or resolution when approached from single disciplines (Boix Mansilla and Duraising 2007). Yet there are numerous challenges to engaging and retaining students in interdisciplinary thinking and learning because of the complexity of working across multiple ways of knowing. Students tend to take the approach of one discipline or subject at a time and do not mix them. Just as C. P. Snow (1964) describes, there seems to be two cultures of students, Science and Arts, who have what McCalman, Muir and Soeterboek (2008: 17) call 'resistance to learning outside their comfort zones'. This forms an obstacle for understanding and engaging in inter-disciplinary thinking, and as a result, students tend to disengage with the com-plexity and ambiguity of integrating multiple disciplines. This challenge is exacerbated if discipline-specialists teaching in interdisciplinary subjects are not familiar or experienced with interdisciplinarity (especially if teaching in such sub-jects for the first time), and so they present students with vague, often tacit and conflicting expectations and assessment criteria based on their own disciplinary approaches. In the face of such challenges, it should be no surprise if students do not engage in interdisciplinary thinking.

Since the role of assessment in engaging learning is well established (e.g. Biggs 2003; Ramsden 2003; Race 2004; Boud & Associates 2010), our aim in this chapter is to examine how assessment can be used to enhance student engage-ment, learning and therefore retention in interdisciplinary subjects, particularly in relation to the development of interdisciplinary thinking. Our main question is: How can we use assessment to engage students in interdisciplinary thinking? We begin with a brief discussion of the objectives of interdisciplinary subjects and the importance of interdisciplinary learning in the broader context of higher educa-tion. We then explore three subsidiary questions that must be addressed when considering how assessment can engage students in interdisciplinary thinking:

(1) what exactly are we assessing and what criteria should we use?; (2) how can we make the criteria concrete and accessible for novices? and (3) what kinds of tasks and assessment types are appropriate for assessing interdisciplinary thinking?

Interdisciplinary learning

In an interdisciplinary subject, students explore, employ, occupy, and integrate multiple perspectives from different disciplines, sub-disciplines and areas of expertise. This is different from what might be called a multidisciplinary subject which merely juxtaposes multiple perspectives on the same topic. Interdisciplinarity involves integrating the perspectives to produce such things as a deeper understanding or illumination, a balanced judgement, viable solution or a product. Boix Mansilla and Duraising (2007: 219) call this developing an interdisciplinary understanding which they define as:

> the capacity to integrate knowledge and modes of thinking in two or more disciplines or established areas of expertise to produce a cognitive advancement – such as explaining a phenomenon, solving a problem, or creating a product – in ways that would have been impossible or unlikely through single disciplinary means.

The objectives of interdisciplinary learning include: general competencies such as written communication or critical thinking; disciplinary and professional skills and knowledge; multi-disciplinary breadth of knowledge of multiple disciplines and fields; and interdisciplinary thinking (Klein 2010: 113). We focus on interdisciplinary thinking as this is perhaps the most difficult aspect to engage students in, and the others have received adequate attention elsewhere. The essence of interdisciplinary thinking is synthesis, integration, balancing and accommodating the insights from multiple disciplines. Just as learning the distinctive ways of thinking is essential for learning in the disciplines (Hounsell and Anderson 2009), learning interdisciplinary ways of thinking is essential for engagement and retention in interdisciplinary learning.

Interdisciplinary learning and contemporary challenges in higher education

Why should we be concerned about engaging students in interdisciplinary thinking? Interdisciplinarity is of growing importance in higher education, and the objectives of interdisciplinary learning align with its broader goals. Becher and Trowler (2001) note that there has been a marked shift in the perceived purposes of higher education towards producing 'highly employable graduates' (Knight 2002: 109) who are 'flexibly skilled' and capable of difficult performances (Shay 2008: 527). This has meant a new emphasis on generic learning outcomes, and expectations that courses will enable students to develop a 'complex set of understanding, skills, efficacy beliefs and metacognition that enriches graduate claims to be highly employable' (Knight 2002: 114). A focus on interdisciplinarity has been seen as one way to enable students to gain the required sophisticated, flexible skills. This is also linked with the increased emphasis on critical thinking, on internationalization, and on solving complex problems.

Critical thinking is one commonly stated graduate attribute of many universities, that is closely aligned with interdisciplinary thinking. Both critical and interdisciplinary thinking enable graduates to flexibly apply their skills to diverse situations, settings and contexts, and to solve problems from multiple perspectives. Furthermore, developing interdisciplinary thinking skills is one way of developing critical thinking. Jones (2006), for example, argues that interdisciplinarity adds a reflexive dimension to critical thinking in that it requires an examination of debates both within a discipline as well as the ways in which others may view ideas that are otherwise commonly accepted.

Also, the objectives of interdisciplinary learning are important in the context of universities' goals for internationalizing university curricula and for developing graduates' global citizenship. The ability to synthesize and integrate diverse perspectives across a range of contexts is central to interdisciplinary thinking and also promotes global engagement and internationalization.

As well as these connections between the objectives of higher education and interdisciplinary thinking, developing interdisciplinary skills is often an explicit learning objective in contemporary universities. University graduates are expected to be able to solve current problems, many of which resist understanding or resolution when approached from single disciplines. On this basis, various universities have stated that their students will graduate with an interdisciplinary understanding. For example, the publication, *Attributes of the Melbourne Graduate* (University of Melbourne 2009), states that graduates of the University of Melbourne should be 'knowledgeable across disciplines' with the ability to 'examine critically, synthesize and evaluate knowledge across a broad range of disciplines'.

As a result of the growing importance of interdisciplinary learning in higher education, there has been a wealth of literature produced on interdisciplinary education, often with a specific focus on higher education (Squires 1992; Boix Mansilla *et al.* 2000; Nikitina 2002; Davies and Devlin 2007; Golding 2009; Mitcham *et al.* 2010), including two textbooks on interdisciplinary studies (Augsburg 2006; Repko 2008).

Interdisciplinarity is especially important in the context of our university. In 2008, the University of Melbourne introduced a landmark curriculum reform known as 'The Melbourne Model' with six broad undergraduate degrees characterized by their emphasis not only on disciplinary depth, but cross-disciplinary 'breadth'. There has always been a range of interdisciplinary subjects offered in cross-disciplinary degrees, but the Melbourne Model has given further emphasis with the addition of at least two types of subject which are explicitly inter-disciplinary: University Breadth Subjects taught by cross-faculty teams and offered to undergraduate students from any faculty, and Interdisciplinary Foundation subjects which are compulsory first-year Arts subjects that integrate several Arts disciplines. The aim is to have graduates who not only have disciplinary expertise, but also understand the broader context and who are able to apply their skills and knowledge to a wide range of situations. These objectives are reflected in the university's statement of graduate attributes and are similar to the graduate attributes of other Australian institutions, as stated above.

Given the importance of interdisciplinarity, the question of concern for the rest of this chapter is: How can we use assessment to help students come to understand and engage with interdisciplinary thinking? There are three main challenges to design assessments for this purpose: The first is figuring out what to assess; the second is to make the criteria accessible and concrete for novices so they are able to engage in what you want to assess; and the third is to devise methods of assessment.

What to assess and what criteria to use?

The assessment of interdisciplinary thinking must start with making the thinking explicit. Students cannot engage in interdisciplinary thinking if they do not know what it is. Scholars in higher education generally accept that good assessment practice involves explicit articulation of assessment criteria (e.g. Brown and Knight 1994; Topping *et al.* 2000; Rust *et al.* 2005; Biggs and Tang 2007). Yet often the criteria most commonly used for interdisciplinary assessment are inadequate. Criteria for high-quality interdisciplinary work frequently employ fuzzy metaphors or are highly abstract, such as: it pushes the boundaries of the disciplines; it all comes together; the whole understanding is more than the sum of its disciplinary parts; or it balances, accommodates and synthesizes different perspectives and ways of knowing. These are too vague for lecturers, let alone students, to use in assessing work.

Fuzzy metaphors tend to be used when assessing interdisciplinary thinking because giving a precise articulation of any thinking is difficult. The problem in specifying clear and precise criteria for assessing interdisciplinary thinking is even more difficult. First, higher education students tend to lack even a novice understanding of interdisciplinary thinking, given the concentration on disciplinary teaching in much of the education system. Second, many staff involved in teaching interdisciplinary subjects (at least at Melbourne) are not expert interdisciplinarians to the same level that they are experts in their disciplines. They do not have an explicit or tacit sense of interdisciplinary thinking and inquiry. Third, as Pace (2009) points out, even experts find it difficult to articulate their characteristic ways of thinking, partly because these have become second nature and automatic to them, and partly because these are 'black boxes' that remain unexamined. Fourth, there are multiple ways of being interdisciplinary, and there are no established ways of thinking involved, as there are in many disciplines.

The solution to this fourfold problem is to make explicit the criteria for high quality interdisciplinary thinking in a way that could be used for assessment purposes. There is a developing literature on identifying interdisciplinary thinking for assessment purposes that is based on interdisciplinary research, reflective practice about interdisciplinary teaching, and empirical analyses of existing assessment criteria (e.g. Boix Mansilla and Gardner 2003; Boix Mansilla 2005, 2006; Boix Mansilla and Duraising 2007). One useful framework, taken from Boix Mansilla and Duraising (2007: 222–33), assembles what is known about high quality interdisciplinary work into specific assessment criteria. We present the framework directly from Boix Mansilla and Duraising (the second and third criteria focus on different aspects of interdisciplinary thinking):

- *Disciplinary grounding:* The degree to which student work is grounded in carefully selected and adequately employed disciplinary insights – that is, disciplinary theories, findings, examples, methods, criteria and forms of communication. Key questions to ask include: Are the selected disciplines appropriate to inform the issue at hand? Are any key perspectives or disciplinary insights missing? Are the considered disciplinary theories, examples, findings, methods, and forms of communication accurately employed, or does the work exhibit misconceptions?
- *Advancement through integration:* The degree to which disciplinary insights are clearly integrated, translated, synthesized or accommodated so as to advance student understanding – that is, the degree to which students use what Nikitina (2002) calls 'integrative structures' that result in more complex, effective, empirically grounded, or comprehensive accounts or products than would have been possible under a single disciplinary framework. Integrative structures could be: conceptualizations, graphic representations, theories or meta-theories, interpretations, explanations, resolutions or solutions, illuminations, models, metaphors, products, policies, narratives, taxonomies, rules or applications (Nikitina 2002; Miller and Boix Mansilla 2004; Boix Mansilla and Duraising 2007; Gardner 2008). Where is there evidence of disciplinary integration such as an integrative structure? Is there evidence that understanding has been enriched by the integration of different disciplinary insights (rather than an association or connection that does not offer any illumination)? Would something be lost if a particular disciplinary insight were missing from the work or if the balance of disciplinary insights were different?
- *Critical awareness:* The degree to which the work exhibits a clear sense of purpose, reflectiveness, and self-critique – that is, framing problems in ways that invite interdisciplinary approaches and exhibiting awareness of distinct disciplinary contributions, how the disciplines are integrated and the limitations of the integration. Does the work show a clear sense of purpose, framing the issue in ways that invite an interdisciplinary approach? Is there evidence of

reflectiveness in the choices, opportunities and compromises involved in interdisciplinary work and in the limitations of the work as a whole, such as what an account fails to explain or what a solution could not address? Does the work present a considered judgement? Does the work show awareness of the tensions and conflicts between the different perspectives without falling back on a simplistic relativism or dogmatism?

How can we make the criteria concrete?

Even though assessment criteria such as those from Boix Mansilla and Duraising give clear and precise criteria for interdisciplinary assessment, they may still be overly abstract so they cannot be easily assessed, and they give little concrete advice to students about what they are expected to do. The second challenge in assessing interdisciplinary thinking is thus to turn the precise assessment criteria into something concrete, observable, and thus assessable.

Labelling or naming the thinking to be assessed, for example, synthesis, is essential but not sufficient. A label is not concrete enough to be assessable or to show students what they need to do, and how they should do it. If we are going to assess interdisciplinary thinking, we have to make it 'visible', concrete and observable (Golding 2011), for example, what exactly does a synthesizer do? Thinking can be assessed on the basis of concrete actions or behaviours, because expert thinkers *do* things that novice thinkers do not. Expert thinkers ask questions while novice thinkers merely shrug their shoulders. Expert thinkers try alternative strategies while novices give up if their first attempt fails. So, the assessment of interdisciplinary thinking requires identifying concrete assessment criteria based on what an interdisciplinary thinker does. These provide criteria that are concrete enough to be assessable and behaviours for students to emulate, thus enabling them to engage in interdisciplinary thinking.

An abstract criterion such as 'integrates different disciplinary insights' can be made more concrete or visible by specifying the sorts of things that would be written, for instance, in a student essay that integrates. Students could more easily engage in integration, and we can more easily assess their ability to integrate, if they finish the following kind of sentences: 'This interdisciplinary understanding is better than our previous understanding because … '; 'It solves x, y and z problems because … '; 'This interdisciplinary understanding has transformed how I approach the issue in the following ways … ', and so on.

An alternative example is with the criterion 'shows reflection and self-critique.' If student work addresses and finishes the following sorts of statement, they will be engaging in interdisciplinary thinking and we have concrete indicators to assess this: 'The problem being addressed is … '; 'My reasons for integrating the disciplines to address this problem are … '; 'A, B and C disciplines need to be involved because … '; 'A limitation of my interdisciplinary approach is … '.

The following example of concrete criteria for assessing interdisciplinary thinking comes from an interdisciplinary global health subject at the University of

Melbourne. In this subject, students learn how to grapple with and solve health problems that involve complex and intertwined medical, social, political, religious, economic and educational factors. High quality interdisciplinary work in this subject would meet the three following criteria and student work can be assessed against these criteria by observing whether they ask and answer the listed questions, whether they give multiple possible answers, and whether they elaborate on these answers.

1 *Shows an understanding of the situation*: What are the dominant factors shaping the current situation? What are the different interests involved? What are the challenges involved? What further information or analyses do I need in order to address and resolve these challenges? What factors and interests are amenable to change? Who are the possible change agents involved?

2 *Identifies relevant 'toolkit' of resources, expertise, people and organizations*: What 'tools' can best address the challenges? What disciplines can provide these tools? Which ones can be mobilized, how and by whom?

3 *Resolves the challenges*: What are the alternatives? Given the nature of the challenges, and all available information and analyses, which is the best solution? Why is this the best solution? Is it feasible and sustainable? What is required to implement it? What would be an effective strategy for implementation? What are its key elements, priorities, timelines? Who can implement this and how might they best do this?

A further example of assessment criteria for interdisciplinary subjects comes from an interdisciplinary history subject. The main aim of this subject is to create an 'ecological' explanation of complex human phenomenon. Students are to create an understanding of everyday life by explaining it in terms of a system of macro-forces involving multiple causes and contexts. High quality ecological explanations would meet the following two criteria:

1 *Analyses the complexity of the issue*: What is the complexity underlying and providing a context for this issue? How are economics, institutions, cultures, values, the environment, social structures, medicine, biology, etc., relevant? How do these factors interact? How do humans interact with these factors? What effect does this reciprocal interaction have on the issue? What argument can be made that supports your interpretation of the interactions and effects?

2 *Imaginatively recreates the issue*: How can the context and the interrelationships be presented as a 'fleshed out' dramatization rather than a bloodless, abstract list of 'the facts of the case'? What would it be like to be involved in this issue? What would the participants feel, think or believe? What narrative can dramatize the technical argument?

These two examples indicate the sorts of questions students are expected to engage with when they do interdisciplinary work, and so they provide concrete criteria that can be used to assess their interdisciplinary learning. More importantly, these criteria and questions can be used as the basis for teaching and learning activities and formative assessment tasks that enable students to gain a better understanding of what constitutes high quality interdisciplinary work and then to engage in high quality interdisciplinary thinking.

How to assess?

Making criteria explicit and concrete helps students to understand what is valued and expected in interdisciplinary learning. Yet there is also the challenge of devising tasks that encourage student engagement with these criteria. We finish this chapter by discussing two kinds of assessment task appropriate to engage students in interdisciplinary thinking.

Isolate different aspects of interdisciplinary thinking for formative assessment tasks

Because interdisciplinary thinking is complex and often novel to students, rather than assessing the totality of interdisciplinary thinking, we argue that students benefit from engagement in assessment tasks that target isolated aspects of this thinking and then give them formative feedback. This can be even more effective if academic teachers first model how they would complete such tasks. The following are possible examples of formative assessment tasks that may be used in interdisciplinary subjects to target specific skills required for interdisciplinary thinking:

- Students analyse the stakeholders involved in: (1) a scientific issue; (2) a legal issue; and (3) a social issue (targets their ability to apply skills across disciplinary contexts).
- A case is presented and students report on several relevant disciplinary perspectives (targets their ability to find, translate and paraphrase multiple disciplinary perspectives).
- A situation or issue is presented and students describe and analyse it from several perspectives (targets ability to apply multiple disciplinary perspectives).
- Students evaluate an argued case for an interdisciplinary decision and identify gaps that would need to be filled to make it a balanced case (targets ability to evaluate interdisciplinary judgements).
- Three disciplinary perspectives are presented about a case, and students devise a balanced position that incorporates all three (targets their ability to make balanced, interdisciplinary judgements).

Once students have formative feedback from completing these smaller assessment tasks, they can complete a larger, final summative assessment task for grading. Completing this task will require them to apply all the interdisciplinary skills they have learned.

Peer and self-assessment for discernment of, and engagement in, interdisciplinary thinking

Because assessment-for-learning, where students are active participants in the learning process, is a useful practice in general (Boud and Associates 2010), it will also be useful for interdisciplinary assessment. Peer and self-assessment in particular, involving students analysing, reviewing and giving feedback, is a particularly useful technique for assessment-for-learning (see, for example, Topping 1998; Sluijsmans 2002; Falchikov 2005; van den Berg *et al.* 2006) that can easily apply to interdisciplinary assessment. Peer and self-assessment are particularly useful in promoting self-regulation and lifelong learning, so using them for interdisciplinary assessment will be very important. To equip students for lifelong learning, we need to help them develop the skills to make complex judgements about their own and others' work (Boud and Falchikov 2006).

Traditionally assessment and feedback have predominately been seen as exclusively the role and responsibility of academic teaching staff (Nicol and Macfarlane-Dick 2006). However, Boud (1990, 2000) questions how students will develop the self-regulation skills needed for life outside of university if formative assessment is left exclusively to teaching staff. Self- and peer assessment encourages reflection and promotes skills in self-assessment as well as enhancing greater meta-cognitive self-awareness (Topping 1998; Liu and Carless 2006). It therefore promotes independent learning and potentially reduces dependence on staff as 'the experts' (Dochy *et al.* 1999). In other words, if students are to learn the self-regulation skills necessary for lifelong learning, they need to be given opportunities to participate actively in the assessment process through formative peer and self-assessment (Boud 2000; Rust *et al.* 2005; Nicol and Macfarlane-Dick 2006).

Peer and self-assessment are also particularly useful for engaging students in interdisciplinary thinking because such assessment practices enable students to gain a better understanding of the assessment criteria (Biggs and Tang, 2007: 187). Even when assessment tasks only target particular aspects of interdisciplinary thinking, and this thinking has been refined into simple and observable criteria, interdisciplinary thinking is still a complex practice and difficult to understand and engage in, and it is even more difficult to do this independently. Peer and self-assessment are necessary for students to be able to move beyond the words of the assessment criteria and be able to discern in practice what counts as interdisciplinary thinking and be able to engage in the thinking expected of them. As part of this process of assessment, students can also be involved in developing or refining the criteria, not just learning to apply them.

Peer review in a student-learning context involves students considering or evaluating the value or quality of their fellow students' work and providing each other with feedback (Topping *et al.* 2000). In the context of interdisciplinary learning, this could involve students reviewing their peers' work guided by the assessment criteria and accompanying key questions (similar to those presented earlier in this chapter). The model used in Golding's classes is that students discuss what interdisciplinary thinking is necessary for a short assessment task (similar to those identified above), and then identify and refine concrete criteria for assessing the thinking needed to complete this task. Golding then models how he would assess and then improve a piece of student work using the criteria developed. Then students complete the same task, get peer feedback, improve their response, and then submit it to Golding for formative feedback about how they can further improve for future assignments.

A self-assessment completed before and after learning is also effective for engaging with and learning interdisciplinary thinking. At the start of an interdisciplinary subject that investigates human–environment interaction at the University of Melbourne, students write their initial answers to such questions as:

- What is the main point of this subject? What are we trying to achieve?
- What does it mean to do interdisciplinary work? Why do we do interdisciplinary work?
- Why is interdisciplinary work important in this subject, given what we are trying to achieve?
- How do we best go about interdisciplinary work?

At the end of their subject course, they write improved answers, and then reflect on how their understanding has developed. This self-assessment method serves several important functions: (1) it provides insight into current student understandings and misunderstandings of interdisciplinarity, which the academic teachers use to design tailored learning activities; (2) it helps students develop a deeper understanding of the interdisciplinary expectations of the subject; and (3) when students revisit the questions at the end of the subject, it demonstrates to students and teachers where interdisciplinary learning has occurred.

Conclusion

Assessment is an effective tool for engagement in any kind of learning, but it is key for interdisciplinary learning. Because interdisciplinary thinking is complex, novel for students (and often academics), while also being tacit and invisible, if we are to engage students in interdisciplinary thinking and retain them in interdisciplinary subjects, our assessment practices must make explicit what is involved in interdisciplinary thinking, and give concrete, explicit guidance to students about how to engage in such thinking. Smaller assessment tasks are important to break up the complex thinking into manageable chunks and give students a chance to get formative feedback. Peer and self-assessment are important to allow students to distinguish what is involved in interdisciplinary thinking and then to engage in it. Pre- and post-assessments allow students to monitor their own interdisciplinary learning, and allow academic teachers to provide targeted learning opportunities.

References

University of Melbourne (2009) *Attributes of the Melbourne Graduate*. Available at: http://www.unimelb.edu.au/about/attributes.html (accessed 1 July 2011).

Augsburg, T. (2006) *Becoming Interdisciplinary*, 2nd edn, Iowa: Kendall Hunt.

Becher, T. and Trowler, P. (2001) *Academic Tribes and Territories*, Buckingham: The Society for Research into Higher Education and the Open University Press.

Biggs, J. (2003) *Teaching for Quality Learning at University*, 2nd edn, Buckingham: The Society for Research into Higher Education and the Open University Press.

Biggs, J. and Tang, C. (2007) *Teaching for Quality Learning at University*, 3rd edn, Maidenhead: Open University Press.

Boix Mansilla, V. (2005) 'Assessing student work at disciplinary crossroads', *Change*, 37: 14–21.

——(2006) 'Quality assessment of interdisciplinary research', *Research Evaluation*, 15(1): 17–29.

Boix Mansilla, V. and Duraising, E. (2007) 'Targeted assessment of students' interdisciplinary work', *Journal of Higher Education*, 78(2): 215–37.

Boix Mansilla, V. and Gardner, H. (2003) *Assessing Interdisciplinary Work at the Frontier*, Interdisciplinary Studies Project, Project Zero, Cambridge, MA: Harvard Graduate School of Education. Available at: www.Interdisciplines.org (accessed 1 July 2011).

Boix Mansilla, V., Gardner, H. and Miller, W. (2000) 'On disciplinary lenses and interdisciplinary work', in S. Wineburg and P. Grossman (eds) *Interdisciplinary Curriculum*, New York: Teachers College Press, pp. 17–38.

Boud, D. (1990) 'Assessment and the promotion of academic values', *Studies in Higher Education*, 15(1): 101–11.

——(2000) 'Sustainable assessment', *Studies in Continuing Education*, 22(2): 151–67.

Boud, D. and Associates (2010) *Assessment 2020: Seven Propositions for Assessment Reform in Higher Education*, Sydney: Australian Learning and Teaching Council.

Boud, D. and Falchikov, N. (2006) 'Aligning assessment with long term learning', *Assessment & Evaluation in Higher Education*, 31(4): 399–413.

Brown, S. and Knight, P. (1994) *Assessing Learners in Higher Education*, London: Kogan Page.

Davies, M. and Devlin, M. (2007) *Interdisciplinary Higher Education*, Melbourne: Centre for the Study of Higher Education.

Dochy, F., Segers, M. and Sluijsmans, D. (1999) 'The use of self-, peer and co-assessment in higher education: a review', *Assessment & Evaluation in Higher Education*, 24(3): 331–51.

Falchikov, N. (2005) *Improving Assessment through Student Involvement*, London: RoutledgeFalmer.

Gardner, H. (2008) *Five Minds for the Future*, Boston: Harvard Business School Press.

Golding, C. (2009) *A Guide for Interdisciplinary Teaching and Learning*, Melbourne: Centre for the Study of Higher Education.

——(2011) 'Educating for critical thinking', *Higher Education Research and Development*, 30(3): 357–79.

Hounsell, D. and Anderson, C. (2009) 'Ways of thinking and practising in biology and history', in C. Kreber (ed.) *The University and its Disciplines: Teaching and Learning Within and Beyond Disciplinary Boundaries*, New York: Routledge.

Jones, A. (2006) 'Re-disciplining generic skills', unpublished PhD thesis, the University of Melbourne.Klein, J. T. (2010) *Creating Interdisciplinary Campus Cultures*, San Francisco: Jossey-Bass and Association of American Colleges and Universities.

Knight, P. (2002) 'The Achilles' heel of quality: the assessment of student learning', *Quality in Higher Education*, 8(1): 107–15.

Liu, N. and Carless, D. (2006) 'Peer feedback: the learning element of peer assessment', *Teaching in Higher Education*, 11(3): 279–90.

McCalman, J., Muir, L. and Soeterboek, C. (2008) *Adventures with Breadth: A Story of Interdisciplinary Innovation*, Melbourne: Centre for the Study of Higher Education.

Miller, M. and Boix Mansilla, V. (2004) *Thinking Across Perspectives and Disciplines*, Interdisciplinary Studies Project, Project Zero, Cambridge, MA: Harvard Graduate School of Education.

Mitcham, C., Frodeman, R. and Klein, J. T. (eds) (2010) *The Oxford Handbook of Interdisciplinarity*, Oxford: Oxford University Press.

Nicol, D. J. and Macfarlane-Dick, D. (2006) 'Formative assessment and self-regulated learning', *Studies in Higher Education*, 31(2): 199–218.

Nikitina, S. (2002) *Three Strategies for Interdisciplinary Teaching*, Project Zero, Cambridge, MA: Harvard Graduate School of Education.

Pace, D. (2009) 'Opening History's "Black Boxes"', in C. Kreber (ed.) *The University and its Disciplines: Teaching and Learning Within and Beyond Disciplinary Boundaries*, New York: Routledge.

Race, P. (2004) *The Lecturer's Toolkit*, 2nd edn, London: Routledge.

Ramsden, P. (2003) *Learning to Teach in Higher Education*, New York: Routledge-Falmer.

Repko, A. (2008) *Interdisciplinary Research: Process and Theory*, Thousand Oaks, CA: Sage.

Rust, C., O'Donovan, B. and Price, M. (2005) 'A social constructivist assessment process model', *Assessment & Evaluation in Higher Education*, 30(3): 231–40.

Shay, S. (2008) 'Assessment at the boundaries', *British Educational Research Journal*, 34(4): 525–40.

Sluijsmans, D. (2002) *Establishing Learning Effects with Integrated Peer Assessment Tasks*, Higher Education Academy. Available at: http://www.heacademy.ac.uk/resources/detail/resource_database/id437_establishing_learning_effects (accessed 1 July 2011).

Squires, G. (1992) 'Interdisciplinarity in higher education in the United Kingdom', *European Journal of Education*, 27(3): 201–10.

Snow, C. P. (1964) *The Two Cultures and a Second Look*, Cambridge: Cambridge University Press.

Topping, K. (1998) 'Peer assessment between students in colleges and universities', *Review of Educational Research*, 68(3): 249–76.

Topping, K., Smith, E. F., Swanson, I. and Elliot, A. (2000) 'Formative peer assessment of academic writing between postgraduate students', *Assessment & Evaluation in Higher Education*, 25(2): 149–69.

Van den Berg, I., Admiraal, W. and Pilot, A. (2006) 'Design principles and outcomes of peer assessment in higher education', *Studies in Higher Education*, 31(3): 341–56.

CRITICAL FRIEND COMMENTARY

David Boud

The rise of interdisciplinary subjects and, more widely, degree programmes that draw from many disciplines, creates new challenges for assessment. Some of the issues to be confronted arise from the notion of interdisciplinarity itself and how it is represented in the curriculum, others are concerns of assessment itself.

Unlike the disciplines that have grown over many years and have developed characteristic cultures and practices of their own (Becher and Trowler 2001), there is no such thing as an interdisciplinary discipline. This means that we have necessarily to consider the interacting complexities of existing disciplinary perspectives. There are many and diverse ways of approaching interdisciplinarity and each present their own challenges for assessment. A subject that involves integrating two disciplinary perspectives is quite different from one that focuses on problems that need many different perspectives (e.g. global warming); the assessment challenges differ also. We should expect to see a very wide range of assessment approaches to accommodate these different intentions. In the same way there is no unitary idea of interdsciplinarity, it cannot be expected that there would be a single view of interdisciplinary assessment.

An important consideration is that neither students nor their teachers come to an interdisciplinary context with discipline neutrality. They have been formed by the epistemologies and cultural practices of the subjects they have studied and they have taken on many of the often implicit dispositions of these disciplines. Students stand apart from this no more easily than their lecturers. This tension points to the important emphasis that Golding and Baik place on self-regulation and assessment that fosters this. One of the aims of higher education is to enable students to question their own perspectives and their own ways of thinking, and interdisciplinary subjects provide a particularly useful vehicle for this reflexivity. Assessment approaches that enable this are required. One would therefore expect to see little of the conventional essay-type task and much more of a reflexive exercise in which students are not only expected to address a complex issue, but to examine the perspectives they bring and seek to represent the different epistemologies and ontologies that they and key writers bring to the topic. It is not a matter of simply adding self- and or peer assessment to the mix but of exploring what is needed beyond students writing something for a tutor to assess.

It is important, however, that they get some critical distance on this. It is hard enough to know what one knows and what one doesn't know in disciplines with which one is familiar; it is much more difficult when crossing disciplinary boundaries. A practice approach to assessment (Boud 2009), and activity in surfacing assumptions could be a necessary precursor to this process. It is only through more complex forms of engagement in assessment tasks that key features of interdisciplinary thinking can be promoted. This raises a major dilemma for interdisciplinary subjects. Their cognitive load on students can easily be higher than an equivalent single discipline subject. Students are not only grappling with the substantive content, but with the different epistemologies of the materials they are engaged with. The demand this creates suggests that great care needs to be taken in adequately scaffolding students for their major assignment, otherwise they will not be able to address the particular interdisciplinary features of the task being asked of them.

References

Becher, T. and Trowler, P. (2001) *Academic Tribes and Territories: Intellectual Enquiry and the Cultures of Disciplines*, 2nd edn, Buckingham: Open University Press/SRHE.

Boud, D. (2009) 'How can practice reshape assessment?', in G. Joughin (ed.) *Assessment, Learning and Judgement in Higher Education*, Dordrecht: Springer, pp. 29–44.

Chapter 12

Assessing employability skills
Understanding employer needs and how to engage with students

Marie Hardie and Norman Day

Introduction: why employability matters

The term 'employability' is widely used in relation to individuals and groups perceived as having barriers to entering the labour market, government programmes aimed at getting people back to work, and in recent years by universities in their programmes to develop skills and relevant experiences for students. There are many definitions, including the one provided by the Enhancing Student Employability Coordination Team (ESECT) at the Higher Education Academy (HEA) (2006: 3) that employability consists of 'a set of achievements – skills, understandings and personal attributes – that make graduates more likely to gain employment and be successful in their chosen occupations, which benefits themselves, the workforce, the community and the economy'.

The graduate employability skills debate, and the issue of how skills are taught and assessed, are set in a climate of: massively increased numbers in UK higher education, up by over 27 per cent from 334,000 in 2004 to 425,000 in 2009 (UK domiciled acceptances) (Universities and Colleges Admissions Services 2011); increasing competition for entry to good graduate opportunities; increased tuition fees; and a 20 per cent graduate unemployment rate in the third quarter of 2010 (Office for National Statistics 2011). From a student perspective, it appears clear that one of the major reasons for coming to university is to enhance career prospects. The National Student Forum (2009) expressed a strong desire for universities to have effective university-wide employability strategies, a prominent careers service and high quality work placement programmes. Such work placement opportunities have been highlighted by Coventry students as influencing factors: 'The unique option of choosing an internship certainly made Coventry University stand out among other universities.' Also highlighted by the forum was the need for more resources to be put into personal development planning and a curriculum that provides opportunities to engage with employers in the classroom.

An important dimension of the graduate employability skills debate centres on whether universities are doing enough to engage with and prepare students for entry to graduate careers. What forms of assessment are used and what part do they play in helping students develop employability skills? Measuring the impact of employability, learning and assessment is complex, not least because those delivering such programmes do not always know, nor can they easily measure levels of competence before and after students undertake employability training. The question of whether they effectively prepare students for success in graduate recruiters' assessment and recruitment processes is also an important consideration. In order to secure a graduate role, students not only need the competencies that employers expect, they need to articulate and evidence these effectively.

Employers and employer organizations are also exerting pressure for universities to improve graduate skill levels. A study of 350 graduate recruiters (Branine 2008) found that 24 per cent were unable to find suitable candidates. Prohibiting factors were cited as poor business awareness, lack of communication skills, shortages of transferable skills and the disparity between academic performance and performance in the selection process. The Confederation of British Industry (2010) highlighted continued levels of dissatisfaction with graduate employability skills, with over 70 per cent of 700 employers surveyed believing that these are the most important criteria in graduate recruitment.

Work by Atkins (1999), Saunders and Machell (2000), Knight and Yorke (2003), and a series of government-commissioned reports, including the Leitch Review on Skills (Leitch 2006) and Higher Ambitions (2009), have placed the debate about higher level skills and the part universities play firmly in the context of the global competitiveness of the UK economy. A series of Council for Industry and higher education reports on international competitiveness have all stressed the need to continue improving the quality and quantity of graduates due to the important part they play in contributing to economic prosperity and global competitiveness. Employability skills and employment rates are likely to remain high profile issues in the years ahead. Under ever closer scrutiny with government requirements to publish clear employability statements, universities are increasingly setting ambitious targets for 'positive destinations' which include the number of graduates who enter graduate jobs.

In this chapter we consider approaches to teaching, learning and assessment in employability programmes and consider aspects of self-, peer and employer assessment. Drawing on two initiatives at Coventry University, the Add+vantage scheme for undergraduates and the Masters Internship for postgraduates, we look at examples of good practice in assessment and the challenges of making this assessment work for all.

Employability skills: what are graduate recruiters looking for and how do they assess and select?

Research undertaken by Jackson (2009), the Confederation of British Industry (2010), and various web providers, including Graduate Opportunities Australia

(2010) highlight a number of important skills. These are: business and customer awareness; communication and literacy; numeracy and IT; self-management; problem solving; team-working. Others commonly cited include analytical skills, critical reasoning, leadership, and emotional intelligence (including self-awareness, strength of character, confidence and motivation), and underpinning all of these should be a positive 'can-do' attitude. 'Soft skills' and work experience are viewed as being important. Displaying 'professional' attributes and being 'work ready' is a theme running through much of the literature on employers' requirements.

Survey data from 700 UK recruiters (Branine 2008) examined changes in the methods of graduate assessment and selection. Results showed that all employers surveyed reported using more 'sophisticated' and 'objective' methods than in the past. Branine concluded that:

> the process of assessing and selecting graduates in the UK has become more person-related than job-oriented, many employers being more interested in applicants' attitudes, personality and transferable skills rather than the type or level of qualification acquired.

(ibid.: 497–513)

Large organizations receive hundreds to thousands of applications for graduate training schemes. Consequently they make use of the full gambit of assessment and recruitment techniques, including psychometric tests, competency-based application forms, telephone interviews, presentations, assessment centres and face-to-face interviews. Small and medium enterprises (SMEs) cannot draw on significant human resource or graduate recruitment teams to select their candidates and therefore often rely more heavily on the curriculum vitae (CV) to construct short lists for interview. Structured university programmes delivered at each level of study, rather than just in the final year, need to help students understand the employment market, recognize and assess the skills required by employers, and understand the methods and techniques they use to assess candidates. They need to provide opportunities for students to become effective in reflecting on their skills and experience.

It is notable that reflection on experience is a newer concept for business students than for those studying subjects such as social work, and the professions allied to medicine. However, its value is gaining momentum, as Mintzberg (2004: 253), writing on the development of management education, states: 'Thoughtful reflection on experience in the light of conceptual ideas is the key to managerial learning.' Reflection can also enable students to become knowledgeable about strengths and weaknesses. As one Coventry University student noted while writing about a work placement experience, 'I need to develop a reflective practice ability to help analyze my strengths and weaknesses so that I can build on my strengths and reduce my weaknesses.'

University employability initiatives: the Add+Vantage Scheme, Coventry University (ACU)

In recent years, many UK universities have developed employability initiatives, either for a wide range of students at all levels, or for more limited numbers, often in the second year of their course. The Add+vantage scheme at Coventry University (ACU), introduced in 2006, was one of the first university-wide accredited employability programmes in the UK offered to all undergraduates in each year of study. Resources were allocated by senior management to support a menu of 150 different employability modules from which students select and undertake one 10 credit module per year of their course, contributing a total of 30 credits to the 360 required for the degree award. Students need to pass at all levels to receive their honours degree.

ACU modules vary from specific skills in IT, marketing and languages, through to generic employability skills in teamwork, communication, leadership, presentation and project management. Also offered are volunteering and work placement modules. Administratively managed by the Careers and Employability Service, teaching is delivered by university academic and professional staff.

ACU teaching and assessment methods

Many employability initiatives developed over the past few years, including the Add+vantage Scheme, are grounded in the latest findings of pedagogical research (Knight and Yorke 2003, 2006). The programme at Coventry aspires to involve learners in the process and, where possible, uses active approaches to teaching, learning and assessment with an emphasis on experiential, problem-centred and work-based learning and work experience.

Cassidy (2006) identifies a number of factors which contribute to the successful teaching and assessment of employability programmes. Among these factors is the importance placed on the way the programmes are delivered. Teaching of ACU students often takes place in smaller groups (15–30 students), creating many opportunities for training, facilitation and a practical skills-based delivery rather than the traditional lecture approach. This allows for the involvement of students in the informal assessment of skills, including peer assessment of CVs, observation of presentations and involvement in assessment centre-type activities. Cassidy also explored peer assessment as a potential strategy for developing employability skills, finding that despite some concerns about the responsibility attached and their ability to be effective, students were positive about being involved in this task.

As an example of educational practice, peer assessment is more generally thought to contribute positively towards the development of employability skills. Falchikov and Goldfinch (2000: 287–322) describe peer assessment as 'engaging with standards and criteria in order to make judgments about the work of peers'. Specific benefits recognized include increased student responsibility and autonomy, evaluative skill development, insight into assessment procedures and expectations of high quality work. Students are also felt to work harder with the knowledge that they would be assessed by their peers. Gibbs (1995) felt that peer review is associated with the development of the ability to make judgements, to supervise one's own work and to encourage responsibility for learning. Commenting on peer assessment, an undergraduate student at Coventry University stated:

> It was really hard at first when the tutors were asking us to comment on other students' work, but I got into it eventually and it taught me an important skill of being critical but also being constructive and sensitive to the needs of my peers.

Cassidy (2006) also found relevant context to be crucial to the success of employability learning. Modules which draw on industry standards, with external assessment from employers and accreditation bodies, are popular in the ACU scheme, with feedback from students highlighting them as relevant and credible. One such example is the ACU IBM (the computer organization) mentoring module for second year computing students, which involves academic tutors, careers advisers and staff from IBM working jointly in the delivery, feedback and assessment of students' performance in the module. Students are assigned an individual mentor from IBM and opportunities are provided to visit the company and explore live projects in which mentors are involved. Key components of assessment include IBM staff assessing student CVs, completion of an IBM graduate application form, a presentation to a panel on an IT-related topic and a 'realistic' job interview using IBM criteria. Many students choose this module because they would like to work for a company such as IBM and see the benefits of having direct contact with a graduate recruiter, inside and outside the classroom, as illustrated by this student:

> The best thing about this module was the contact with the company. It made me work harder on my CV and the presentation that I gave to them. I was very nervous during my assessed interview but the tips they gave me at the end were really helpful. I think there should be more modules like this.

The development and assessment of CVs form an important component in many ACU modules. A survey of all graduate vacancies (predominately SMEs) to Coventry University Careers Service in 2009–10 noted that over 65 per cent of companies requested a CV as the selection starting point. Students are encouraged to become reflective learners in the production and development of this document, engaging with their peers and tutors and developing skills in self-assessment, to enable them to be clear about what they offer employers and to be able to present this information in a professional and dynamic way. Staff teaching these techniques create opportunities within the group for peer assessment of CVs, reviewing application forms, observing presentations, and in conducting mock interviews.

Due to the range of specialist and generic employability skills modules offered in the Add+vantage programme, a wide variety of assignment briefs are used. Strengths, weaknesses, opportunities, threats (SWOT) analysis, report writing, individual and group presentations to peers and/or to employers, self-reflective journals, action planning and writing motivational statements are frequently used to help students recognize and record career understanding. In many modules students are expected to produce a job application against a real advert, produce a CV tailored to their career aspirations, and develop competence-based responses to application and interview questions.

ACU modules are assessed in a variety of ways. Some mirror the requirements of the professional organizations, for example, CISCO, CIM (Chartered Institute of Management) and RSA (for computer literacy), SAGE (computerized book-keeping) and Tee line (shorthand), while others subscribe to the standards of specific companies that are involved, such as IBM. Modules developed over the past two years place work experience and/or other employer involvement at the core. These build on the aspirations of many students to explore the opportunities and standards in specific career areas, for example, in Psychology, Criminology, and Applied Research. Because these modules relate very specifically to individual career plans, students engage with the teaching and assessment process in a positive way.

Jackson (2009), who undertook a comprehensive and international review emphasizing some of the problems associated with defining and interpreting employability competencies, concluded that certain skills require competency in others, creating a 'web of synergistic relationships'. Employers will often seek combinations of skills which will vary according to the organization and job role environment, referred to as constellations (Male 2005). In the ACU Five Life Skills module (Level 3), students are involved in an 'assessment centre' activity, which aims to replicate a 'tough day at the office'. Activities include participation in and managing a meeting with peers, taking a difficult decision faced by the team, resolving team member conflict, and writing a short summary communicating a piece of complex information. This module helps develop greater understanding of the importance of communication skills, problem solving and teamwork as individual competencies, but also emphasizes the synergies between them. On completion of the module, students undertake a presentation to the group and tutors, reflecting on both their development through the course and of the role played within the 'tough day' simulation. Module evaluation in October 2010 showed a satisfaction rating of 97 per cent. Students report this module as challenging but beneficial, as illustrated by this student:

> I joined this module because I hope to secure a job on a graduate training scheme and I know that I will need to do assessment centre activities. The workshops throughout the course were very practical and focused directly on recognizing important graduate skills. The actual assessment activity was very hard and I felt under pressure but it gave me a taste for what it might be like when doing it for real.

The importance of work experience in employability learning and graduate recruitment

Work by Berman and Ritchie (2006) and High Fliers Research (2011) has increasingly shown that employers want graduates with work experience. This and other forms of work-based learning are strongly advocated as effective means of enhancing employability (Moreland 2005). *The Times* 100 top UK graduate recruiters (High Fliers Research 2011) found that 60 per cent of employers believe that candidates without previous work experience are highly unlikely to be successful in finding a job or to receive a job offer for their organization's graduate programmes. According to the report, employers want evidence that applicants have practical experience; organizations commented that, irrespective of the graduate's academic achievements, it would be very hard to demonstrate the skills and competencies required without prior work experience. With this in mind, many universities, including Coventry University, have developed pro- grammes at undergraduate and postgraduate level to increase the opportunities for structured work placements and modules which prepare students for place- ment. These modules are popular and evidence has emerged that success rates on these modules are higher than average. The pass rate for the undergraduate work experience modules in the ACU scheme averaged at 92 per cent in 2009/10 compared to the scheme average of 84 per cent. Students are engaged by responding to work-related problems and 'real-life' scenarios to develop their business and commercial awareness and professional communications skills. The assessment methodology for work-based modules explicitly addresses the requirement for students to show employers how they are critically reflecting upon their learning experiences outside the classroom and is captured through diaries, short reflective reports and assessed presentations.

Postgraduate Masters Company Internship module: Coventry University Business School

Providing work-related experience in higher education can be taken a step further through the idea of providing internships; one such example at postgraduate level is the Masters Company Internship. Taken in place of the traditional dissertation, and carrying 50 of the 180 credits required for the Masters award, internship students spend 8–12 weeks in a host company, working independently on a real business project. Project support is provided through a university academic supervisor and a workplace mentor.

The module aims to provide students with the opportunity to: apply theory to practice; work on a real organizational issue identified by the host company; work independently; develop both hard and soft personal skills; enhance employability skills and prospects; gain experience of a competitive recruitment process; reflect on their experience and learning as part of their personal development; and provide UK and overseas work experience for home and international students. The module provides students with an opportunity to develop their employability skills and a means to demonstrate and evidence these to employers. Entry to the internship module is optional but selective, the recruitment process designed as with undergraduate programmes to replicate that typically used by employers with CV submission, presentation and panel interview. In the region of 400 students per year are prepared for the selection process with a range of interventions including workshops, lectures and practice sessions, supported by a virtual learning environment (VLE). Through this process, formative assessment is undertaken using both peer and academic staff feedback. Approximately 300 of these students go on to apply formally for the module, 63 per cent of whom have a 30-minute interview. Students were initially uneasy with providing constructive and critical feedback and some academic staff had reservations in providing feedback in the area of recruitment. To address this problem, frameworks have been developed which outline the key areas on which comments are to be made. This system has worked effectively and each year the number of students applying for the module has increased, as has the number of selected students. In the academic year 2009–10 in excess of 65 students completed an internship – a figure expected to rise to over 80 in 2010/11. Although the module is staff resource-intensive, there has been senior management support for the work due to the outcomes in relation to student employability.

Module requirements and assessment

Module assessment has three weighted elements (marked out of 100): (1) submission of a 7000-word management report (75 per cent); (2) a 2500-word reflective piece (15 per cent) in which the student reflects on their personal learning and development; and (3) employer assessment (10 per cent). Bandings for the report and reflective piece are: Fail below 40 per cent; Pass 40–59 per cent; Merit 59– 69 per cent; Distinction 70 per cent and over. When initially introduced, assessment was based solely on the management report and although students were required to include a short reflective piece this was not assessed. Following feedback from students, employers and the external examiner, the current assessment process was developed. Employers wanted to provide feedback on the students, their performance and the impact of the work and students wanted to hear how the employers rated them. It was, however, interesting that those employers wanted to do this within an assessment framework provided by the university. Subsequently the employer framework was developed to include the key aspects highlighted by their input.

Management report

Assessment for the internship report follows the conventional structure to that of the Masters dissertation, with the exception of the 30 per cent emphasis on the project conclusions, recommendations and contribution. Students are expected to identify recommendations which are realistic and achievable in relation to the strategy, operations and resources of the organization. Included within the assessment framework is a literature review pertinent to the research, a relevant project plan, data collection and research findings. Types of projects identified by organizations have included: Analysis of Market Potential in East Africa; Development of a Business Marketing Strategy; Identification and Evaluation of Business Prospects; Critical Review and Analysis of Financial Procedures; Introduction of Product Costing; Diversity Monitoring; and Introduction of Accounting and Internal Control Systems.

Reflective piece

Students are free to write their 2500-word reflective piece on any aspect of the internship. Guidance is provided through a taught workshop and students have an opportunity to submit a short piece for formative assessment. Marks at Merit and Distinction are awarded for work revealing a deep level of insight and learning from the reflective process with a symbiosis between theory and practice. Reflections demonstrate that the student has a sound basis for being a reflective professional in their chosen career path.

Employer assessment

Employers provide a mark against a range of predetermined criteria which have been developed and refined from programme evaluation and employer input. Criteria include among others:

- *student performance*: Communication skills; time management and punctuality; observed interpersonal skills (how well the student related to other colleagues in the office/team); overall enthusiasm and motivation; observed analytical skills; ability to work on their own initiative.
- *the management report*: Quality of submitted work; predicted benefits of the project; recommendations to your organization; overall level of performance.

Student engagement feedback

The internship module has become a key feature of the business programmes with students highlighting the opportunity to complete an internship as one of their reasons for choosing Coventry for their programme of study. Evaluation and feedback from students and employers on all aspects of the process have been essential in developing and improving the module. Following the selection process, focus groups and one-to-one interviews have been undertaken with students who were both accepted and rejected for the module. All students highlighted the value of the employability skills workshops, the opportunity to have preparation and feedback sessions on CVs, and to undertake presentations and a formal interview. Many students indicated that the workshops had enabled them to improve their skills sufficiently to successfully obtain part-time work outside of the university. To date, the module has a 100 per cent pass rate, with average marks across cohorts lying at the higher end of the banding between Merit and Distinction.

Qualitative analyses of students' reflective work using the NVIVO8 software have been ongoing since 2006. The conceptual framework developed from this work has identified five key themes: (1) feelings of anxiety and uncertainty before commencing the project: 'I was scared and apprehensive about what lay ahead'; (2) the challenge of doing a real piece of work: 'Every mistake would have an after-effect and every success a benefit attached'; 'This was the real world and the comfort of university was suddenly gone'; (3) the opportunity to apply theory to practice: 'It gave me the opportunity to apply everything I had learnt in the classroom'; (4) impact: 'Before, I was a shy lad, my internship made me very confident'; 'I was asked questions on the internship project at numerous job interviews'; (5) mentor and academic supervisor support: 'She allowed me to test theories in business life ... I realized that giving an employee freedom gets the best out of them.'

It is within the reflective accounts that we see the impact on the students of undertaking an internship captured in the following comments: 'Writing the reflective account makes me realize how the last few months have changed me'; 'Looking back at the experience, I now grasp the fact there were some things about myself which I wasn't aware of.' Through the reflective piece students are able to consider their personal development from the perspective of engaging with employers and real business issues and not just from an academic perspective. Without exception they highlight the element of fear and the subsequent feeling of confidence that allows them to 'feel the fear and do it anyway'. Other comments include: 'If I was going to turn down every opportunity I get, when would I learn? How would I prove to myself that I have a "can do" spirit?'; 'The internship started with an idea, but I later realized that this turned out to be a huge step forward in my life.' In addition to learning from the assessment criteria, students have also learnt the value of what can be gained from the process itself: 'I know that reflecting should be an ongoing process as it is a valuable tool to improve my knowledge and understanding ... it will become a constant activity in my future, both at the workplace and in my personal activities.' A typical comment made by students in their module feedback can be summed up as follows: 'The internship was the most important module of my study.'

Conclusion

The issue of universities preparing students for graduate employment will remain high on the agenda in the current economic climate. The pressure on universities from stakeholders to demonstrate and evidence the outcomes of the activities they use to engage students in the spectrum of employability will only increase. With rising UK tuition fees, a key feature of marketing undergraduate and postgraduate programmes to potential students and their families is likely to include the opportunities provided for students to engage with the 'world of work' and the graduate success rate in obtaining appropriate employment. In this chapter, we have discussed two successful Coventry University employability initiatives, the Add+vantage scheme for undergraduates and the Masters Internship for postgraduates. These initiatives provide examples of how students can be engaged and assessed across a range of related factors identified by employers as required in the marketplace. Factors range from preparing for the practical recruitment process of applying for work, through the development of both *soft* interpersonal and a variety of *hard* technical skills and the provision of work experience placements to successfully managing and completing real projects for business. The authors believe that key factors leading to the success and the quality of employability initiatives include offering programmes which are credit-bearing with wide-ranging and innovative assessment methods. Integral in this process are students self- and peer assessing, academic staff assessing the academic quality of work, and employers assessing knowledge, skills and impact of the qualities they are seeking. Assessment is aimed at bridging the gap between academic theory, practical application and the development of skills valued by employers. The challenge facing Coventry University and other institutions will be to increase the opportunities open to all students, both in the classroom and in the workplace, which will allow them to develop, apply and evidence the necessary skills and facilitate successful transfer from university into the workplace.

References

Atkins, M. J. (1999) 'Oven ready and self basting: taking stock of employability skills', *Teaching in Higher Education*, 4(2): 267–80.

Berman, J. and Ritchie, L. (2006) 'Competencies of undergraduate business students', *Journal of Education for Business*, 81(2): 205–9.

Branine, M. (2008) 'Graduate recruitment and selection in the UK: a study of the recent changes in methods and expectations', *Career Development International*, 13(6): 497–513.

Cassidy, S. (2006) 'Developing employability skills: peer assessment in higher education', *Education and Training*, 48(7): 508–17.

Confederation of British Industry (2010) *Ready to Grow: Business Priorities for Education and Skills*, Education and Skills Survey 2010, London: CBI.

Enhancing Student Employability Coordination Team (2006) *Pedagogy for Employability Learning*, Series 1, York: Higher Education Academy.

Falchikov, N. and Goldfinch, J. (2000) 'Student peer assessment in higher education: a meta-analysis comparing peer and teacher marks', *Review of Educational Research*, 70(3): 287–322.

Gibbs, G. (1995) *Assessing Student Centred Courses*, Oxford: Oxford Centre for Staff Development.

Graduate Opportunities Australia (2010) *Survey of Graduate Employers in Australasia*. Available at: http://www.graduateopportunities.com/career_advice/top_10_skills_employers_seek (accessed 3 August 2011).

High Fliers Research (2011) *The Graduate Market in 2011: Annual Review of Graduate Vacancies and Starting Salaries at Britain's Leading Employers*, London: High Fliers Research. Available at: http://www.highfliers.co.uk/download/ GMReport11.pdf (accessed 3 August 2011).

Higher Ambitions (2009) *The Future of Universities in a Knowledge Economy*, London: Department for Business, Innovation and Skills. Available at: http:// www.bis.gov.uk (accessed 3 August 2011).

Jackson, D. (2009) 'An international profile of industry-relevant competencies and skills gaps in modern graduates', *International Journal of Management Education*, 8(3): 29–58.

Knight, P. T. and Yorke, M. (2003) 'Employability and good learning in higher education', *Teaching in Higher Education*, 8(1): 3–16.

——(2006) *Employability in Higher Education: What It Is – What It Is Not*, Learning and Employability Series 1, York: Higher Education Academy.

Leitch, S. (2006) *Review of Skills, Prosperity for All in the Global Economy: World Class Skills*, London: The Stationery Office.

Male, S. (2005) 'Development and validation of an instrument to assess the generic competencies of engineering graduates', unpublished paper, Perth: University of Western Australia.

Mintzberg, H. (2004) *Managers not MBAs: A Hard Look at the Soft Practice of Managing and Management Development*, San Francisco: Berrett-Koehler.

Moreland, N. (2005) *Work-related Learning in Higher Education*, York: Higher Education Academy.

National Student Forum (2009) *Annual Report*, London: Department for Business Innovation and Skills.

Office for National Statistics (2011) *Labour Force Survey: Graduates in the Labour Market*. Available at: http://www.statistics.gov.uk/cci/nugget.asp?id=1162 (accessed 3 August 2011).

Saunders, M. and Machell, J. (2000) 'Understanding emerging trends in higher education curricula and work connections', *Higher Education Policy*, 13(1): 287–302.

Universities and Colleges Admissions Services (2011) *Data Summary*, Cheltenham: UCAS. Available at: http://www.ucas.ac.uk/about_us/stat_services/stats_online/ data_tables/datasummary (accessed 3 August 2011).

CRITICAL FRIEND COMMENTARY

Mantz Yorke

Assessment of academic work is a complex undertaking – and is more complex than many appreciate. As is acknowledged in the chapter by Hardie and Day, the complexity is greatly increased when it comes to assessing achievements other than the academic, such as those typically seen as fitting under the heading of 'employability' or 'professional expertise'.

Hardie and Day's chapter offers two curricular models that appear to satisfy academic and employer requirements while, perhaps most importantly, actively engaging students. In assessing employability-related achievements there are two competing requirements: (1) the need to specify intended learning outcomes (often in some detail) in order to signal to students what they should aspire to achieve, to provide a framework for assessment, and to provide evidence for quality assurance purposes; and (2) the need to respond to the 'situatedness' of achievements in work-related settings of various kinds. The first is inflected with tightness of specification; the second with the need to make broad judgements (save where the development of competences is professionally mandatory). Summative assessments built into modules related to the development of students' employability tend to contain elements of both tightness and looseness (the latter term is not used in a pejorative sense). Philosophically, there is a tension between realist and relativist approaches to assessment (Yorke 2011).

Where professional organizations are involved, there is often a need for the assessment to conform to those bodies' specific requirements – and with justification where, for example, public safety depends upon demonstrated competence. Such assessments are manifestly 'tight' and realist. On the other hand, *how* one goes about one's work is a more subjective matter in which the person's achievement has to be gauged with reference to the context, the capacity to cope with whatever comes their way, the student's personal style, and so on: effectiveness in relation to 'soft skills' can be demonstrated in a variety of ways. Assessment of 'soft skills' is necessarily judgemental and relativist. Other kinds of employability-related achievement can be roughly partitioned along these lines.

Cross-cutting the realist/relativist distinction are the kinds of assessment that are undertaken. These include analytical work on case material (sometimes prior to workplace experience, and in effect asking questions like 'what would you have done?'); judgements of actual performance in simulations or in the workplace; and reflective evaluation of simulation or workplace experience. Academics and employers are differently placed with respect to the kinds of achievement on which they can make grounded judgements. There is also the issue of what can actually be warranted, as regards student achievement, where the time and resources available for assessment are limited.

While academics and employers, such as those involved in the modules mirroring the expectations of professional organizations and companies, may appreciate the realist/relativist distinction in assessment (if not in these particular terms), curricula at module and programme level disregard it when they assimilate disparate achievements into a single index, such as the grade awarded for the module as a whole and the honours degree classification. In this assimilation, information of potential value to a stakeholder is lost. The Higher Education Achievement Report, mooted in Burgess Group (2007) and currently undergoing trials, has some potential to mitigate the problem.

Assessment of employability-related achievements is underdeveloped in higher education, and is not easy. As research papers are wont to comment, further work on the topic is needed.

References

Burgess Group (2007) *Beyond the Honours Degree Classification: Burgess Group Final Report*, London: Universities UK.

Yorke, M. (2011) *Assessing the Complexity of Professional Achievement*. Available at: http://learningtobeprofessional.pbworks.com/f/CHAPTER+A10+FINAL.pdf (accessed 3 August 2011).

Chapter 13

Getting the context right for good assessment practice

Lynne Hunt, Sara Hammer and Michael Sankey

Introduction

This chapter provides a case study about what happened to promote good assessment practices at a regional university in Australia. It provides a 360° perspective on the top-down, middle-out and bottom-up strategies that were used to get the context right for quality assessment. The argument is that good assessment practice is a whole-of-university responsibility. A simple story illustrates this – self-plagiarism became a topic of discussion at the University's Learning and Teaching Committee. The question was: What should be done when a student's turnitin.com report indicates considerable overlap with previous assignments completed by the student? The outcome of the deliberations suggested that higher education students should demonstrate evidence of growth and development through assignments. Of necessity, this will result in some overlap and higher order application of previous assignments. Second, if the overlap is extensive, then there is something wrong with the systematic design of assessment in the overall degree programme. In brief, staff teaching in the same programme should be aware of assessment tasks in other modules or units and avoid duplication. At the heart of this discussion lay a presumption that universities have a responsibility to facilitate coherent student learning journeys. This provides the starting point for this chapter, which argues that good assessment practice in universities is more than the outcome of individual efforts to design meaningful student assignments. It also requires systematic and university-wide strategies that assure and support quality assessment.

The emphasis on a systemic, whole-of-university approach implies that this chapter is as much about context as it is about assessment *per se*. This is because

> Effective change is embedded in context and comes when those involved make it their own through use and adaptation to local histories and contexts. Enhancements of practice are produced by a complex array of individually and collectively induced incentives, histories and values. A measure of control at the ground level is a condition of success.
>
> (Bamber *et al.* 2009: 2–3)

Case study methodology

The chapter deploys a case study methodology in order to share practice because: 'Case studies may provide ideas, suggestions, or imagery that might sensitize outsiders to issues they may have not considered, particularly with regard to the process of institutional change' (Wals *et al.* 2004: 347). This case study is based on a university that conducted a whole-of-university change management project, known as the Programme Revitalization Project, which was designed to enhance learning and teaching systems and processes across the board. It has particular import for student retention and progression because one aim of the change management project was to sustain revenue flows through enhanced student retention. Enrolling and keeping students is more difficult in regional universities like this one which specializes in widening access to higher education. It has particular challenges. For example, many students live in remote areas. Indeed, some 80 per cent of the students at this university study online and by distance education. The university has significant numbers of non-traditional students. Often, they are the first in their families to study for a degree, and many are older students involved in family and work responsibilities. The change leadership task was to improve the student learning journey for this student population, in particular, by enhancing coursework and assessment.

Bamber *et al.* (2009) caution against the use of case studies as best practice examples because of the unique influence of local circumstance on outcomes. In their view, case studies should be informed by theory: 'Without explicit concepts and theory to illuminate, cases would simply be narratives, more-or-less interesting stories. With a theoretical lens they can help the reader to see enhancement initiatives in a new, more analytical way' (ibid.: 5). In this case study change leadership was informed by empowerment theory, which Labonté (1990a: 64) described as a murky concept, 'vacillating between politically conservative models of self-empowerment and social action models of political change'. For him, empowerment means 'to gain or assume power'. It is a transformative approach that operates at three levels (Labonté, 1990b: 73):

- *intrapersonally*, associated with self-efficacy;
- *interpersonally*, as the construction of knowledge and analysis based on personal and shared experiences;
- *within communities*, as the cultivation of resources and strategies that assist in transformation.

The identification of levels of empowerment facilitates analysis of what needs to be done to get the context right for quality assessment. Much of the literature to promote assessment, for example, Suskie (2009), is focused on enhancing self-efficacy. It directs attention to matters over which individual lecturers have influence, such as providing students with clear goals, using a variety of formative and summative assignments, use of marking grids and provision of meaningful feedback to students that leads to their growth and development. This chapter shifts attention to Labonté's level three which Hunt (2006: 64) described as a community development model of change: 'A key point is that the promotion of teaching and learning in universities requires organizational reorientation through a process that engages the hearts and minds of staff. In short, process is as important as product.' Accordingly, the focus in this case study is on the processes and strategies deployed to enhance assessment rather than on the outcome of innovative assessment practices, many of which are described on the university's exemplar website.

In this case study, change leadership was informed by the twin philosophies of cross-institutional planning and the student learning journey. The chapter, therefore, starts with a working definition of each before going on to describe a whole-of-programme approach to assessment that is linked to the mapping of graduate qualities and skills. Further, it identifies specific strategies such as: an external review of assessment practice at the university; strategic planning; assessment policies; project management methodology; the use of templates and guidelines; professional development for staff; and enhanced support for students for the development of academic learning skills.

Approaches to change

According to Hunt and Peach (2009), cross-institutional planning traverses the traditional barriers between academic and administrative services and challenges inward-looking organizational silos in order to achieve a change-capable culture. It is an approach that represents a paradigm shift towards 'holistic, systems thinking and cross-disciplinary knowledge' and to a world view based on 'participation, appreciation and self-organization' (Sterling 2004: 49–50) – a process particularly suited to change leadership in universities, where academic staff are accustomed to individual autonomy and academic freedom.

In this case study, cross-institutional planning was informed by the concept of students' learning journeys (SLJ), which is an outcomes-based approach that explores students' journeys through their degree programmes from the perspective of students as shown in Figure 13.1.

It is a holistic approach designed to get the context right for student learning. It is also a plural concept – students' learning journeys – which gives rise to flexible and diverse responses rather than a 'one-size-fits-all' strategy. A key argument in this chapter is that while individual lecturers can improve assessment in their own courses, a whole-of-university response is required to create coherent learning journeys for students because 'changing only an element at one level may have limited, local and provisional success ... because the rest of the system is not touched and established patterns prevail over the single change' (Bamber et al. 2009: 3).

Assessment review

The Programme Revitalization Project described in this case study was preceded by an external review of the university's assessment practices. This arose from

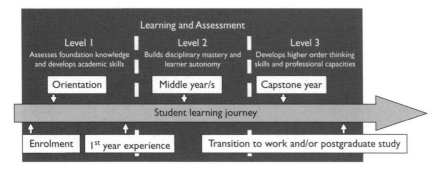

Figure 13.1 The student learning journey

evidence of poor assessment and from the emergence of separate faculty policies and procedures associated with assessment which risked a fragmented and complex time for students studying across faculties. The outcomes and recommendations of the review were organized under eight headings, most of which were associated with getting the context right. Indeed, the report explicitly recorded the need for a holistic approach:

> It is important to read the recommendations as an integrated whole rather than as isolated components. Thus, for example, less use of examinations and strengthening of risk management concerning plagiarism are related ... So, too, providing some form of feedback on every assessment (including examinations) is linked to the overall design of a course (and programme) as well as to management of staff time.
>
> (Assessment Working Group 2006: 5)

Commendable though an integrated approach may be, addressing the outcomes of the report within a hermetically sealed framework of improving only assessment practices still risked marginalized or limited outcomes. However, shortly after the review, the university embarked on a year of whole-of-university change in order to put the university on a firm financial footing and direct resources to the core business of research and teaching. The outcomes of the review were rolled into these new processes, providing a much broader context for change.

The Change Leadership Project

Getting the context right

The university-wide change leadership initiative was organized as four projects: (1) Facilities; (2) Academic Profile; (3) Student Management; and (4) Corporate Services. Only the Academic Profile project directly concerned academic matters. It had two phases, the first being to reduce the number of degree programmes offered by the university, resulting in a workable platform for quality enhancement of coursework and assessment.

The Programme Revitalization Project (PRP) that lies at the heart of this case study was the second phase. Its objective was to enhance learning, teaching and assessment to facilitate the SLJ and enhance retention. The university provided the top-down framework for action and its Academic Development Unit (ADU) provided the middle-out drive for change. The aim was to get the context right for bottom-up initiatives by faculty staff that make a difference to assessment where it matters – at course level. PRP was divided into ten sub-projects. All sub-projects had an impact on assessment practice insofar as they established the direction of change. The Technology Enhanced Learning sub-project, for example, facilitated the development of online assessment and a broad curriculum project directed attention to internationalizing the curriculum and associated assessment practice. However, this chapter will focus on just six of the sub-projects because they were central to getting the context right for quality assessment practice. The six sub-projects are: Human Resources and Management; Teaching Excellence; Assessment; Professional Development; Academic Learning Skills; and the Course and Programme Management System incorporating graduate qualities and skills. Each member of the ADU staff was invited to provide leadership for one of these. Each was charged with setting goals against which they reported every month to their colleagues in the ADU and to faculties. Ultimately, the outcomes were reported up to the University's Learning and Teaching Committee and, from there, to faculty Learning and Teaching Committees. It was designed as an empowering process of transparency and engagement to build a change-capable culture supportive of teaching excellence.

Organizational reorientation included new ADU work patterns so that some of their time was devoted to university-wide tasks such as the development of resources and templates, while most of the working week was allocated to faculties to complete the tasks established in annual Faculty Learning and Teaching Action Plans. This set a context of negotiation, flexibility and goal achievement. Organizational change extended beyond enhanced support for teaching and assessment to ensuring that learning and teaching matters were appropriately integrated into the university's strategic plan, and that budgets flowed to learning and teaching activities. Much of this work was led through the Human Resources and Management (HRM) sub-project and directed by a member of the Vice-Chancellery team to provide high-level leadership for institutional change. Tasks included collaboration with the Buildings and Facilities department to plan spaces that facilitate students' learning and engagement with the Human Resources Department to ensure that learning and teaching achievements feature in appointment, promotion and annual performance appraisal processes. Activities such as these are many steps away from discussion of assessment but, unless students are supported in their learning and unless teaching staff see their engagement with learning and teaching as career building, initiatives to improve assessment risk falling on stony ground.

Good assessment:

1. is an integral part of the teaching and learning process;
2. is designed to guide students' learning and provide opportunities for personal development planning and the documentation of students' achievements through e-portfolios;
3. addresses the diversity of students' backgrounds, experiences and learning styles;
4. is fair and equitable;
5. informs students of progress through timely, constructive feedback that enhances learning;
6. adopts a criterion-referenced approach;
7. demonstrates alignment between learning objectives, learning activities and assessment tasks;
8. assesses identified graduate qualities and skills, along with disciplinary and professional knowledge;
9. includes clear assessment criteria linked to learning objectives and provided to students at the same time as assessment tasks;
10. is moderated in accordance with policy and, where relevant, contractual arrangements with institutional partners;
11. is designed to take into consideration students' overall workload; and
12. is manageable from a staff workload perspective.

Figure 13.2 Key features of quality assessment practice

The integration of teaching into career building prospects required some formulation of expectations including the development of Good Teaching Guidelines. Figure 13.2 identifies the key features of quality assessment practice noted in the Guidelines, which were developed through a process of back-mapping to current policy. It became a way of making policy transparent. It also revealed the need for significant re-writing and simplification of assessment policies, including the removal of artificial hurdles to students' successful completion of assessment requirements.

The Teaching Excellence sub-project provided the capacity-building for staff to enhance their careers through teaching. It simplified a number of disparate teaching award processes into a streamlined approach incorporating faculty and university awards aligned to national teaching awards criteria. This also entailed coordinating dates so that it became possible for staff members or teams to continuously build their teaching portfolios to ever higher demands within the space of a year. Teaching awards were included in criteria for promotion, and staff now have the opportunity to weight their applications to recognition of teaching as well as research outcomes. In brief, the corporate work of the HRM sub-project was supported by the capacity-building work of the Teaching Excellence sub-project.

The institutional reorganization to get the context right for quality teaching, learning and assessment had so far included the development of Faculty Learning and Teaching Action Plans, the reorganization of ADU work, embedding teaching in career-building strategies including promotion and performance appraisal, documenting clear expectations about good teaching and assessment practice and the provision of opportunities to develop career milestones through teaching awards.

The next task was to make this stick. For example, it became apparent that some academics serving as supervisors in performance appraisal processes might not themselves be skilled in asking questions pertaining to learning, teaching and assessment. Accordingly, a list of possible questions was developed as a resource, housed on the website of Human Resource Management and included in supervisor training. These were closely aligned with the Good Teaching Guidelines so that staff received consistent messages about expectations and opportunities.

This discussion about getting the context right for good teaching and assessment shows how all university departments have a role to play. Other activities included collaboration with the Buildings and Facilities Department to speed the provision of a Learning Commons (Schmidt and Kaufman 2007) which incorporates a Learning Centre that students can visit for extra assistance with academic learning skills. The university's quality assurance department negotiated widely to develop an annual cycle of Course and Programme Review, which includes reference to the Good Teaching Guidelines and analysis by a course teaching team of the outcomes of their assessment processes. The key point is that quality assessment is now embedded in business-as-usual practices. It has become routine, part of the wallpaper of quality university teaching.

The Assessment and Graduate Qualities sub-project

The Assessment and Graduate Qualities sub-project targeted aspects of 'getting the context right' that are specific to assessment. This involved developing templates, guidelines, and quick-fix, bite-sized 'How to' flyers including an assessment checklist. It provided resources about criterion-referenced assessment, feedback, moderation and designing assessment for students living with disability. The flyers are available online and in hard copy in staff rooms around the university. Some were converted into display banners. Saturation coverage was the key to raising awareness of the importance of quality assessment. An exemplar website provided opportunities for faculty staff to model good assessment practice and the University's Visiting Learning and Teaching Scholar Programme attracted national and international expertise for professional development workshops. All were interviewed to provide a web-based resource that is now available open-source.

Biggs' (2003) model for aligning assessment with learning objectives, graduate skills and teaching activities forms the basis of the templates and guidelines. These define the university's graduate qualities and skills and provide a breakdown of each that assists academics to customize to their own degree programme. The templates help staff to identify and assess different levels of learning outcomes. The documents adopt a whole-of-programme perspective, charting a process of disciplinary mastery through which students develop foundational knowledge and skills before progressing to advanced levels of application, analysis and evaluation (Morgan *et al.* 2002). The templates are empowering because they scaffold a process that facilitates staff engagement in programme design, evaluation and review. They are based on good practice principles that enhance the SLJ, including accountability, authenticity, coherence, equity, reliability, transparency and validity (Sadler 2005; Nicol and Macfarlane-Dick 2006). Some are designed to address contemporary issues such as the increased diversity and internationalization of the student cohort and feature some of the most recent thinking on the purposes of assessment in higher education (Boud 2009). These resources also emphasize the enduring value of designing assessment for learning as well as for the accreditation of learning and focus particularly on the provision of appropriately targeted and timely feedback on student progress. These practices are designed to engage students and facilitate their progression through their degree programmes.

The development of resources and templates is a necessary, but not sufficient, condition for getting the context right for good assessment practice. Certainly the templates scaffold the process of thinking about assessment across whole degree programmes, but the risk is that they will be ignored. What made them stick were requirements to comply with revised policies about embedding graduate qualities and skills in the curriculum. This is enforced through accreditation requirements. Faculty Learning and Teaching Action Plans, which attracted additional funds, were devised to direct ADU support to staff undertaking the alignment of assessment with learning objectives and graduate qualities and skills. This was facilitated by the reorganization of ADU work patterns and given initial impetus by the PRP that required faculties to focus on the top 15 programmes that accommodate approximately 80 per cent of all students. It was a 'best bang for buck' process that was project managed with clear goals and accountability for outcomes. This context of top-down policy direction, facilitated by middle-out organization including guidelines and templates, gave rise to local, bottom-up initiatives. For example, two faculties began their own Course Revitalization Projects, in which the ADU representatives worked with the Associate Dean (Learning and Teaching), heads of school and course coordinators to revise course materials in accordance with the now established good practice principles. The ultimate motivation for all arose from Australian Government requirements to embed and assess graduate qualities and the university's pending quality assurance review.

The Programme Revitalization sub-project

The Programme Revitalization Project facilitated the development of an integrated model of professional development that provides a context of continuous support for teaching staff. It begins with three-hour, facilitated online courses for staff employed on casual contracts to ensure that they have the skills for marking student assignments and providing appropriate feedback. New full-time staff must complete a two-day induction to learning and teaching, which is organized as one day of face-to-face professional development with follow-up action learning projects designed to bring direct benefit to students. Opportunities for self-development have been created through open source, online foundation modules which, if the staff member chooses to complete assignments, may contribute to progress through the Graduate Certificate in Tertiary Teaching, a formal qualification that staff members may study without fee payment. Online resources such as the Exemplar Website and How-to flyers together with the Visiting Scholar Programme form part of the integrated professional development model; so too does a comprehensive programme of communities of practice, all of which are supported by a series of professional development workshops including Tailored Professional Development that responds to requests from faculty staff for point-of-need learning.

The university in this case study is known for its effective use of communities of practice (AUQA 2010), which provide what Labonté (1990b: 73) described as opportunities for 'the construction of knowledge and analysis based on personal and shared experiences'. Staff meet monthly at informal get-togethers that are purposefully but loosely structured according to Etienne Wenger's model of building community, sharing practice, and building domain knowledge (McDonald and Star 2008: 3). The fluidity and regularity of these sessions make them ideal fora to address problems quickly (Wenger and Snyder 2000: 141). For example, the university's strategic goal of delivering greater flexibility to students through the adoption of a blended learning model put pressure on academic staff to upgrade their learning technology skills. The Faculty of Arts Learning and Teaching Community of Practice responded to this by providing guest presenters and by sharing online assessment practices.

The Academic Learning Skills sub-project

Any 360° approach to enhancing assessment must support both staff and students. The university in this case study specializes in blended learning opportunities that aim to accommodate equitably the needs of students studying on campus or by distance education. As a consequence, online resources to facilitate the development of students' academic learning skills were well established before the advent of PRP. These included an innovative home-grown programme, called AWARE, that enables students to self-diagnose gaps in their academic learning skills. PRP attracted additional funds to fine-tune and advance academic learning skills support for students. The on-campus Learning Centre was relocated to the library to provide greater visibility and accessibility. This meant that its services in support of numeracy and literacy skills could be integrated more closely with the library's resources designed to enhance students' information literacy. Further, the university developed a Virtual Learning Centre that aligned with on-campus support services.

Course and Programme Mapping System

A key outcome of the Programme Revitalization Project was the development of the Course and Programme Mapping System (CPMS), shown in Figure 13.3.

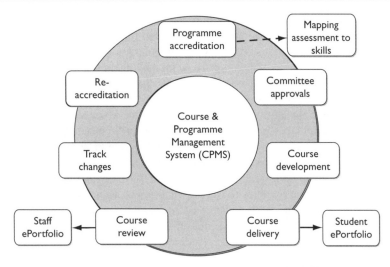

Figure 13.3 The Course and Programme Mapping System (CPMS)

This online system was designed to make it difficult for staff to get things wrong. Rather than asking staff to learn detailed policy and procedure about course and programme development, expectations are built in to the online environment so that staff are now required to complete fields associated with the alignment of learning objectives, assessment and graduate qualities and skills. As a change in leadership process this risked being maligned as a draconian and centralized imposition on academic freedom – corporatization at its worst. Yet in the new order of quality and teaching standards, this system makes it easy for staff to get things right. It also provides freedom for staff members to make changes to their courses because the CPMS has built-in approval processes. From the perspective of students, this is important because faculties are positioned to monitor changes and, for example, to check how alterations in assessment in one course might influence another. It is especially important when staff wish to make changes to the now compulsory field of graduate attributes because these need to be managed across students' whole degree programmes. The CPMS also accommodates links to staff and student ePortfolios. This means, for example, that there is an automatic feed of completed graduate qualities and skills to students' portfolios that assists them to collate evidence of their assessed achievements for current and future employment.

Conclusion

This chapter has documented a holistic approach to the management of university assessment that includes cross-institutional planning and collaboration and a project management methodology based on sub-projects associated with human resource management, teaching excellence, assessment, graduate qualities and skills, professional development, academic learning skills and the CPMS that incorporates processes to facilitate the alignment of assessment with graduate qualities and skills. It has noted the development of assessment templates and guidelines and organizational reorientation facilitated by the development of Faculty Learning and Teaching Action Plans that attracted additional funding to get the jobs done. The aim of the chapter is to provide a case study of transformative practices designed to get the context right for quality teaching, learning and assessment. These are summarized in Figure 13.4, which provides an integrated image of the separate processes described in this chapter.

For some, the case study may be too corporate – organizational intervention that impedes academic freedom to develop assessment as individual lecturers see fit. However, the point of the chapter is to describe the praxis arising from a vision to enhance students' learning journeys. This shifts attention to whole-of-university responsibility for ensuring students' continuous growth in learning through quality assessment practices. Further, the chapter describes the development of the CPMS infrastructure that makes it difficult for staff to get things wrong. This addresses contemporary trends in higher education to greater accountability for standards. The university in this case study can now demonstrate the alignment of learning objectives with graduate qualities and assessment, and it provides staff with the freedom to make changes to assessment within the

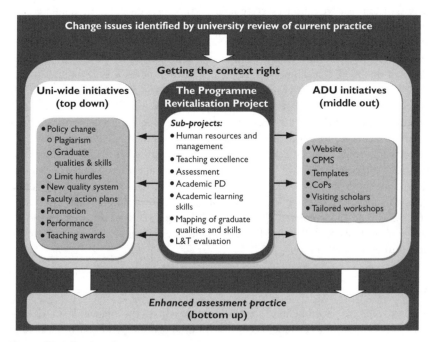

Figure 13.4 Getting the context right for assessment

framework of clear approval processes that facilitate consistency across whole degree programmes for students.

The holistic approach advocated in this chapter has a long history that bears repeating because fragmented change leadership strategies detract from students' learning journeys and give rise to situations in which university learning education 'is (merely) the sum of the student's experiences of a series of discrete, largely unrelated ... classes' (Barr and Tagg 1995: 7). It is an approach that has much in common with learning organization theory (Tagg 2003) because it recognizes the need for structural and cultural reorientation for change to be effective. Hunt and Peach (2009) noted that there is considerable consensus in the literature about how to manage holistic change, noting that effective strategies are multidimensional, systematic and participative. This chapter has identified practical initiatives to enhance university assessment practices that are based on these principles, noting that this adds up to whole-of-university responsibility for enhancing assessment practices.

References

Assessment Working Group (2006) *Assessment Working Group Report*. Available at: www.usq.edu.au/learnteach/topics/~/media/USQ/learnteach/ADS/Assess-WorkGroupReportpdf.ashx – 2009-07-19 (accessed 3 February 2011).

AUQA (2010)*AUQA Good Practice Database*. Available at: http://www.auqa.edu.au/gp/search/detail.php?gp_id = 3175 (accessed 3 February 2011).

Bamber, V., Trowler, P., Saunders, M. and Knight, P. (2009) *Enhancing Learning, Teaching, Assessment and Curriculum in Higher Education*, Maidenhead: Open University Press.

Barr, R. B. and Tagg, J. (1995) *From Teaching to Learning: A New Paradigm for Undergraduate Education*. Available at: http://ilte.ius.edu/pdf/barrtagg.pdf (accessed 2 February 2011).

Biggs, J. (2003) *Teaching for Quality Learning at University*, 2nd edn, Maidenhead: The Society for Research into Higher Education and Open University Press.

Boud, D. (2010) *Assessment 2020: Seven Propositions for Assessment Reform in Higher Education*, Sydney: Australian Learning and Teaching Council.

Hunt, L. (2006) 'A community development model of change: the role of teaching and learning centres', in L. Hunt, A. Bromage and B. Tomkinson (eds) *The Realities of Change in Higher Education: Interventions to Promote Learning and Teaching*, Abingdon: Routledge, pp. 64–77.

Hunt, L. and Peach, N. (2009) 'Planning for a sustainable academic future', in iPED Research Network (eds) *Academic Futures: Inquiries into Higher Education and Pedagogy*, Newcastle-upon-Tyne: Cambridge Scholars Publishing.

Labonté, R. (1990a) 'Econology: health and sustainable development', paper presented at Integrating Health and Environment Conference, Canberra, Australia.

——(1990b) 'Empowerment: notes on professional and community dimensions', *Canadian Review of Social Policy*, 26: 64–75.

McDonald, J. and Star, C. (2008) 'The challenges of building an academic community of practice: an Australian case study', in *Proceedings of the HERDSA 2008*

International Conference: Engaging Communities, 1–4 July 2008, Rotorua, New Zealand: HERDSA.

Morgan, C. K., Watson, G. K., Roberts, D. W., McKenzie, A. D. and Cochrane, K. W. (2002) 'Structuring the curriculum for different years of undergraduate programs', paper presented at the Conference of the Australian Association for Research in Education, Brisbane, December. Available at: http://www.aare.edu.au/02pap/mor02051.htm (accessed 3 February 2011).

Nicol, D. J. and Macfarlane-Dick, D. (2006) 'Formative assessment and self-regulated learning: a model and seven principles of good feedback practice', *Studies in Higher Education*, 31(2): 199–218.

Sadler, D. R. (2005) 'Interpretations of criteria-based assessment and grading in higher education', *Assessment and Evaluation in Higher Education*, 30(2): 175–94.

Schmidt, N. and Kaufman, J. (2007) 'Learning Commons: bridging the academic and student affairs divide to enhance learning across campus', *Research Strategies*, 20(4): 242–56.

Sterling, S. (2004) 'Higher education, sustainability and the role of systemic learning', in P. Blaze Corcoran and A. E. J. Wals (eds) *Higher Education and the Challenge of Sustainability: Problematics, Promise and Practice*, Dordrecht: Kluwer Academic Publishers, pp. 49–70.

Suskie, L. (2009) *Assessing Student Learning: A Common Sense Guide*, 2nd edn, San Francisco: Jossey-Bass.

Tagg, J. (2003) *The Learning Paradigm College*, Bolton: Anker.

Wals, A. E. J., Walker, K. E. and Blaze Corcoran, P. (2004) 'The practice of sustainability in higher education: a synthesis', in P. Blaze Corcoran and A. E. J. Wals (eds) *Higher Education and the Challenge of Sustainability: Problematics, Promise and Practice*, Dordrecht: Kluwer Academic Publishers, pp. 347–8.

Wenger, E. C. and Snyder, W. M. (2000) 'Communities of practice: the organizational frontier', *Harvard Business Review*, January–February: 139–45.

Further resources

Assessment Website. Available at: http://www.usq.edu.au/learnteach/topics/assess (accessed 3 August 2011).

Communities of Practice. Available at: http://www.usq.edu.au/cops (accessed 3 August 2011).

Course and Programme Mapping System. Available at: http://www.usq.edu.au/learnteach/qualpolplan/cpms (accessed 3 August 2011).

Programme Revitalization Website. Available at: http://www.usq.edu.au/learnteach/prorevital.htm (accessed 3 August 2011).

CRITICAL FRIEND COMMENTARY

Sue Thompson

Changing assessment practices cannot happen in isolation; strong and research-informed leadership is needed to manage a planned, multi-faceted, whole-university change management initiative as described in this chapter.

Getting the context right for change in assessment requires creating the conditions that will bring about transformational change.

The systemic approaches that are the focus of this case study have parallels with the strategic approach to transformational change taken by the Re-engineering Assessment Practices in Higher Education (REAP) project which has demonstrated successful large-scale re-engineering of assessment practices through a framework based on articulated principles and a model of self-regulation that engages students as active partners in assessment. REAP's approach includes policies and strategies to support and guide changes in practice, initiatives to support enhanced course design and new thinking in departments and faculties, and enhancements to quality assurance processes aligned to these new policies and practices. Nicol and Draper (2009) use REAP as a case study to propose a blueprint for constructing a large-scale project that generates transformational organizational change across a higher education institution.

In locating this chapter's case study change initiative within a theoretical framework of empowerment, the authors recognize the critical importance of engaging staff. Promoting a 'change-capable' culture that engages staff and enhances the student learning experience requires cultivating quality leadership at all levels of the university (Fullan and Scott 2009). The case study in this chapter is particularly interesting for its integrated 'top-down', 'middle-out', and 'bottom-up' approaches. Differences in disciplinary cultures can act as barriers to transformational change and heads of department, programme leaders and deans working from the 'middle out' have a pivotal role in the enhancement of learning, teaching, assessment and curriculum where departments and programme teams are the key organizational units when it comes to change (Trowler *et al.* 2003).

The discussion about the development of 'change-capable' culture that lies at the heart of this chapter accords with the approach to change leadership adopted by the UK Change Academy, a partnership of the Higher Education Academy and the Leadership Foundation for Higher Education, which brings together cross-institutional teams to think creatively about and develop a major change initiative. A number of UK higher educational institutions have developed their own Internal Change Academies, a model which has been instrumental in developing cadres of change agents and in enhancing ownership and understanding of change as a process (Oxley and Flint 2010).

The whole-of-programme approaches to assessment outlined in this chapter are seen as key to enabling a coherent and integrated student experience. This reflects similar approaches that are being used and researched elsewhere such as PASS (Programme Assessment Strategies) (Programme Assessment Strategies 2009–11) and TESTA (Transforming the Experience of Students Through Assessment), two national UK projects that are investigating programme-level assessment environments.

The conceptualization and design of professional development support and the use of collaborative spaces described in this chapter provide engaging models for securing involvement of academic staff in thinking about and implementing innovative assessment and teaching practice. The focus is on supporting and developing staff to engage students in new ways as part of the learning process. This raises interesting questions about the student perspective and how getting the context right for good assessment practice creates the conditions that support and engage students as active partners in assessment.

References

Fullan, M. and Scott, G. (2009) *Turnaround Leadership for Higher Education*, San Francisco: Jossey-Bass.

Nicol, D. J. and Draper, S. A. (2009) 'Blueprint for transformation organisational change in higher education: REAP as a case study', in T. Mayes, D. Morrison, H. Mellar, P. Bullen and M. Oliver (eds) *Transforming Higher Education Through Technology Enhanced Learning*, York: Higher Education Academy.

Oxley, A. and Flint, A. (2010) 'Learning from internal change academy processes', *Educational Developments*, 10(3): 25–8.

Programme Assessment Strategies (2009–11) *Higher Education Academy Funded National Teaching Fellowship Project*. Available at: www.pass.brad.ac.uk (accessed 16 May 2011).

Trowler, P., Saunders, M. and Knight, P. (2003) *Changing Thinking, Changing Practice*, York: LTSN Generic Centre.

Chapter 14

Technology-supported assessment for retention

Ormond Simpson

Introduction

It is a common saying in education that 'assessment drives learning' although it is not clear who first coined the phrase. Perhaps the phrase might be more accurately stated as 'feedback drives learning'. Indeed, as Hattie and Timperley (2007) note, feedback can improve learning both at school and university level, more than any other factor. Of course, and importantly, feedback and assessment are not the same. In this chapter, I will use the term feedback to mean information given to a student about their learning progress but which does not count towards their grade for their course or module, and assessment to mean the process by which a student's work is marked and counted towards their final course grade. In which case, there ought perhaps to be a corollary to the first statement above to say 'assessment also drives drop-out', at least in distance learning.

Some evidence for that statement comes from a study of student progress through course modules at the Open University in the United Kingdom. Figure 14.1 is a 'rivergram' showing progress through a Science Foundation course, where the width of the river at any point is proportional to the percentage of students who are still active at that point. The lines labelled 'TMA01, TMA02', and so on are where tutor marked assignments (TMAs) occur (there are six assignments in the course with a final exam).

The rivergram can be seen as a stream flowing right to left with students as the salmon travelling upstream left to right and leaping up weirs at each assignment. It can be seen that there is substantial drop-out before each weir or assignment – some 38 per cent before the first one with only 2 per cent bypassing it and returning to take the second assignment. There is similar drop-out before subsequent assignments, and after only three assignments some 48 per cent of the students have entered the exit stream and have dropped out of the course.

Of course, this is only indirect proof that assignments can cause drop-out. There may have been events between assignments which may have caused drop-out, which was then only picked up by the non-appearance of the subsequent assignment. However, data from Open University withdrawal surveys supports

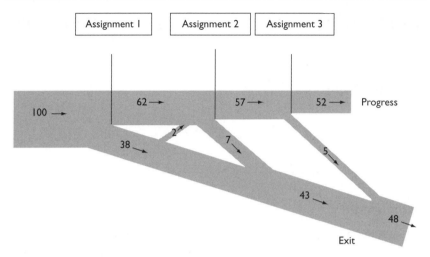

Figure 14.1 A 'rivergram' of the percentage of active students on a Science Foundation course at the UK Open University

this picture of assessment-generated drop-out. So if feedback drives learning but assessment can cause drop-out (and may possibly be one of the biggest causes of drop-out), are there ways in which the feedback and assessment strategies can be redesigned to reduce drop-out and thus increase student retention? In particular, are there ways in which technology can be used to make feedback and assessment more retention-friendly?

Student retention in the UK

Before tackling that question, it is useful to examine the phenomena of student retention and drop-out, which are complex and multi-factorial events and can be measured in a number of ways. The simplest measures, however, may be the overall graduation rates of higher education institutions. In UK full-time higher education, these vary from around 95 per cent (for Russell Group universities) to around 70 per cent for universities who accept many students from widening participation backgrounds. The average UK graduation rate is around 82 per cent. The average graduation rates for part-time and distance higher education are much lower, however – at 39 per cent (part-time students), 46 per cent (London University International Programme students) and 22 per cent (Open University students) (Higher Education Funding Council for England 2009) (see Figure 14.2).

The difference in graduation rates is striking, with part-time students at the same institutions as their full-time equivalents graduating at less than half their rate. Where part-time study is combined with distance and open entry, as in the Open University, the graduation rate is only around a quarter of the full-time equivalent.

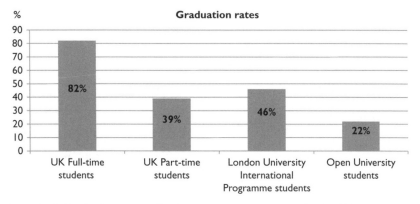

Figure 14.2 Graduation rates of higher education institutions in the UK
Source: *Higher Education Funding Council for England* (2009).
Note: The last three figures are calculated over 11 years.

There could be many reasons for these discrepancies, but the most obvious may be the simplest. Both part-time and distance students are likely to be far less engaged with their institutions than full-time students, a phenomenon described as transactional distance (Moore 1991). In other words, part-time and distance students are likely to have far less contact with their institution, its staff and other students than their full-time equivalents, and such contact is likely to be through less rich media than face-to-face meetings, for example, via telephone, email or virtual learning environments (VLEs). Given that feedback and assessment are often the most important points of contact between students and their institutions, the question posed previously can be rephrased – can assessment and feedback reduce the transactional distance between students and institutions, increasing student engagement and thereby increase student retention?

Why is student retention important? Before answering this question, there is a paradox to unpack. Most higher education institutions pay lip service to student retention. Yet there may also be a deep-seated ambivalence to it as well. As Johnston and Simpson (2006: 30) note, 'the biggest barrier to student retention is the institution itself' and even where institutions set up retention projects, there is evidence that they fade away after only a few years (Tinto 2009, cited in Simpson 2010). An example of this ambivalence may be the UK Open University which sometimes appears to be two institutions uncomfortably sharing the same campus. There is the 'Open' – all about supporting students and keeping them in, and the 'University' – all about academic standards and (using assessment) sifting students out, a phenomenon which Halsey, Heath and Ridge (1980: 216) called 'the paradox of the title'.

Thus, the obverse of student retention – student drop-out – becomes a topic rather like poverty. Everyone is against poverty but most people seem to accept that it will always exist whatever you do, whilst some believe that it has to exist in order to incentivize the general population (Dorling 2010). Similarly some academic staff may believe that their primary role with respect to students is to

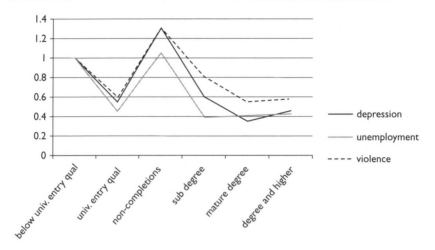

Figure 14.3 The probability of suffering various effects among different groups according to educational experience

Source: Bynner and Egerton (2001).

'weed out the unfit' and ensure that only those students proficient from the start are allowed to qualify – what Simpson (2009) calls the 'Darwinista' tendency. Other staff may take the view that students are destined to pass or fail and that their role is only to provide adequate teaching opportunities – the 'Fatalista' opinion (ibid.).

Yet student drop-out may be a huge but hidden cost to society. There is evidence that dropping out of full-time higher education has deleterious effects on students and subsequently on society as a whole. Figure 14.3 is derived from data collected by Bynner and Egerton (2001) and shows the probability of suffering depression, unemployment and (for women) partner violence, among various groups according to their educational experience.

Non-completers of higher education suffer markedly higher probabilities of depression, unemployment and partner violence than either graduates or A-level completers. This does not prove that dropping out is the cause of those effects as the reverse might be true, that students become depressed for some reason and then drop out. However, it seems more likely that an event has an effect, rather than vice versa, and of course such students were not too depressed to get into university in the first place.

If drop-out does cause these effects, then there may be long-term problems for both the students who dropped out and for society as a whole. Professor Emeritus Lord John Layard, founder of the Centre for Economic Performance at the London School of Economics, suggests that depression is the biggest single mental illness in UK society and has costs running into billions of pounds (Layard *et al.* 2007). With UK higher education participation at around 45 per cent of the age group and drop-out rates running at around 20 per cent, some 9 per cent of the entire 18-year-old age cohort may be affected by increased levels of depression, costing UK society possibly millions of pounds.

There appears to be no equivalent evidence about the effects of dropping out on part-time and distance students. It can be hoped that the supposed lower level of student engagement in those areas of higher education has the positive effect that dropping out is less damaging than full-time drop-out. But that may change with the introduction of markedly higher fee levels in UK universities. A recent report commissioned by the UK government (Browne 2010) has recommended that UK universities be allowed to raise their tuition fees to up to £9000 a year for full-time students with pro rata rises for part-time and distance students. This is likely to increase the indebtedness of part-time and distance students with possibly negative subsequent effects on them when they drop out.

Cost-benefits of assessment and feedback

The reason for the digression above is that assessment and feedback are usually seen as costs in higher education, mostly in terms of staff time. Thus, there is often pressure to minimize these costs, especially the cost of feedback; perhaps sometimes it is seen as non-essential as it does not contribute towards formal assessment. However, it is vital to remember that if assessment and feedback can be designed in ways to increase student retention at reasonable investment cost to an institution, then there may well be a positive financial return on that investment to that institution.

The return for any institution of such an investment will depend on how that institution is funded. For institutions funded largely from student fees (as seems likely in the UK in future), it can be shown that the extra institutional income generated by n extra students from a total of N students completing a year (and so continuing on to the following year) will be:

$$£[n(F - S - V/N) - N*P]$$

where the student tuition fee is £F, there is fixed institutional student overhead of £V per year plus a student-related expense of £S per student per year and the cost of a retention-focused activity is £P per student.

To illustrate how this might work, take a hypothetical example of an institution where there is an increase in retention of 10 students from a population of 1000 students (i.e. a 1 per cent increase in retention) due to an increase in feedback costing £20 per student. In this case the student tuition fee is assumed to be £6,000, the institutional student-related expense is £200 and the overhead £500,000. Then the extra institutional income will be:

$$£[10(6,000 - 200 - 500,000/1,000) - 20 \times 1,000] = £33,000$$

Since the cost of this change in assessment is £N*P = £(20 × 1,000) = £20,000, this particular activity makes a surplus of £(33,000 − 20,000) = £13,000, an annual return on investment of 65 per cent.

The point of this hypothetical example is merely to suggest that there could well be cases where enhancements in feedback and assessment strategies which increase student retention may be financially self-supporting, or even profitable to the institution. Thus, arguments that increasing feedback is too expensive may need to be cost-analyzed and possibly rebutted. In addition, given the negative effects of drop-out suggested earlier, there may be large but unquantifiable gains to the retained students and society as a whole.

Assessment, feedback and retention

Given the argument above, it is a little curious that there seems to be relatively little research into how assessment and feedback can improve retention. Here it is important to draw a distinction between the aims of 'enhancing students' learning experience' (a quote from the stated aims of the UK Higher Education Academy 2011) and increasing student retention as the two are not necessarily the same. It is perfectly possible, for example, to find that students' learning experience has been improved among the survivors of a cohort, while ignoring the fact that much of the cohort has already dropped out. Thus, critics of the National Student Survey of student opinion note that while the Open University is consistently near the top of the survey, the survey only goes to the students surviving to their equivalent of the second year. The Higher Education Funding Council for England (2009) statistics suggest that this is roughly 30 per cent of the students who started, so the sample is rather biased. With the caveat in mind that learning experience is not necessarily the same as student success, the main findings about feedback, assessment and retention come from the following areas.

Formative feedback

Formative feedback is feedback to students on work that is not graded or used for assessment except sometimes in a qualifying sense, i.e. it must be completed to allow summative assessments to be submitted. In their book, *Retention and Student Success in Higher Education*, Yorke and Longden (2004) argue strongly for the retention value of formative assessment because of its capacity to enhance student learning. There is also evidence from studies in the United States such as Black and Wiliam (1998), Kluger and De Nisi (1996), and a number of others. Despite the reservation above about enhancing student learning, the number and thoroughness of the studies suggest that there must be a retention effect, however difficult it is to measure.

In addition, Gibbs and Dunbar-Goddet (2007), in a survey of UK degree programmes, found that the timeliness, volume and quality of feedback most closely predicted how far students took a 'deep' approach to their studies. They noted that in studies in the USA a deep approach was found to be the best predictor of student engagement, and that educational practices which increased

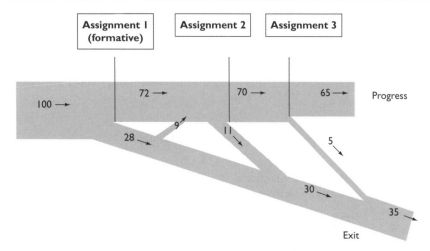

Figure 14.4 A 'rivergram' of the percentage of active students on a rewritten Science
　　　　　Foundation course with a formative assignment at the UK Open
　　　　　University

engagement also increased retention. Although this extended sequence is not
definitive, it is nevertheless a strong addition to the accumulated evidence for
formative feedback and retention.

Finally there is also evidence from the UK Open University in the form of
another 'rivergram'. The Science Foundation course whose assignment submission rivergram was illustrated in Figure 14.1 was subsequently rewritten and a
formative assignment was introduced as Assignment 1. The revised rivergram is
shown in Figure 14.4.

It can be seen that fewer students drop out before the first (now formative)
assignment – 38 per cent versus 28 per cent – and that more students return to
the second assignment having skipped the first – 9 per cent versus 2 per cent.
Thus, there are more students on the 'progress channel' at every stage than in
the pre-formative course – 72 per cent versus 62 per cent, 70 per cent versus
57 per cent, and so on. It is not possible to compare the overall retention rates
of the two courses as their contents and exam strategies were different, but
nevertheless the overall pattern of more students carrying on at every stage is
clear.

Finally, it is important to note that grading formative assignments may reduce
their value. Black and Wiliam (1998) found that assignments with feedback and
marks, or marks only, led to less learning than assignments with just feedback.
Similarly, Kluger and De Nisi (1998) found that performance feedback actually
depressed future performance in one-third of all the feedback research they
studied. In a further one-third, the feedback had no effect and only in one final
third did performance increase. They suggested that feedback must be focused
on building learners' self-efficacy, and closing the gap between their goals

and current performance. Feedback pointing out poor performance, suggesting the performance is 'wrong' or that the goals are unclear, often led to a subsequent deterioration in performance. Gibbs (2010) argued that the Open University loses much of the effectiveness of its assessment strategies by its policy of marking all its students' assignments, even those which are purely formative.

'Meta-cognitive awareness' in feedback and assessment

'Metacognitive awareness' is the idea that students need to be able to make the same judgements of assignments that tutors make. That means students being able to see exemplars of different grades, getting some idea of what grade they might get for a particular assignment and – where possible – being able to enter a dialogue with tutors and other students about those grades. As Sadler (1989: 19) notes:

> The indispensable conditions for improvement are that the student comes to hold a concept of quality roughly similar to that held by the teacher, is able to monitor continuously the quality of what is being produced during the act of production itself, and has a repertoire of alternative moves or strategies from which to draw at any given point. In other words, students have to be able to judge the quality of what they are producing and be able to regulate what they are doing during the doing of it.

Both Hattie (2009) and Gibbs (2010) believe that metacognitive awareness of assessment is an important factor in learning and consequent retention. Indeed, Hattie (2009), in his meta-survey of more than 50,000 studies, rated 'self-reporting of grades' (i.e. students should be able to assess their learning for themselves at every stage) as the most important factor in student success out of the 130 factors. Gibbs (2010) quotes findings from the Scottish 'Re-engineering Assessment Practices in Scottish Higher Education' (REAP) study which found worthwhile improvements in first year performance and retention on a whole range of courses through simple mechanisms such as marking exercises.

At its simplest, meta-cognitive awareness could be developed through enhanced worked examples of assignments: that is examples where the thought processes behind the example are explained as well as the answer itself. For instance, in a maths worked example, it will be best to explain why certain lines of working are not pursued as well as the final working which is. Sometimes such worked examples give the impression of a clear route to the solution when there are byways which have to be explored on the way. Similar examples could be developed even in more discursive subjects such as sociology, although the example would be more about the line and strength of the argument.

Such examples are reasonably simple to generate. Yet institutions sometimes seem very resistant to provide these, perhaps through a fear that students will model them too closely. However, there is little doubt that students warmly welcome such models. In a survey of UK Open University 'taster packs' (used to give intending students a 'feel' for the course they are interested in), it was the specimen assignments (containing a typical example of a student's assignment with a tutor's comments and grade) which were more valued by students than the specimen course material itself (Adams *et al.* 1989).

Self-assessment questions

A type of formative feedback with a long history in distance education is the 'self-assessment question' or SAQ. These are short questions in a distance education text designed to self-test a student's understanding of the previous paragraphs or pages of material. The answers are given either immediately after the question or at the end of the text. In many ways, SAQs fulfil Hattie's (2009) specification for 'self-reported grades' – in his research the most effective form of learning. But of course the problem is that there is always a temptation for the student to glance straight to the answer without testing themselves in any way, or to skip the SAQ altogether. It may be that the answer will lie in better design of SAQs together with emphasizing the research findings on their value to students, or in the form of electronic text which only allows students to proceed if they have attempted the SAQ. But this then is likely to restrict SAQs to multiple choice questions which are then subject to the criticism by Gibbs (2010) as encouraging only shallow learning – see 'surface and deep learning' below.

Ipsative assessment

A more recent development that may have an effect on retention is 'ipsative assessment' (Hughes 2011). This is assessment or feedback which compares a student's achievement not with an absolute standard, but with their previous performance. The suggestion is that this is more congruent with Dweck's (1999) findings that students who are praised for effort are more likely to increase their efforts than students praised for their achievement. One example of ipsative assessment is from UK Dyslexia Action in their postgraduate course for specialist teachers. Students are required to read a set text and then have several weeks to complete an online assessment consisting of a computer-marked multiple choice test. They can have as many attempts at the test as they wish, and at each try are told whether their answers are right or wrong, but nothing else. Course tutors can offer help at any point before the deadline at which a threshold has to be reached. Results so far suggest that most students achieve the threshold and find the process motivational, often improving their scores beyond the threshold (Goodwin 2011, pers. comm.). However, further research is needed into how ipsative assessment can be applied and what the effect on retention, if any, might be.

Motivational feedback and assessment

To be effective in increasing retention, all forms of feedback and assessment will need to motivate students' learning. As Anderson (2003) notes, motivation is the best predictor of student retention – reduced motivation leads to drop-out. Thus, retention services need to address this by clarifying and building on motivation-reducing issues. However, there seems to have been little research into what might constitute motivational feedback and assessment, it possibly being assumed that the need to get a good grade is sufficient motivation in itself. But as Wigfield, Eccles, Roeser and Schiefele (2009) suggest, learning motivation is a multiple of the assumed possibility of accomplishing a task times the perceived value of that accomplishment. If either of those quantities are zero, then the multiple (the learning motivation) is zero. This suggests that feedback tasks need to be carefully graded so that students believe their chances of success are high.

Technology, assessment and retention

Given the individualized (and therefore expensive) nature of the assessment and feedback strategies needed to enhance retention, are there ways in which the power of information technology can be harnessed to reduce costs, increasing the possibility of positive financial returns and therefore the likelihood of implementation of such strategies? There may be several possibilities: I have selected three examples further to the previous ipsative example.

Computer-marked assessment

There is a long history of the use of technology in assessment in distance education. The UK Open University first introduced computer-marked assignments (CMAs) in the early 1970s. Initially these were multiple choice questionnaires which students completed by pencilling in boxes on forms that were returned by post to the Open University, and marked using an optical reader. Feedback to students was given in the form of a simple grade, returned again by post. There could be up to 12 CMAs in a course module, collated with up to eight tutor-marked assignments (TMAs) to give the overall module grade.

Later, attempts were made to give more sophisticated feedback through standard responses to wrong answers returned to students. More recently 'interactive CMAs' (iCMAs) were introduced in the Science Faculty (Jordan 2011). These were online and gave students instantaneous feedback using the 'OpenMark' software developed at the Open University. The use of such software enabled the feedback to be more sophisticated – in particular, wrong or inadequate answers could be given specific feedback (ibid.).

As well as in numerate subjects, CMAs have been used for assessment in the Open University in subjects where there may be no right or wrong answers, such as in the humanities and social sciences. Of course, such subjects are usually assessed through discursive methods using complex language, such as essays, but as yet there is little sign of a technology that can do any more than spot possible plagiarism.

Polling

Another recent technological development in feedback is 'polling software'. This is the online or texting equivalent of asking for a show of hands. A multiple choice or free text quiz can be designed using the software which can then be inserted, for example, as a slide in a PowerPoint presentation. Students are invited to respond to the quiz either on the internet or by texting their answers to a phone number. Either way their answers can then be shown graphically in the same presentation, the histograms for (say) 'yes' 'no' or 'I don't know' building up as students answer. A number of systems exist such as *Poll Everywhere* (http://www.polleverywhere.com). A short video showing an example of the use of *Poll Everywhere* can be viewed on http://www.facultyfocus.com/wp-content/uploads/images/polling-1orlando.mp4?c=FF&t=F101004a (accessed 13 May 2011).

Audio and video feedback

Another example of the innovative use of technology in assessment is from the Open Polytechnic of New Zealand, where a webcam above the tutor's desk is used to video the marking of an assignment. The resulting video can be placed in the institution's virtual learning environment or copied onto a DVD and posted to the student. Ice, Curtis, Phillips and Wells (2007) used a mix of recorded audio and text feedback in an online course and found an extremely high student satisfaction with embedded asynchronous audio feedback as compared to asynchronous text-only feedback.

All these technological developments from computer-marked assessment to polling to audio and video feedback may well enhance a student's feedback and assessment experience. Nevertheless, the evidence for the effects of such technology on retention remains unclear and there is a need for controlled and validated experiments to establish retention effects. However, such experiments are difficult to design.

Surface and deep learning

Multiple choice tests and feedback systems of these kinds have been frequently criticized, most notably by Gibbs (2010) who suggests that they lead to 'shallow learning' rather than the desired 'deep learning'. There does not seem to be strong evidence offered for this assertion and it might be argued that for potential drop-out students, any kind of successful initial learning may increase their confidence and motivation, thereby reducing their likelihood of dropping out. After all, to take the metaphor literally, throwing non-swimmers in at the deep end is unlikely to produce successful swimming. Starting at the shallow end is rather more likely to produce eventual success at the deep end.

Conclusion

There seems to be surprisingly little evidence that clearly connects summative assessment strategies with increasing student retention. If anything, it appears that assessment can sometimes drive drop-out rather than retention. There is better evidence for the value of formative feedback in increasing retention, particularly in the form of Hattie's (2009) 'self-reporting grades'. In essence, it would appear that in order to enhance student retention in higher education, both formative feedback and assessment need to be essentially motivational. While the evidence for the motivational and retention value of formative feedback seems quite strong, a great deal of work remains to be done in evaluating the ways in which assessment can be made less likely to be a cause of drop-out and more of a positive factor in student retention.

Technology may offer some useful ways forward, but as yet there is little clear evidence for the effects of using technology in feedback and assessment in increasing student retention. While computer-marked assessment and feedback using multiple choice questions have become quite sophisticated, it is not easy to see how technology can be applied to subjects which are assessed by more discursive methods such as essays. Multiple choice questions have in any case been criticized on the grounds that they may encourage shallow learning. But other possibilities are beginning to develop, such as ipsative assessment, polling and video/audio feedback. However, whatever new methods appear, it will be important to evaluate them not only for retention effectiveness, but also for cost-effectiveness in order to overcome objections about the possible price tags attached.

References

Adams, C., Rand, V. and Simpson, O. (1989) 'But what's it really like?: The Taster Pack idea', *Open Learning*, 4(3): 42–3.

Anderson, E. (2003) 'Retention for rookies', paper presented at the National Conference on Student Retention, San Diego, California.

Black, P. and Wiliam, D. (1998) 'Assessment and classroom learning', *Assessment in Education*, 5(1): 7–74.

Browne, J. (2010) *Securing a Sustainable Future for Higher Education: An Independent Review of Higher Education Funding and Student Finance*. Available at: www.independent.gov.uk/browne-report (accessed 4 August 2011).

Bynner, J. and Egerton, M. (2001) *The Wider Benefits of Higher Education*. Available at: http://www.hefce.ac.uk/pubs/hefce/2001/01_46.htm (accessed 9 March 2011).

Dorling, D. (2010) *Injustice: Why Social Inequality Persists*, Bristol: Policy Press.

Dweck, C. S. (1999) *Self-Theories: Their Role in Motivation, Personality, and Development*, Philadelphia: Taylor & Francis.

Gibbs, G. (2010) 'Does assessment in open learning support students?', *Open Learning*, 5(2): 163–6.

Gibbs, G. and Dunbar-Goddet, H. (2007) *The Effects of Programme Assessment Environments on Student Learning*. Available at: http://scholar.google.co.uk/scholar?q=Gibbs,+G.+%26+Dunbar-Goddet,+H.+%282007%29+The+effects+of+-programme+assessment+environments+on+student+learning&hl=en&as_sdt=0&as_vis=1&oi=scholart (accessed 19 March 2011).

Halsey, A., Heath, A. and Ridge, J. (1980) *Origins and Destinations: Family, Class and Education in Modern Britain*, Oxford: Clarendon Press.

Hattie, J. (2009) *Visible Learning: A Synthesis of Over 800 Meta-Analyses Relating to Achievement*, Abingdon: Routledge.

Hattie, J. and Timperley, H. (2007) 'The power of feedback', *Review of Educational Research*, 77(1): 81–112.

Higher Education Academy (2011) Website. Available at: http://www.heacademy.ac.uk/ (accessed 9 March 2011).

Higher Education Funding Council for England (2009) Website. Available at: http://www.hefce.ac.uk/pubs/hefce/2009/09_18/ (accessed 19 January 2011).

Hughes, G. (2011) 'Towards a personal best: a case for introducing ipsative assessment in higher education', *Studies in Higher Education*, 36(3): 353–367.

Ice, P., Curtis, R., Phillips, P. and Wells, J. (2007) 'Using asynchronous audio feedback to enhance teaching presence and students' sense of community', *Journal of Asynchronous Learning Networks*, 11(2): 3–25.

Johnston, V. and Simpson, O. (2006) 'Retentioneering higher education in the UK: attitudinal barriers to addressing student retention in universities', *Widening Participation*, 8(3): 28–36.

Jordan, S. (2011) 'Using interactive computer-based assessment to support beginning distance learners of science', *Open Learning: The Journal of Open and Distance Learning*, 26(2): 147–64.

Kluger, A. and De Nisi, A. (1996) 'The effects of feedback intervention on performance: a historical review, a meta-analysis and a preliminary feedback intervention theory', *Psychological Bulletin*, 119: 254–84.

——(1998) 'Feedback interventions: toward the understanding of a double-edged sword', *Current Directions in Psychological Science*, 7(3): 67–72.

Layard, R., Clark, D., Knapp, M. and Mayraz, G. (2007) *Cost-Benefit Analysis of Psychological Therapy*, Centre for Economic Performance Discussion Paper 829, London: Centre for Economic Performance, London School of Economics and Political Science. Available at: http://eprints.lse.ac.uk/19673/ (accessed 9 March 2011).

Moore, M. G. (1991) 'Distance education theory', *American Journal of Distance Education*, 5(3). Available at: http://www.ajde.com/Contents/vol5_3.htm#editorial (accessed 20 January 2011).

Sadler, D. R. (1989) 'Formative assessment and the design of instructional systems', *Instructional Science*, 18: 119–44.

Simpson, O. (2009) 'Theories of student support', presentation at the London University International Programme. Available at: www.authorstream.com/Presentation/ormondsimpson-405222-theory-distance-student-support-motivation-retention-learning-support2-narrated-education-ppt-powerpoint/ (accessed 9 March 2011).

——(2010) '22%: can we do better?', report to the Open University Centre for Widening Participation. Available at: www.ormondsimpson.com (accessed 9 March 2011).

Wigfield, A., Eccles, J., Roeser, R. and Schiefele, U. (2009) *Development of Achievement Motivation*. Available at: http://www.robertroeser.com/docs/publications/2009_Wigfieldetal_Motivation.pdf (accessed 19 March 2011).

Yorke, M. and Longden, B. (2004) *Retention and Student Success in Higher Education*, Maidenhead: Open University Press.

CRITICAL FRIEND COMMENTARY

Mark Childs

Retention rates are an issue for institutions all across the education sector. One in 10 students drop out in their first year and fewer than eight in 10 complete their studies; statistics that remain consistent year on year (National Audit Office 2007: 5). Assessment does indeed form a barrier to progression, yet with the Darwinistas and Fatalistas driving the role of assessment in institutions, there may be little room for flexibility in removing these barriers in the way of students. Other common reasons for withdrawal can perhaps be more readily addressed within our institutions than changing assessment. A common cause of drop-out among students is a lack of integration; either failure to form strong social bonds within peer groups, or a lack of sense of connection with the institution. A student feeling homesick or isolated will be more prone to be deterred from continuing when another issue arises, such as a low mark in an assessment (ibid.: 46).

One way in which students can be integrated to a larger extent is through the design and delivery of the curriculum. Activity-led learning (ALL) is particularly effective at engaging students and helping them feel that they are an integral part of the institution (Wilson-Medhurst and Glendinning 2009). In studies of ALL at Coventry University, the feedback from lecturers and students is especially positive when discussing how much better they have got to know each other, since collaborating on activities fosters far better interaction between lecturers, support staff and students than the passive reception (and delivery) of lectures.

Ormond Simpson mentions giving feedback in the form of audio, and this has been shown to provide not only more in-depth and nuanced information to students while still taking less time to do (Rotherham 2009). It also promotes a stronger sense of social cohesion (Ice *et al.* 2007). Even students who do not find audio particularly helpful due to language difficulties still report their greater sense of being 'cared for' by their lecturers on receiving feedback through audio (Childs *et al.* 2010).

Of course, a great boon to social inclusion is the use of online social networks. There is a danger, however, in buying into Prensky's (2001: 1) 'digital natives' viewpoint and assuming that all students are accustomed to, or even like, Web 2.0 technologies. Nevertheless, facilitating online and offline opportunities for learners to form connections with their peers and the institutions, and actively identifying students at risk of becoming isolated, could do much to enhance students' feelings of involvement. Examples of this can be seen in many institutions. For example, at Leicester College, transition from first to second years of the part-time Foundation Degree in Photography and Video was increased to 100 per cent through encouraging blogging over the summer vacation (Stone 2011). At the Open University, students who otherwise would not meet are given the opportunity to have an experience of co-presence through the institution's provision of an island in Second Life™ (Peachey 2011).

These new technologies continue to increasingly break down barriers between students, and between students and staff, as well as maintain social ties with friends and family back home once students are at their place of learning, and so will help to reduce these feelings of isolation and alienation. If higher education can take advantage of these trends, they may do much to overcome the barriers in Simpson's rivergram. In short, social network technologies will act as salmon ladders in learners' continued movement upstream.

References

Childs, M., Oliver, M. and Bate, S. (2010) 'Providing feedback using audio', paper presented at the Association for Learning Technology Conference, Nottingham, UK, 7–9 September 2010.

Ice, P., Curtis, R., Phillips, P. and Wells, J. (2007) 'Using asynchronous audio feedback to enhance teaching presence and students' sense of community', *Journal of Asynchronous Learning Networks*, 11(2): 3–25.

National Audit Office (2007) *Staying the Course: The Retention of Students in Higher Education*, Report by the Comptroller and Auditor General, London: National Audit Office, 26 July 2007.

Peachey, A. (2011) 'Can a tiger wear a turban and still be a student?', Research Seminar at University of Worcester Island, 19 May 2011.

Prensky, M. (2001) 'Digital natives, digital immigrants', *On the Horizon*, 9(5), October 2001, NCB University Press. Available at: http://www.marcprensky. com/writing/Prensky%20-%20Digital%20Natives,%20Digital%20Immigrants%20-% 20Part1.pdf (accessed 19 July 2011).

Rotherham, R. (2009) *Review of the Sounds Good Project*. Available at: http://www. jisc.ac.uk/media/documents/programmes/usersandinnovation/sounds%20good% 20final%20report.doc (accessed 19 July 2011).

Stone, L. (2011) *HELLO Project (Higher Education Lifelong Learning Opportunities)*, ELESIG Midlands Seminar Series, University of Northampton, 19 May 2011.

Wilson-Medhurst, S. and Glendinning, I. (2009) 'Winning hearts and minds: implementing activity led learning (ALL)', in *Proceedings of the Learning by Developing Conference*, 12–13 Feb. 2009, Laurea, Helsinki. Available at: http://markkinointi. laurea.fi/julkaisut/d/d07.pdf.

Chapter 15

Issues and strategies for student engagement through assessment in transnational higher education

Glenda Crosling

Introduction

This chapter discusses assessment in transnational higher education (TNHE) and its impact on the engagement and retention of students. While the features of student engagement, retention and assessment discussed in the other contributions in this book apply in TNHE, the perspective explored in this chapter is that curriculum and assessment are intertwined and need adequate attention in TNHE so that they reflect the offshore situation and student cohort. The underpinning approach is that to engage students, studies must be relevant to students' lives and future aspirations.

In TNHE where education programmes are often designed in one country and delivered to students in another, the relevance of the programme for students and thus their engagement cannot be assumed. Focusing on the foreign branch campus form of TNHE (a full campus of a university physically located 'offshore' in a different country from the 'parent' university), the discussion addresses the need for curriculum and assessment to be contextualized to the local setting. The chapter concludes with strategies to ensure that curriculum and assessment are localized accordingly, facilitating students' engagement and retention in their studies. The author's experience over a number of years in TNHE in various capacities frames the views and strategies on student engagement and assessment that are discussed.

Transnational higher education

Before discussing assessment and student engagement in TNHE, the nature of TNHE requires clarification. TNHE refers to the expansion of higher education beyond national boundaries, with students physically situated overseas from the parent institution (Edwards *et al.* 2010). Many higher education institutions have participated in TNHE over recent times (McBurnie and Ziguras 2007), and there are a large number of examples of such institutional mobility. This includes universities from Australia, the USA, the UK and other countries opening branch campuses in many developing countries (Varghese 2009). TNHE is a global trend, drawing on the eagerness of developing countries for educated populations in order to fuel their economic and social development. While in the past students from developing countries may have been international students in higher education systems in developed countries, TNHE means that students can take the educational programmes offered by established universities in their region, or in their own country, through a range of forms. One common form is the 'franchise', or the 'twinning' programme, based on contractual arrangements in other countries with foreign partners (Bodycott and Walker 2000; Dunn and Wallace 2003; Edwards *et al.* 2010). Another form, mentioned earlier, is 'parent' institutions establishing campuses in other countries, commonly named foreign branch campuses, which is this chapter's focus. However, the literature for 'twinning' programmes is drawn on in the discussion because, as well as differences, there are similar issues for both.

Whatever the TNHE form, a major outcome is vastly increased diversity in the backgrounds, previous educational experiences and expectations of the institution's students and academic staff. While international students are an established part of higher education, the concept of an institution actually located in an offshore setting with local as well as international students to that setting, and academic staff who are not local to the language and culture of the home institution, brings additional diversity to the equation of quality education.

There are rewards for institutions engaging in TNHE, such as increases in the university's overall student numbers, so that at a surface level more students are able to engage with higher education studies. As Varghese (2009: 23) points out, what in the past was a relatively low number of students crossing borders for higher education has increased recently; nearly 2.9 million students took part in 2006 and the number is expected to increase to 7.2 million by 2025. However, with the advent of student caps on numbers and immigration restrictions, there may be increased interest by institutions in achieving financial advantages by *going to* other countries as foreign branch campuses, rather than students *coming* to them across borders as international students. Furthermore, institutions that engage in mobility may project themselves as innovative in that they are responding to global changes and needs. There may also be intrinsic and extrinsic benefits in terms of providing a service for the developing regions of the world, thereby contributing to global well-being and the development of mutual trust and respect with the countries in which their TNHE programmes operate.

However, concomitant risks exist for institutions with no guarantees for success. First, setting up TNHE arrangements is costly, especially for a branch campus, and costs may not be recovered, nor profit generated, if the programme/s do not attract enough students. Furthermore, reputational damage can result if the educational quality suffers (Edwards *et al.* 2010) due to the outsourcing of some operations or their transference to another country, as can potentially occur in the case of foreign branch campuses. Thus, it can be argued that both educational quality and institutional reputation are relevant to assessment and student engagement in TNHE operations, especially considering student diversity and programme quality.

Edwards *et al.* (2010), for instance, reviewed Australian Universities Quality Agency (AUQA) audit reports of higher education institutions and identified the potential for reputational and quality risks if offshore staff are inadequately inducted into their university's values, academic expectations, policy and curriculum developments. They stress the importance of student assessment in TNHE programme quality, pointing out that systematic moderation of student assessment in courses and subjects is required to ensure equivalence of high standards at home and abroad. However, the distance and communication that are integral to TNHE, including foreign branch campuses, may impact on the effectiveness of operations, with such issues perhaps exacerbated in the context of a large degree of diversity in the backgrounds of students and academic staff.

Curriculum, assessment and transnational higher education

The risks faced by institutions with franchise or twinning arrangements that are outlined in the literature include student assessment (McNicoll *et al.* 2003). For example, in discussing Asian offshore partners of an Australian university, McNicoll *et al.* identify issues of distance and communication as contributing to tensions in, among other elements, the excellence in programme delivery. These issues also apply to foreign branch campuses and to the quality of assessment. Because assessment is key in student learning, these are important factors as they impact on student engagement in foreign branch campuses.

Assessment in TNHE also needs to be contextualized to the dangers of what may be seen as cultural imperialism, which refers to the simple passage of educational programmes (including the curriculum and assessment) from one country to others in a colonial-like manner, with very little, if any adaptation to meet the local situation. Such programmes may lack relevance to students' lives and future aspirations. This situation exemplifies McBurnie and Ziguras' (2007: 62) comments that since its emergence in the 1980s, 'transnational higher education in South East Asia has commonly involved very little effort to respond to the particular needs of the offshore students in different countries'. Student assessment cannot be divorced from this situation; for example, a lack of sensitivity in assessment tasks that require students to investigate study points of particular relevance to the home university country, but which are not significant in the offshore country.

McBurnie and Ziguras (ibid.: 66) also maintain that ideally, 'teaching staff in each location need to have input into course design'. Students can detect the status of staff within the institution in terms of respect, autonomy and responsibility, impacting on the teachers' involvement and engagement in the educational programme. It can impact on students' engagement in their learning (Crosling 2011) in that engaged teachers demonstrate enthusiasm in planning their teaching appropriately for the programme's particular student cohort. Furthermore, engaged teachers would be more likely to seek and respond to student responses to the course design which includes the teaching and learning approaches. This engenders a sense of co-creation by staff and students in the course design, with the advantage of further entrenching student engagement in the educational programme.

Input into course design and assessment is important as it is well recognized that assessment has a significant, if not determining, impact on the quality of student learning (see, for example, Race 2004). Biggs' (1999) well-accepted views on constructive alignment of the curriculum explain the interwoven role of assessment in education programmes, also emphasized in outcomes-based education. For quality education, assessment needs to be aligned to the course and subject learning outcomes, and to the teaching and learning approach. Integral to this process are the students and, by implication, their study engagement. Joseph Schwab's (1973) views on curriculum development (including assessment) further exemplify the importance of its contextualization to the major participating parties, which Schwab identifies as the student, the teacher, the subject content, and of particular relevance to this discussion, the milieu. Clearly, there are implications at this point for tensions related to distance and communication in TNHE and in foreign branch campuses, where the design is undertaken in one national setting, and delivered by teachers to students in another, with limited adaptation for the offshore milieu and student cohort. It also brings to mind the relevance of the notion of 'glocalization', in simple terms seen as thinking globally and acting locally, where boundaries lessen in importance because of transnational movement. As people and processes interact across borders, the global melds with the local (Roudometof 2005). Swyngedouw (2004) discusses glocalization as a more radical response of deeply and bitterly disempowered people in a geographic location asserting their own visions and strategies that are alternative to those of the dominant power.

Relating this more specifically to higher education, Thomas (2002) draws on the work of Bourdieu and Passeron (1977) and institutional habitus, pointing out that there is much international research and theory relating to factors involving the individual, the social and the organizational that impact on student retention in higher education. Thomas (2002) identifies that student engagement is strongly influenced by inclusive teaching, learning and assessment. If these are not inclusive, students from the non-dominant culture in the educational setting may be alienated. Thomas also centralizes assessment in the academic experience, and Crosling, Thomas and Heagney (2008b) highlight the importance of teaching and learning in student engagement. Relating these views to an offshore foreign branch campus setting, student alienation can occur if the educational programme and its assessment do not reflect the milieu's situation and concerns. Furthermore, the teaching staff may be alienated if their milieu is not reflected in the subject matter and teaching approach (Crosling 2011).

This is not an unexpected perspective. The reports on TNHE from AUQA reviewed by Edwards *et al.* (2010) point out that an internationalized curriculum is required. Stella and Liston (2008), in reviewing AUQA audit reports, state that the curriculum should integrate an international, intercultural or global dimension into the purpose and functions of tertiary education. Consequently, courses including assessment should reflect cultural sensitivities and international perspectives, such as contextualization of cases. This does not imply compromising assessment standards, but rather increasing relevance for the offshore setting in mode and content. For cultural diversity, valuing and appreciating international models and perspectives in a discipline are required. In assessment, the academic staff in the offshore setting may interpret the materials, tasks and requirements differently, disadvantaging offshore students (ibid.). The reports examined by Stella and Liston point out that regular comparative analysis of onshore and offshore student performance is required in TNHE to ensure equivalence of student learning outcomes, as well as mechanisms to ensure the effectiveness of moderation.

Student learning in TNHE: an internationalized curriculum

As discussed previously, students in each TNHE location need to see the relevance of their studies to their situations in order to engage. Curriculum internationalization has been put forward to achieve this (Edwards *et al.* 2003; Crosling *et al.* 2008a). However, making the curriculum relevant to all students in all locations is not achieved simply by tagging on local perspectives. As McBurnie and Ziguras (2007) state, the core education needs to be internationalized, including the assessment of students. Such an emphasis indicates that it is a pressing need with implications for the educational programme's quality (ibid.: 66).

Student diversity must be considered in relation to the curriculum, including assessment. While student diversity applies in any teaching situation, its impact is heightened in TNHE since, as McBurnie and Ziguras point out, all classes contain students with differences of prior life, educational and work experience, age, gender, ethnicity and motivation for study. However, the diversity may be magnified when the academic staff/ teachers are also diverse. Consequently, lecturers and tutors who are engaged with their students need to take the opportunity to tailor their teaching to their students' needs. This means providing a range of ways to approach study, so students can 'engage with teachers, with each other and materials in the most effective way for them and for the task' (ibid.: 66), for instance, building into the educational programme opportunities for collaborative learning in a particular setting if students demonstrate a preference for this.

Specific issues regarding assessment in TNHE are that student and staff educational backgrounds and expectations may differ from the assumptions embedded in the curriculum, which reflect those of a more developed education system. For instance, while the educational systems of many South-East Asian countries are developing quickly, there may be a mismatch of expectations in that some students from these systems still may conceive of education as a process of learning and reproducing information, rather than understanding, interpreting and applying it through critical analysis. Students from some linguistic and cultural backgrounds may organize their thinking and writing differently from the western preference for a deductive, writer-responsive form with the natural preference to, for instance, take a circular, rather than linear form (Vance and Crosling 1998). There may be issues in terms of use of non-standard English, or the use in academic writing of the local variety of spoken English, which incorporates non-standard features (Crosling 1996).

McBurnie and Ziguras (2007) offer an important perspective involving customizing the curriculum and its teaching, learning and assessment for the TNHE setting. Following Biggs (1999), they suggest that transnational educators should not adhere too closely to perceived historical divergences between Asian and Western learners, but instead use strategies that transcend local cultures and are universally effective. According to McBurnie and Ziguras (2007: 72), 'a bland curriculum arising from a globalized educational programme can be resisted by tailoring teaching and learning strategies to the local context, and by employing empowered local lecturers and tutors'. Indeed, in citing the New Zealand document, *UNESCO and Council of Europe (2001) Code of Practice in the Provision of Transnational Education*, Ziguras (2007: 18) argues that TNHE 'should encourage the awareness and knowledge of the culture and customs of both awarding institutions and receiving country among the students and staff'. The benefits of this are clear:

> By embedding a course in several local contexts in which it is taught, students in each teaching location begin to gain from the course's transnational character and lecturers and students alike are encouraged to reflect on the curriculum in terms of various differences and similarities of experience at global, national and local levels. Internationalizing the curriculum in this way is much easier if offshore teaching staff have input into curriculum development and review processes.
>
> (ibid.: 18)

An example of such tailoring is the offshore campus developing its own strengths within the curriculum; these draw on and are based on their relevance to the offshore setting (Crosling 2011), such as a focus on local marine biology in science in a coastal area.

Strategies for contextualizing assessment to the TNHE setting

In TNHE, several factors require consideration in the assessment and engagement of students. First, student engagement will be compromised if students feel alienated from a curriculum that has been designed for another setting. The risk is that the assessment outcomes for the students in the offshore setting may not be representative of their abilities and achievements. Second, offshore teachers may also feel alienated and experience lack of ownership over the educational programme if it is merely transferred to them for delivery from the parent university. With limited, if any, input these teachers may not themselves be engaged in their teaching, in turn, intensifying the chances of their students lacking involvement and engagement. Consolidating these factors, assessment as the realization of the learning experience for students may not effectively provide guidance and direction for them in their learning. Overall, the curriculum including the teaching and the assessment in TNHE ought to be contextualized for maximum impact on the engagement of students.

The strategies below provide approaches to contextualize the curriculum and the assessment to the offshore setting and student cohort.

Recognition of the TNHE location and student cohort in the curriculum and assessment

In order to enhance the relevance of the educational programme for students, the values and expectations of quality education that are embedded in the curriculum and assessment need to match with those held by the academic staff in the offshore setting. This can be achieved by inducting offshore staff into the university's academic values and expectations as a basis for appreciating the values that underpin the curriculum and the assessment, so that these values can percolate through the teaching and learning programme to their students. This enables the offshore students to appreciate the aim and purpose of their curriculum as well as the assessment tasks. For instance, staff offshore may be unfamiliar with the university's vision, mission and educational goals which encapsulate global principles for higher education and guide the curriculum, assessment and teaching and learning, as well as the university's graduate attributes.

While onshore these concepts may be pervasive and assimilated incidentally, but this is less likely offshore where staff may hold a range of alternative expectations and values. For example, critical and analytical approaches to teaching and learning may be unclear and staff may teach in a way that is incompatible with the assessment requirements for their subjects and courses. This is potentially an unfair situation for the students offshore who may experience different requirements from those embedded in the assessment tasks. Furthermore, exposure of the onshore staff to alternative ways that, for example, critical analysis may be understood cross-culturally broadens their perspectives. It also contextualizes the responses that their own onshore international students may initially take to such requirements, thereby contributing to educational quality.

Staff offshore may be unfamiliar with the university policies and procedures about assessment and other education quality issues, and how they shape appropriate practice. Induction will provide the basis for shared values, expectations, best practice and student-centred teaching and learning. Furthermore, staff sharing in these understandings will feel an increased sense of inclusion, involvement and engagement with their institution and in their teaching, and be more likely to teach with enthusiasm and commitment and help their students to engage in their studies (Crosling 2011).

Collegial relations, or shared communities of practice (Dunn and Wallace 2003) of academic staff across locations, lay the foundation for the inclusion of offshore staff in education matters. Such arrangements provide the platform for offshore staff to advocate awareness of the offshore context and students in curriculum and thus assessment. The availability of Information and Communication Technology (ICT) lessens the distance between onshore and off-campus academic staff and facilitates collegial relations of staff teaching a subject or a course. While perhaps not as effective as face-to-face communication, ICT does enhance the possibility of the transferral and induction into the organization's tacit as well as explicit knowledge (Wenger *et al.* 2002). This practice enables the development of a common purpose, facilitating the sharing of concerns, achievements and resolution of problems before they escalate. Furthermore, staff in both the parent university and the TNHE setting can learn inter-culturally about one another, again broadening understanding. In such a climate, awareness of the situations offshore and onshore can be promoted, laying the groundwork for collaborative involvement in curriculum development and assessment so that the needs of students in the TNHE setting can be integral to assessment practices.

Following the implementation of the previous two points, the operation of groups of onshore and offshore academic staff teaching a subject can further shared understanding of the curriculum and assessment. Operating in an inclusive and collegial way and utilizing ICT, such groups enable the participation of offshore staff in the management of subjects and courses so that the characteristics of the offshore location and student cohort can be discussed and built into the curriculum, teaching and learning and assessment approaches. Typical outcomes could be the inclusion of local examples in the range of assessment tasks, which draw on and reflect the TNHE location and characteristics. Another example may be recognition of the offshore students' learning preferences for communal learning such that group work assignments may be included in the assessment protocol. For TNHE students, this creates a sense of inclusion rather than exclusion in that their particular situation is reflected in the course and its assessment, thus authenticating the assessment tasks. It also enables staff in the parent university setting to learn cross- and inter-culturally, for example, by raising the awareness of the responses of diverse groups of students to an assessment task and of the provision of formative student feedback for improvement, as well as the adaptation of teaching on the basis of assessment outcomes.

Putting in place a sound, multi-faceted programme for assessment moderation

The first phase in developing moderation draws on the previously discussed collaborative academic staff approaches for onshore and offshore staff, jointly establishing assessment tasks and criteria. If the subject management groups mentioned previously are effective, the assessment tasks should be inclusive for all students regardless of location and backgrounds. The next step is ensuring all examiners have shared understanding of the interpretation of the assessment criteria. By involving collaboration and perhaps using typical models of excellent, fair and poor levels of achievement, the meaning and the levels for different grades are established. For instance, if one assessment criterion is 'critical analysis', discussion can expose different views on its realization in students' work across locations as the basis for developing a set of shared and inclusive response modes, while maintaining the criterion's integrity.

Based on the previous step, commonalities in the interpretation of criteria can be developed and circulated to students. This may be in the form of a rubric providing guidance for the achievement levels for the criteria. Inclusive for all staff, this establishes commonality among diverse teaching staff and guides students from diverse backgrounds and in offshore settings about the expectations at different achievement levels. To provide equitable assessment experiences for offshore students, it is important that the purpose of the assessment tasks and their link to learning outcomes are explicit. Following completion of the marking for the assessment piece, a sample of the papers for each grade should be moderated to ensure that shared interpretations of the criteria prevail.

Feedback for students

It is important to provide adequate constructive feedback on students' written work as outlined in the previous point, allowing enough time for reflection and for addressing the assessor's comments before the next assignment is submitted. This helps students close the gap between their expectations of the requirements and those of their examiners. Staff can be encouraged to provide assessment feedback sessions in the mainstream teaching programme, outlining areas of strength and areas for improvement, including appropriate approaches to achieve improvement. Students in the class can be asked to reflect on their own work in relation to the comments and consider adjustment of their approaches for higher achievement. Providing students with examples of appropriate and less appropriate responses authenticates the exercise for students.

At a higher level, the assessment results in terms of grade distributions across the different locations in which the subject operates need to be reviewed and tracked. Any discrepancies in patterns should then be further investigated and, if required, reviewed in relation to student progression and retention rates. For instance, variance in grade distributions could stem from any of the points raised in this section concerning staff and students, or extend as deep as student selection or entry pathways.

Development of inclusive assessment protocol

It is necessary to recognize the different characteristics of students from diverse linguistic, cultural and ethnic backgrounds in the TNHE setting, and so provide a fairer evaluation of their academic performance. Where English is not their first language, students may use non-standard grammatical and syntactic forms in their writing in assignments and exam responses. There are several implications of this: first, academic staff in the parent university assessing or moderating such work may mark it down because of what they see as poor English. Importantly, students need to be aware that standard English is required. If students' written work frequently exhibits non-standard expression, this needs to be included as a proportion in the grading system. If it is part of the assessment criteria, guidance for students to meet this requirement needs to be included in the teaching and learning process (Crosling 1996). While universities stipulate a level of English required for admission to studies, academic language and conventions may be the issue rather than English language ability. Students need to be aware of the expectation in their assessment and supported to function along the required lines in their work.

Second, students from a range of linguistic and cultural backgrounds may organize their ideas and written responses differently from the expectations of their teachers. For instance, they may use a circular, inductive or reader-focused form, rather than linear, inductive or writer-focused, as preferred in the Western setting. Examiners of such work may mark it down because their access to the main ideas is foiled, and because it does not meet their cultural expectations. Examiners need to be provided with cross-cultural training so that they can appreciate different modes in which ideas may be presented. They are then positioned to be able to decide on their requirements. Furthermore, if a particular form of writing is expected, this needs to be transmitted explicitly and clearly to students as a requirement, and they need to be provided with guidance if required.

Third, if oral presentations and verbal responses are assessment components, diverse students may be disadvantaged because of spoken language pronunciation that differs from their assessors' expectations. If the assessors have had limited contact with a range of accents, they may label these as poor English and disadvantage students in marking, and miscommunication may occur. Furthermore, students may misinterpret an examiner's colloquial comment, which reflects home country mores, as a criticism. Cross-cultural awareness training for assessors and students should be provided in this circumstance (Crosling and Martin 2005). Issues of students' poor English pronunciation can be addressed with instruction, as well as techniques to lessen the emphasis on spoken language (for example, the use of prosodics, rhythm, timing, and so on).

Students in offshore settings with diverse linguistic and cultural backgrounds may hold expectations of study approaches that differ from those of the institution and their teachers. For instance, they may not expect to operate as independent learners and so not appreciate suitable approaches for study and assessment success. This has implications across the spectrum of their study, including study management, argument development in response to issues and topics, integrating written study material, information and data, and organizing their responses and expression in assignment tasks. Academic induction programmes set the scene for students to understand and ultimately to operate successfully within the expectations and academic transition programmes across the early semesters of their study in order to consolidate and reinforce such understandings (Crosling 2003).

Students from diverse linguistic, cultural and educational backgrounds may have differing expectations of the use of published material from that reflected in Western academic discourse. Without violating ethical standards, it is important to acquaint such students with the role of published material in the development of an argument, and importantly, the underpinning reasons for this. Examples in teaching of appropriate usage provide a forum to educate students. Annotated models of previous students' assignments which demonstrate a range of responses to tasks on different topics are useful, and can be built into the mainstream teaching programme, again educating students about expectations.

Conclusion

This chapter addresses transnational higher education in terms of student engagement and assessment with particular relevance for educational programmes designed for one location and cohort of students, but delivered in another. The conclusion suggests that efforts need to be taken to create an inclusive environment for both the offshore academic staff and students so that, without compromising standards, their interests, learning preferences and needs can be acknowledged and addressed in curriculum and assessment. This lays the basis for the enhancement of the educational experience for students in TNHE settings, with ensuing benefits not only for the individual students, but also for the institution as its understandings of students and staff diversity are widened and built into educational operations and programmes.

References

Biggs, J. (1999) *Teaching for Quality Learning at University*, Buckingham: Society for Research into Higher Education and Open University Press.

Bodycott, P. and Walker, A. (2000) 'Teaching abroad: lessons learned about inter-cultural understanding for teachers in higher education', *Teaching in Higher Education*, 5(1): 79–94.

Bourdieu, J. and Passeron, J. C. (1977) *Reproduction in Education, Society and Culture*, London: Sage.

Crosling, G. (1996) 'International students writing in English: improvement through transition', *Prospect: A Journal of Australian TESOL*, 11(1): 50–7.

——(2003) 'Connecting new students: a faculty academic transition programme', *Widening Participation and Lifelong Learning*, 5(1): 40–2.

——(2011) 'Defining identity, engaging teachers and engaging students: "education strengths" in a foreign branch campus', in L. Thomas and M. Tight (eds) *Institutional Transformation to Engage a Diverse Student Body*, Bingley: Emerald Publishers, 245–252.

Crosling, G., Edwards, R. and Schroder, W. (2008a) 'Internationalizing the curriculum: the implementation experience in a Faculty of Business and Economics', *Journal of Higher Education Policy and Management*, 30(2): 107–21.

Crosling, G. and Martin, K. (2005) 'Student diversity and group work: a positive combination for curriculum internationalization', in E. Manalo and G. Wong-Toi (eds) *Communication Skills in University Education: The International Dimension*, Auckland: Pearson Educational, pp. 136–49.

Crosling, G., Thomas, L. and Heagney, M. (2008b) *Improving Student Retention in Higher Education: The Role of Teaching and Learning*, London: RoutledgeFalmer.

Dunn, L. and Wallace, M. (2003) 'Teaching offshore in Asia: into the unknown', unpublished manuscript.

Edwards, J., Crosling, G. and Edwards, R. (2010) 'Outsourcing university degrees: implications for quality control', *Journal of Higher Education Policy and Management*, 32(3): 303–15.

Edwards, R., Crosling, G., Lavazeric-Petrovic, S. and O'Neill, P. (2003) 'Curriculum internationalisation: a typology', *Higher Education Research and Development*, 22(2): 183–92.

McBurnie, G and Ziguras, C. (2007) *Transnational Education*, London: Routledge.

McNicoll, Y., Clohessy, J. and Luff, A. (2003) *Auditing Offshore Partnerships: Lessons from Reviewing Nursing and Psychology Courses Offered in Singapore*, Melbourne: Faculty of Medicine, Nursing and Health Sciences, Monash University.

Race, P. (2004) 'What has assessment done for us – and to us?', in P. Knight (ed.) *Assessment for Learning in Higher Education*, London: RoutledgeFalmer, pp. 61–74.

Roudometof, V. (2005) 'Transnationalism, cosmopolitanism and glocalisation', *Current Sociology*, 53: 113–35.

Schwab, J. (1973) 'The Practical 3: translation into curriculum', *School*, August: 501–22.

Stella, A. and Liston, C. (2008) *Internationalization of Australian Universities: Learning from Cycle 1 Audits*, Canberra: Australian Universities Quality Agency.

Swyngedouw, E. (2004) 'Global or glocal? Networks, tensions and rescaling', *Cambridge Review of International Affairs*, 17(1): 25–48.

Thomas, L. (2002) 'Student retention in higher education: the role of institutional habitus', *Education Policy*, 17(4): 423–42.

Varghese, N. (2009) 'GATS and transnational mobility in higher education', in R. Bhandari and S. Laughlin (eds) *Higher Education on the Move: New Developments in Global Mobility*, New York: IIE/AIFS Foundation Global Education Research Reports, pp. 7–27.

Vance, S. and Crosling, G. (1998) 'Integrating writing with the curriculum: a social constructionist approach', in J. F. Forest (ed.) *University Teaching: International Perspectives*, Boston: Garland Publishing, pp. 361–92.

Wenger, E., McDermott, R. and Snyder, W. (2002) *A Guide to Managing Knowledge: Cultivating Communities of Practice*, Boston: Harvard Business School Press.

Ziguras, C. (2007) *Good Practice in Transnational Education: A Guide for New Zealand Providers*, prepared for the Education New Zealand Trust. Available at: http://www.educationnz.org.nz/secure/eeidfReports/ENZ010-GoodPracticein TransnationalEducationFINAL.pdf (accessed 15 August 2011).

CRITICAL FRIEND COMMENTARY

Ron Edwards

In addressing the relationship between TNHE and assessment, this chapter is timely as much of the international education literature has focused on theory and principle. While assessment must be driven by theory, it is inherently practical. Teachers have to write the assessment pieces and the students have to complete them. Assessment is also highly political. It gives academics power over students. How many readers have reminded inattentive students that the topic is 'in the exam'? Power resides with those who write the exam. While consideration of assessment in the internationalization process of TNHE is essential, it is also fraught with difficulty. Some of the difficulties are outlined below. All these practical difficulties are assisted by the clear articulation of theory, principle and policy supplied in Glenda Crosling's chapter. In all, the chapter provides an excellent platform to approach assessment in TNHEs.

The chapter addresses the vital issue of assessment and its impact on student engagement in TNHE. A significant aspect of this is who writes the exam paper. This is a core question in the matter of assessment in international education. The answer reflects power relationships and how effectively the university has embedded internationalization. The chapter addresses the situation where, if the home campus staff member has written the assessment independently, perhaps without divulging the contents to colleagues in branch campuses and twinning partnerships, there is potential for home country culture and biases to be reflected in the assessment items. The home country culture may be more individualistic, assertive, status conscious and have a shorter time horizon in everyday decision-making than the host country culture. Higher standards of living and Western ways of doing things may also influence the way the assessment is written. All these factors are likely to be unconsciously incorporated into the way the curriculum is delivered and the assessment set and marked. As indicated in Glenda Crosling's chapter, they add to the potential that students studying offshore will be disadvantaged and limit the university's capacity to offer a genuinely international education.

In this chapter, Glenda Crosling expresses the importance of collegial meetings of those teaching the curriculum to avoid ethnocentric approaches to assessment. This approach is in line with emerging practice in TNHE. Staff on the offshore campuses and other forms of TNHE can share in designing questions and preparing marking guides. Open discussions allow them to highlight differences in expectations and interpretation. The result may be assessment pieces that are accessible for all students undertaking the course, whatever their cultural background. As the chapter also emphasizes, collegial meetings contribute to the development of trust and mutual respect between onshore and offshore staff. Some may be initially concerned that the integrity of the exam may be compromised by teaching staff beyond the direct control and oversight of the parent university. Academics are not all equally trusting, especially when there is little personal contact with the offshore teacher and where staffing changes mean there is little opportunity to build trusting relationships. Consequently, there may be resistance to sharing the exam paper, leaving open the possibility of culturally laden examination papers. Collaboration can ameliorate or even circumvent such situations.

Importantly, the chapter discusses the impact of assessment practice on student engagement in the TNHE setting. The strategies put forward to promote this are practical and can be implemented. While implementation may be problematic initially, efforts need to be made so that the full academic potential of students in offshore settings can be catered for, as well as for their teachers. Glenda Crosling's chapter is a valuable addition to the literature on TNHE.

Conclusion

Christine Broughan and Steve Jewell

This book has demonstrated that student engagement and development can be enhanced through assessment. Throughout the book contributors have shared their, often warts and all, stories about various theoretical and practical ways in which this may be realized. There is no doubt that assessment sharpens the minds of students more than any other activity we ask them to do and as such it represents a powerful tool by which to engage and retain them. However, we should also remember that assessment is a critical factor in the exclusion and attrition of students and therefore the cost of getting it wrong is significant. What lessons can we draw from the book in terms of the optimum conditions required to ensure that assessment contributes to the enduring watermark of first-rate higher education provision for all?

Several contributors have emphasized the need to understand the market conditions under which we are operating. We are living through a time of unprecedented change where the landscape of higher education has been transformed forever. The massification and internationalization agendas are opening up the markets and government demands for employability skills are shaping provision. The terrain is qualitatively different and we need to adapt existing assessment tools or develop new ways of doing things in order to remain fit for purpose.

Furthermore, what becomes apparent throughout the book is that a 'whole of university' strategy is required that supports the notion of effective learning and assessment. We need to reduce the gap between the rhetoric of what is written in policy or promised to students in prospectuses and the reality of their experience on the ground. Development of assessment policy should be an iterative process, constantly reinventing itself and making use of the latest in innovation and technology. The impact that this will have on academic staff should not be underestimated.

Staff development activities that inspire and nurture the adoption of more imaginative and inclusive methods of assessment that are timely and relevant are fundamental to achieving a cultural shift away from outmoded practices that inure. It is vital that staff have confidence in the pedagogy behind assessment methodologies so that they can make informed decisions to suit the needs of their students and therefore optimize the developmental benefits that assessment might hold. If there is no such thing as a 'typical' student, then the freedom to choose from a comprehensive menu of possible assessment styles is essential in order to move away from the 'one size fits all' approach, and begin to embrace diversity in ways that seek to ensure that the same students are not repeatedly disadvantaged.

The messages about what students want from assessment are largely consistent among the book's contributors. Students want learning-focused assessment that is student-centred; evidence suggests that adopting these fundamental principles encourages students to rise to the challenge and engage in their learning in a meaningful way. In addition, students want choice when it comes to assessment design and flexibility in terms of negotiating *what* is assessed and *when*.

Authentic assessment that is designed to develop students as learners is clearly more valid than assessment regimes that are based on the dubious assumption that a submission of *x* number of words is somehow related to the degree of learning that has taken place. However, this type of assessment requires a more holistic approach that negates the use of reductionist 'checklists' and contributes to the dismantling of traditional teacher/student hierarchies. To this effect, the book highlights the need to support students in their learning through peer and tutor mentoring, and while students generally embrace the notion that assessment in higher education is, and should be, different to their previous learning environments, students need to be provided with opportunities to develop their assessment literacies.

The value of feedback in the assessment process cannot be underestimated. In order to encourage the learner to be reflexive, sufficiently engaged and more confident in their ability to think critically, creatively and innovatively, feedback needs to be appropriately timed, dialogic and meaningful. Some authors suggest that the economies of scale and scope required by higher education will mean that effective feedback can only be achieved using technologies and/or peer assessment. Certainly greater levels of interoperability between assessments need to be accomplished in order to encourage a more holistic view of student learning.

Assessment has often been cited as a reason why students tend to leave their courses early, and while we will be beholden to the vicissitudes of consumer demand, we need to ensure that assessment continues to challenge, empower and shape our students. Assessment can act as a formidable enemy or powerful ally in achieving the central tenets of what higher education means. There is a possibility that the near future will see a step change in the way that assessment is used to engage and develop students. The triple helix relationship between higher education, government and business appears stronger than ever before and assessment should be used astutely to bind together the needs of all three. The global race for education will be won by the agile and those not encumbered by competing policies, outdated systems and inappropriate resources. We hope that this book has demonstrated how assessment can empower both staff and students in a community of learning fit for the twenty-first century.

Index